REVOLUTION AT QUERETARO

The Mexican Constitutional Convention of 1916–1917

Latin American Monographs, No. 33
Institute of Latin American Studies
The University of Texas at Austin

Revolution at Querétaro

The Mexican Constitutional Convention of 1916–1917

by E. V. NIEMEYER, JR.

PUBLISHED FOR THE INSTITUTE OF LATIN AMERICAN STUDIES
BY THE UNIVERSITY OF TEXAS PRESS, AUSTIN AND LONDON

Library of Congress Cataloging in Publication Data

Niemeyer, Eberhardt Victor, 1919–
  Revolution at Querétaro.

  (Latin American monographs, no. 33)
  Bibliography: p.
  1. Mexico—Constitutional history.
  2. Mexico. Congreso Constituyente, 1916–1917.
  I. Texas. University at Austin. Institute of
  Latin American Studies. II. Title. III. Series:
  Latin American monographs (Austin, Tex.) no. 33.
  JL1215 1917.N53   342'.72'029   73-20203
  ISBN 0-292-77005-7

This work is affectionately dedicated to J. Lloyd Mecham, Professor Emeritus of the University of Texas, and his colleagues, past and present, of the university's Institute of Latin American Studies—Professor Nettie Lee Benson, the late Carlos E. Castañeda, the late Charles W. Hackett, and Professor Lewis Hanke—all of whom stimulated my interest in Latin America.

CONTENTS

ILLUSTRATIONS

PREFACE

A constitution has significance to the extent that it serves as a basis for the social and economic development of a people in an atmosphere of political freedom and tranquillity. Since its promulgation, the Mexican Constitution of 1917, with the demands of the revolutionary upheaval of 1910 incorporated into its provisions, has been the legal foundation for the greatest transformation experienced by the Mexican people since the Conquest. Honored and obeyed, dishonored and disobeyed, many times amended, it still serves as the instrument for achieving the national purpose, although some provisions describe a goal for the future rather than an effective reality. Nevertheless, its status is sacred, strengthened during fifty-five years of existence.

So much for the Constitution of 1917—for this is neither an analysis of that document nor an account of its evolution from 1917 to 1972. Rather, it is a focus on the assembly that wrote the constitution. Strangely enough, no study in depth of the remarkable convention which produced the Constitution of 1917 has appeared in English. Social scientists have studied Mexico from one end to the other, have analyzed Mexican institutions, and have written much about Mexico and the Mexicans, but they have overlooked the Constitutional Convention of 1916–1917. It should not have been this way. As early as 1933 Professor Frank Tannenbaum wrote, "The Constitutional Convention of 1917 was the most important single event in the history of the Revolution."[1] In 1952 Professor Ward M. Morton pointed out that "the radical nature of the reforms incorporated in the Mexican

[1] Frank Tannenbaum, *Peace by Revolution: Mexico after 1910*, p. 166.

Constitution of 1917 and the consequent controversy have tended
to obscure the constitution-making assembly."[2] In 1968 Professor
Charles C. Cumberland wrote, "The Convention which produced the
Constitution of 1917 has unfortunately escaped the attention of serious
scholars even though it was one of the most dramatic and important
assemblies of the 20th century."[3] A year later Professors James W.
Wilkie and Albert L. Michaels could still write, ". . . there is no published scholarly study of the Convention and the men who drafted the
Constitution."[4] Cumberland, however, has somewhat ameliorated the
situation by devoting a chapter to the Constitutional Convention in his
outstanding, posthumously published book on the Constitutionalist
movement.[5]

This book does not pretend to be a systematic analysis of the Constitutional Convention of 1916–1917 or a definitive biographic study
of those delegates who played major roles in the deliberations. Rather,
it is an attempt to record the unfolding of ideas expressed during the
debates on the most distinctive articles of the constitution and to show
how the ideals of the Mexican Revolution were written into fundamental law. It is an attempt to document the humanitarian concern of
the delegates for their fellow countrymen and to show the strong determination that existed at Querétaro to lay the foundation for a more
just and equitable future for Mexico. Finally, it is an attempt to shed
some light on the delegates themselves, on who they were and where
they came from, on their idiosyncrasies and attitudes, on their individual contributions to the writing of the Constitution of 1917.

Many persons have helped me to make this work possible. I will always be grateful to them. I owe a lasting debt to Srta. Emma Villaseñor of Mexico City, who made available source material unobtainable
elsewhere, and who, together with her father, Ing. Adolfo Villaseñor
Norman of Zacatecas, talked with me at length about the convention

[2] Ward M. Morton, "The Mexican Constitutional Congress of 1916–1917," *Southwestern Social Science Quarterly* 33, no. 1 (June 1952): 7.

[3] Charles C. Cumberland, *Mexico: The Struggle for Modernity*, p. 357.

[4] James W. Wilkie and Albert L. Michaels, eds., *Revolution in Mexico: Years of
Upheaval, 1910–1940*, p. 288.

[5] Charles C. Cumberland, *Mexican Revolution: The Constitutionalist Years*, chap.
9.

and the delegates; to Lic. Antonio Martínez Báez of Mexico City; to Professor Karl M. Schmitt of the University of Texas, who made helpful suggestions in the preparation of the manuscript; to Professor Lyle C. Brown of Baylor University, who furnished material from his own extensive collection on the revolution, read the chapters, made invaluable criticism, and—above all—encouraged me to undertake this task; and to my wife, Lala, who stayed after me to complete the job, only to be rewarded with the burden of typing the manuscript.

E. V. NIEMEYER, JR.

REVOLUTION AT QUERETARO

The Mexican Constitutional Convention of 1916–1917

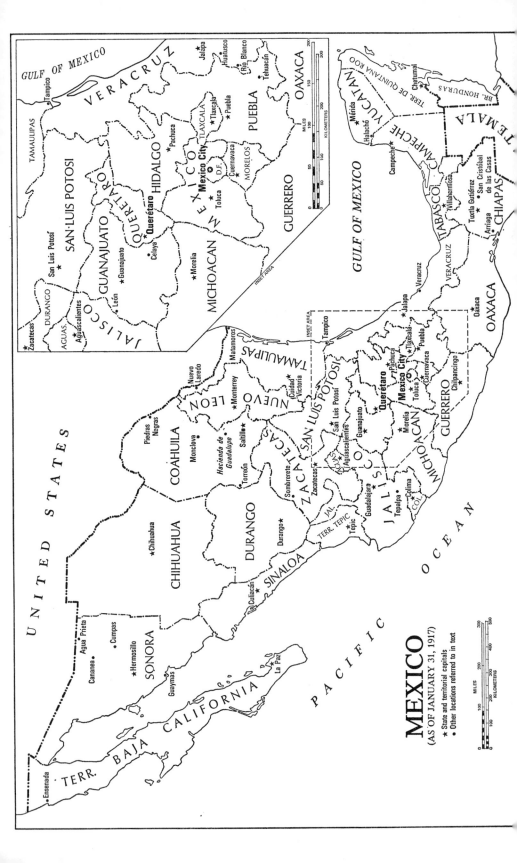

MEXICO
(AS OF JANUARY 31, 1917)

★ State and territorial capitals
● Other locations referred to in text

1. 1857 to 1917: Background for a Revolutionary Constitution

I meditated a moment at the departure of the Congreso Constituyente. I saw the grand parade of ideas as if they were centuries on the march. And then I understood that the work of the men of the Revolution, among whom I was an imperceptible unit, would make a new *patria*, one great and strong . . . and that we were face to face with the greatest transformation of a people toward real liberty.

Ramón Frausto (Guanajuato)
Fernández Martínez Album

To arms! Great liberties are never won on one's knees, nor by kissing the soles of the tyrant's feet, but by fighting nobly, like a man, with the law and arms in hand.

Francisco Figueroa (Guerrero)
Fernández Martínez Album

A S SOON AS THE DELEGATES to the Constitutional Convention of 1916–1917 had taken the oath of office on November 30, 1916, Gen. Francisco J. Múgica (Michoacán)[1] mounted the podium and, echoing Cato, exclaimed, "Carthage must be destroyed, there is the enemy in whom we must sink the dagger of the Revolution up to the hilt."[2] His prophetic words sounded the keynote of a revolutionary assembly that ended a cycle of the most diverse events and phenomena in Mexican

[1] At the first reference to a delegate to the Querétaro Convention, he is identified by the state from which he was elected. For a listing of delegates mentioned in this work, see Appendix F.

[2] *Diario de los debates del Congreso Constituyente, 1916–1917*, I, 377. Unless otherwise stated, I am responsible for all translations.

history. The period opened with the promulgation of the Constitution of 1857; it continued with the bloody War of the Reform, foreign intervention, and empire; and, following the peace-and-order dictatorship of Porfirio Díaz, the period concluded with that catastrophic upheaval known as the Mexican Revolution and with the promulgation of the first practical and viable constitution in the nation's history: the Constitution of 1917. To understand the intensity of Múgica's feelings and those of fellow delegates who shared his views, to understand what had to be destroyed and why, it is necessary to review the events of the preceding sixty years. Issues which were hotly debated in the course of drafting the Magna Carta of 1917 concerned the national problems of the period.

From the end of the colonial era to 1857, the central theme of Mexican political life was the struggle between two opposing factions: conservatives and liberals. Conservatives predicated their stand on the continued predominance of the Roman Catholic church, a landowning oligarchy, a centralist government controlled from Mexico City, and a military establishment. Liberals sought greater freedom, both individual and economic, and equality; curbs on the power of the Church and its clergy; effective control of the military; and a federal system of government, both in theory and in practice. Coming to power through revolution in 1853, the liberals began to implement a farreaching program of reforms.

Three important measures embodied this program. The Ley Juárez of 1855 deprived military and ecclesiastical courts of all jurisdiction in civil suits, confining these tribunals to military and religious matters respectively. The Ley Lerdo of 1856 sought to make real property more available for national development by depriving civil and ecclesiastical bodies of the right to own and acquire such property, except that which was needed for purposes of worship. The Ley Iglesias of 1857 sought to limit abuse in the collection of fees for clerical services. These decrees, especially the Ley Lerdo, expressed the essence of nineteenth-century liberalism.

In 1856 a convention (composed of moderate and left-wing liberals, but no conservatives) proceeded to draw up a constitution. Operating in an atmosphere of complete freedom, this body produced the Constitution of 1857, which enumerated the Rights of Man as guarantees of individual liberty against an overbearing government. The constitution also provided for a unicameral congress, composed of members elected indirectly by popular vote, with powers superior to those of the executive; a judicial system with popularly elected judges; and a federal system of national and state governments. Although the delegates rejected as too radical Ponciano Arriaga's sweeping proposal for agrarian reform, they did declare that education was free, and they incorporated the provisions of the Ley Lerdo, thus incurring the wrath and unyielding opposition of the Church, which refused to accept any challenge to its pervasive and heretofore dominant role in Mexican life.

Signed on February 5, 1857, and promulgated a week later, the Constitution of 1857 was denounced immediately by most of the clergy and conservatives alike. Even President Ignacio Comonfort, who had sworn to uphold this fundamental law of the land, declared it to be unworkable. Subsequently, Mexico drifted rapidly into anarchy. If the Constitution of 1857 had made an inauspicious start, however, the document gained in stature in the years immediately following, for it became the symbol of republican Mexico, the standard around which Mexicans would rally to battle reaction and foreign intervention, to uphold national honor and dignity.

From 1857 to 1867 a bloody religious civil war between liberals and conservatives engulfed Mexico. Under the leadership of President Benito Juárez, the liberals fought to preserve gains won since 1853 and to strike new blows against the Church in the form of provisions for the separation of Church and State, suppression of convents, nationalization of church properties, religious toleration, and regulations governing religious activities. A coalition of clergy and conservatives stubbornly resisted, only to be driven from Mexico City in late 1860. Although the War of the Reform had ended in victory for the liberal forces, peace was still elusive. Defeated in battle, the clergy still sought to recoup their losses, to preserve the supremacy of the Church in Mexico. Intriguing with Napoleon III of France, who had visions of another French empire in the New World, the clericals turned to a system of government that had offered protection and support in other countries and other epochs, one they had long endorsed: monarchy.

Archduke Maximilian of Austria, perhaps the most tragic figure in Mexican history, sat on the throne of the Second Empire from 1864 until his defeat and subsequent execution in 1867. Sustained by French arms and with little or no mass support, he struggled continuously with obdurate church prelates determined to preserve clerical privilege. Although a liberal at heart, Maximilian was an alien sitting on an artificial throne; thus he lasted only three years before succumbing to a stubborn Benito Juárez and his republican supporters, who rightly considered themselves to be the true government and who fought without quarter.

Collapse of the empire and restoration of the authority of the Constitution of 1857 throughout the republic marked the removal, at least temporarily, of the Church and its discredited prelates from positions of influence. Also, it sounded the end of the influence of the conservative party in nineteenth-century Mexican politics. Firmly in power at last, the victorious liberals under Presidents Juárez (1867–1872) and Sebastián Lerdo de Tejada (1872–1876) attempted, under a democratic system, to rehabilitate a nation devastated and exhausted by almost fifteen years of continuous warfare. Despite obstacles, business conditions improved; a railroad connecting Veracruz with Mexico City was constructed; public education received extensive support; and basic freedoms and rights were respected. A monumental act occurred on October 5, 1873, when the most important of the Laws of the Reform were written into the constitution. This was an act which signified public acceptance of the following measures: separation of Church and State, civil marriage, prohibition of the acquisition of real property by religious institutions, substitution of a simple promise to tell the truth for the religious oath, and voidance of religious vows.[3] The period 1867–1876 was the golden age of the Constitution of 1857, the period of its most faithful observance, as the Mexicans strove to make their political system work. Had political and economic institutions continued to develop under a liberal, democratic spirit, the

[3] J. Lloyd Mecham, *Church and State in Latin America*, p. 375.

nation might have evolved with greater economic and social justice. Unfortunately this did not occur. To understand what happened in the following years is to understand the causes of the Mexican Revolution of 1910. Only in terms of the iniquity of the *porfiriato* (1876–1911) can the revolution, the first social upheaval of the twentieth century, be adequately explained.

The *porfiriato*, which began with Porfirio Díaz's takeover of the government in 1876 through a traditional coup d'état, ushered in a new era in Mexican history—thirty-five years of authority, order, and progress. Save for the period 1880–1884 (when in obeisance to the constitution he permitted a devoted partisan, Manuel González, to hold the presidency), Díaz served as chief executive until his forced removal from office in 1911. His rule for three and one-half decades was accompanied by the most phenomenal material growth and prosperity in Mexican history. In response to extensive railroad construction, a judicious management of the nation's finances, and peace and stability, foreign capital flowed into Mexico. Mining, industry, agriculture, and commerce developed at an unprecedented rate. In a relatively short time, a complete capitalistic system was imposed on an undeveloped society; thus the country, which had been feudal in nature and torn by internecine warfare since independence, became a modern nation. Under Porfirio Díaz, Mexico entered the twentieth century with an established international credit rating, a well organized banking system, security of life and limb for a growing middle class, and increasing development of natural resources. Exemplifying the blessings of peace and extensive foreign investment, Mexico represented the model Latin American nation.

The picture, however, deceived the observer. Social, economic, and political conditions belied the appearance of peace, evolution, economic growth, and democratic practice. Almost imperceptibly at first, but more clearly in later years, the Porfirian system tightened its grip on Mexico and revealed the high price being paid for national development. National problems which surfaced or became exacerbated during the period indicated basic shortcomings and the danger that, unless corrected, they would lead to unrest and violence.

First, Mexico suffered under an inequitable land system. The Ley

Lerdo and the Constitution of 1857 had, it was believed, stressed economic liberalism and free enterprise, conditions necessary for the development of private property. Unfortunately, when the large estates
of the Church and property held corporately by Indian groups were
divided, the tenants did not always become the owners; in many cases
title passed to members of a rising middle class and to *hacendados*.
Concentration of land ownership, with resulting exploitation of small
landowners, quickened under the land laws of 1883 and 1894, which
removed restrictions on the sale of land. Under government authorization, survey companies received as the price for their services one-
third of all vacant lands they located and surveyed. With callous dis-
regard for the rights of the occupants, whole rural communities were
dispossessed of lands they and their people had worked for centuries.
So great was the concentration of land in the hands of a few *hacendados* that by 1910 almost nine-tenths of the rural families had no
land at all.[4] Had the *latifundios* produced sufficient food to feed the
populace, the situation might have been mitigated. Unfortunately, this
did not occur, because owners increasingly turned to the production of
commodities for export. Instead of continuing a feudal system, the
porfiriato developed a rural capitalism based on large estates oriented
toward the international market and employing wage labor.[5] In the
rich sugar-producing area of Morelos, *hacendados*, bent on increasing
their acreage, steadily dispossessed *campesinos* of their lands between
1880 and 1910. Whole villages disappeared, as residents were driven
off their lands to work as day laborers on the haciendas. Resistance to
this destruction of free, communal life provoked bitter clashes between
campesinos and *hacendados*. When Emiliano Zapata assumed leadership of the agrarian discontent in Morelos in 1909, he set in motion a
movement soon to gain national significance, one which vividly expressed two basic goals of the Mexican Revolution: land and liberty.[6]
By coincidence, Andrés Molina Enríquez, a lawyer and anthropologist,

[4] Moisés González Navarro, *El Porfiriato: La vida social*, vol. 4 of *Historia
moderna de México*, ed. Daniel Cosío Villegas, p. 212.
[5] Fernando Rosenzweig et al., *El Porfiriato: La vida económica*, vol. 7 of *Historia moderna de México*, ed. Daniel Cosío Villegas, p. 315.
[6] John Womack, Jr., *Zapata and the Mexican Revolution*, pp. 9, 43–54.

published in that year his famous study of Mexican social problems, *Los grandes problemas nacionales*. In his analysis of the agrarian problem, the author foresaw the revolution, advocated division of the large estates, and called for restoration of the Indian system of communal ownership. He would later advise delegates to the Constitutional Convention of 1916–1917, as they sought a solution under law to the problem of rural property rights.

Second in seriousness was the plight of rural and urban labor. Workers did not receive their just share of the national product; neither were they organized to demand it. The prevailing theory of classical capitalism presupposed that wealth trickled down to the masses. This did not occur in Porfirian Mexico. Wages did increase some 60 percent between 1876 and 1910, but prices of basic foodstuffs more than doubled during the same period. In the midst of unprecedented prosperity for the privileged few, the masses toiled at near-starvation wages. On the great haciendas peonage held workers in bondage. In the factories child labor, low wages, and long hours of work under unsanitary conditions prevailed. Throughout Mexico the labor force lived in ignorance and misery, degradation and disease, inebriation and despair; workers were increasingly victimized by an exploitative economic and social system.[7]

The philosophy that sanctioned this system, that aided and abetted its practice, derived from the positivism of Auguste Comte. Brought to Mexico in the 1860's by Gabino Barreda, who was later to become a noted educator, positivism emphasized science in place of metaphysics in education, strong government with limitations on individual freedom, order, and progress. The doctrine served Díaz well in his efforts to achieve peace, stability, and economic development. The intensity of the drive for order and progress was surpassed only by the ruthlessness with which it was carried out. For the impoverished masses, the doctrine of positivism proved disastrous; individual rights and interests—rights to water, to land, to a livable wage—were sacrificed for the betterment of society, that is, the development of the nation. Influenced strongly by social Darwinism, the positivists con-

---

[7] González Navarro, *El Porfiriato*, pp. 216–239, 280–297.

sidered the masses to be expendable. By 1900 a small, influential clique surrounding Díaz, the *científicos*, had come to dominate Mexican political and economic life. They promoted, often to their own selfish interests, the exploitation of the nation's resources. Foreign investors and corporations allied themselves with this oligarchy in order to gain lucrative concessions. A decade later, the odium of all who had not benefited from this monopoly of political and economic power, this system which benefited the few at the expense of the many, was directed against the dictatorship and the *científico* group within it.[8]

Another characteristic of the Díaz period, one which exacted retribution during the period of the revolution, was the remarkable recovery of the Church. The anticlerical fervor of the reform period gave way to an accommodation of Church and State under Porfirio Díaz. Although the Laws of the Reform were not repealed, they were enforced only sporadically in different regions or not at all. Under such an arrangement, the Church recouped much of its wealth while regaining power and prestige. Surreptitiously, it recovered property. Once more priests put business before religion, openly displayed their contempt for the laws regulating public religious acts, and entered the educational system with renewed vigor. In a real sense, the Church became a bulwark of the dictatorship: its prelates and clerics believed that their own best interest depended on the continuance of Porfirian rule.[9]

Finally, the Díaz system tore to shreds the practice of democracy that had distinguished the period 1867–1876. Paying lip service to the Constitution of 1857, Díaz succeeded in gaining control of the government by conciliating opposing liberal and conservative elements, by playing off supporters and rivals against each other. After the four-year administration of Manuel González, Díaz began a second term in 1884 and did not relinquish the office until forced to do so in 1911. During this period he personified government authority in Mexico. His administration was perpetuated by an obedient congress; a servile judiciary that dispensed justice for the benefit of the

[8] Karl M. Schmitt, "The Mexican Positivists and the Church-State Question, 1876–1911," *A Journal of Church and State* 8 (Spring 1966): 200–213.
[9] Mecham, *Church and State*, pp. 376–379.

wealthy, the foreigner, and the influential; sycophantic state governors; fraudulent elections at all levels; and an absence of contending political parties. For all practical purposes, democratic government had ceased to exist in Mexico by 1910, when an apathetic electorate returned Díaz to office for the seventh consecutive term. Especially ironic was the fact that thirty-four years earlier the old dictator had taken over the presidency on a no–re-election platform. Díaz had succeeded very effectively in emasculating the Constitution of 1857 while constructing a personalist dictatorship, one which checked democratic development. The blame, however, did not rest with Díaz alone. As Daniel Cosío Villegas, the dean of Mexican historians, has explained, Mexicans had lost faith in the ideal of liberty and had sacrificed it on the altars of peace and material progress. They had renounced political freedom, albeit temporarily, to enable Díaz to provide the country with the economic impulse needed to achieve national development. Once they had turned it over to Díaz, however, the people would recover their liberty only after an exhaustive struggle. The Constitution of 1857 failed to operate because of a change in the Mexican's sense of values, in his philosophy of life, in his public morality.[10]

Under these circumstances, rumblings of discontent, first heard around 1900, became more audible as the decade advanced. The cry for justice and reform found expression in the program of the Mexican Liberal party (MLP), issued on July 1, 1906, from St. Louis, Missouri, where the framers had sought refuge from vigilant Mexican authorities. Influenced by socialism and by the anarchist ideas of Ricardo Flores Magón, members of the MLP represented a new breed of liberals, far to the ideological left of the nineteeth-century reformists and more prone to advocate violence as the means to an end. Based on class struggle, the MLP proposals advocated land reform, rights for labor, protection of the Indian, strict enforcement of anticlerical measures, constitutional revision, and overthrow of the Díaz regime. Printed in the MLP organ, *Regeneración*, which circulated clandestinely throughout Mexico, the call for change and socioeconomic betterment had a stirring effect on those who would later

[10] Daniel Cosío Villegas, *La Constitución de 1857 y sus críticos*, pp. 194–195.

play prominent roles in the Constitutional Convention of 1916–1917, who would write basic MLP proposals into the new law of the land.[11]

By 1910, pressures of discontent presaged the end of the dictatorship. The glitter of peace, prosperity, and material progress, so impressive to those who gathered in Mexico City in September to celebrate the centennial of the War for Independence, could no longer conceal the weakness of the supporting structure. A large-scale strike of copper-miners had broken out at Cananea, Sonora, in 1906; and in 1906–1907 the textile workers had struck at Río Blanco, Veracruz.[12] Both strikes involved violence; and other strikes followed, especially in the mining and industrial centers in northern Mexico. Brutal suppression had embittered the proletariat against capital (especially foreign capital) and against the dictatorship that encouraged and protected it; land hunger and the misery of a rural proletariat contrasted with the *latifundio* and the opulent life of many *hacendados*; favoritism toward foreigners outraged Mexicans who were given the status of second-class citizens in their own country; meaningless adherence to democratic practices maintained a corrupt bureaucracy and negated the principles of constitutional government; an economic crisis that began in 1907 adversely affected all the social classes; and the Church, once more rich and powerful as a result of the laxity of enforcement of anticlerical laws, was considered as an ally of the dictatorship. All of these conditions made social upheaval inevitable.

Stimulated by overwhelming social and economic injustices, political unrest toppled the Díaz dictatorship. The MLP program of 1906 clearly expressed socioeconomic discontent, but a little book written by Francisco I. Madero, *La sucesión presidencial en 1910*, was more influential in arousing the political agitation that brought the Díaz

[11] For a concise account of the Flores Magón brothers' activities from 1900 to 1906 and the objectives of the MLP, see Lyle C. Brown, "Los liberales mexicanos y su lucha en contra de la dictadura de Porfirio Díaz, 1900–1906," in *Antología MCC, 1956*, pp. 89–136. For the text of the MLP proposals and the degree to which they were later incorporated into the Constitution of 1917, see James D. Cockcroft, *Intellectual Precursors of the Mexican Revolution, 1900–1913*, pp. 239–245.

[12] González Navarro, *El Porfiriato*, pp. 316–336.

regime to an end. Authored by the scion of a wealthy Coahuilan family and published in 1908, the book attacked the evils of dictatorship, called for effective suffrage, and demanded an end to the practice of re-electing high government officials. It is significant that Madero gave little attention to the need for socioeconomic reform. Nevertheless, *La sucesión presidencial en 1910* had a tremendous effect. Madero had openly criticized a regime that had been in power for thirty-two years and that seemed impregnable. Soon Mexico seethed with political activity that neither Díaz nor his administration could contain. Although Madero abhorred violence, he sounded the call to revolution in October, 1910, with his Plan of San Luis Potosí. Lamenting the subservience of the legislative and judicial branches to the executive and declaring that the principles of separation of powers, state sovereignty, municipal self-government, and civil rights "only exist in writing in the Constitution," the plan denounced the recent election of Díaz as fraudulent, declared that he and government officials were illegally holding office, and empowered Madero, as provisional president, to make war on the regime. Like his book, Madero's Plan of San Luis emphasized political reform, which he believed must precede social and economic betterment. He did, however, strongly attack the *científicos*, whom he accused of "rapidly and unscrupulously squandering the national resources."[13]

Seven months after Madero had issued his call to revolution, the Díaz administration collapsed, and the old dictator was driven into exile. Then to a triumphant Madero and his followers fell the impossible task of restoring order, maintaining stability, and bringing about reform under a democratic process. After a transitional period of four and one-half months under an interim government, Madero was duly elected president of Mexico and inaugurated on November 6, 1911. When he took office, tension and unrest gripped the country. Armed bands were active in several states, and opportunists plotted open rebellion. Torn between those who sought political and socioeconomic reform and those who sought a return to the world of

[13] For the text of the Plan of San Luis Potosí, see Manuel González Ramírez, ed., *Planes políticos y otros documentos*, pp. 33–41.

Porfirio Díaz, Mexico drifted uncertainly into a new period in its national history. Believing in an evolutionary approach to agrarian reform, Madero underestimated the magnitude of the problem. He did order the survey and sale of national lands; and Congress in December, 1911, passed a bill providing for the purchase of privately held lands for resale in small plots. The partition of *ejidos* among *campesinos* and the distribution of national lands to villages without lands were undertaken. Important as these measures were, they really skirted the problem of providing a great quantity of land for the landless masses in a short period of time. Although the concepts of ejidal restoration and expropriation as methods of carrying out agrarian reform stem from the Madero period, very little land was returned.[14] Madero's fifteen months in office were marked by frustration and despair. Mexico could not make the transition from dictatorship to democracy without violence and bloodshed. Inept at governing, incapable of overcoming the elements of the Díaz regime that obstructed him and his administration at every turn, beset by unrest and uprisings, Madero was a tragic failure.

A coup d'état overthrew Madero and his government in February, 1913. Emerging as the strong man of the movement was Gen. Victoriano Huerta. Madero had entrusted him with the defense of the capital at the beginning of the *decena trágica*, but the general betrayed the president and took him prisoner on February 18. After forcing Madero and Vice President José María Pino Suárez to resign on the following day, Huerta became president with the approval of a supine Congress. On the twenty-second his subordinates murdered Madero and Pino Suárez. This bloody act, carried out three days after the ambitious Huerta's assumption of presidential power, destroyed any claim to legitimacy the new government might have had; and it stigmatized Huerta as the archvillain of Mexican history. Many have branded Huerta's counterrevolutionary regime as regressive, as an attempt to return to the Age of Díaz. Huerta and his advisers recognized, however, the need for some reform; they knew that there could be no turning back to the conditions of the *porfiriato*. But during his

<hr/>

[14] Charles C. Cumberland, *Mexican Revolution: Genesis under Madero*, pp. 213–219.

seventeen months in the presidency, Huerta was too occupied with preserving his government to effect any reforms.[15]

First to repudiate Huerta was Governor Venustiano Carranza of Coahuila. On his own initiative and with his cause reinforced by the default of other state and national leaders, Carranza launched his campaign to overthrow the usurper and to avenge the fallen Madero. News of Madero's arrest reached Saltillo on February 18. Carranza immediately convoked the state legislature, which issued a decree disavowing Huerta and vested extraordinary powers in the governor. On the same day Carranza issued a circular condemning Huerta's assumption of the presidency as illegal and stating that the orderly process of government had broken down. Appealing to all patriotic citizens for support, he announced that he was assuming leadership of the country in accordance with Articles 121 and 128 of the Constitution of 1857.[16] The boldness of his action, however, belied the lack of forces available to undertake any type of military campaign; in the beginning the army was still with Huerta. Carranza had nothing and was even denied the use of his state capital, Saltillo. His scattered units lost their first battles. His only recourse was to retreat and to formulate a plan of action for the future. This was the Plan of Guadalupe. The plan was drawn up at the hacienda of the same name, which is located approximately sixty miles north of Saltillo, and signed on March 26, 1913, by seventy-one revolutionaries of minor military rank, all irregulars in the force grouping around Carranza. This plan, banner of the Constitutionalist movement that it engendered, marked the beginning of a long march that ended at

---

[15] Michael C. Meyer, *Huerta, A Political Portrait*, pp. 176–177. This work is a well-documented reappraisal of Victoriano Huerta and his government.

[16] Article 121: "Every public official, without exception, shall before entering on the discharge of his duties, take an oath to maintain this constitution and the laws arising thereunder." Article 128: "This Constitution shall not lose its force and vigor even though its observance be interrupted by rebellion. In case that through any public disturbance a Government contrary to the principles which it sanctions be established, its force shall be restored as soon as the people shall regain their liberty, and those who have participated in the Government emanating from the rebellion or have cooperated with it shall be tried in accordance with its provisions and with the laws arising under it."

Querétaro three years and eight months later with the installation of a constitutional convention that would draft the Constitution of 1917.

Simple and to the point, the plan disavowed Huerta and the legislative and judicial branches of the federal government as well as all state governments that continued to recognize him after thirty days.[17] Designated First Chief of the Constitutionalist Army, Carranza was to be temporarily entrusted with the executive power. Upon occupying Mexico City, the First Chief was to call for general elections and turn over the office to whoever was subsequently elected president.

Had Carranza been the strict Constitutionalist he claimed to be, he would have denounced Huerta in the name of one of Madero's cabinet members, whose succession to the presidency was provided by law. For this he has been branded by some as another opportunist on the stage of Mexican history, motivated more by a thirst for power than by a desire to avenge Madero.[18] Yet Carranza had the courage and determination to denounce the usurpation and to lead the struggle for the restoration of Mexican honor. Propriety, if not strict legality, was on his side.

Failure to mention a social or economic program to nurture the great movement begun by Madero accentuates the purely political character of the Plan of Guadalupe. According to Alfredo Breceda, Carranza's private secretary, the First Chief dictated the plan to him and then asked him to call the other revolutionaries to discuss it. The great majority were in accordance with the wording, but a vociferous minority of young reformers wanted to include provisions to break up the large estates, guarantee rights for the workers, put an end to peonage, and abolish the hated *tiendas de raya*. Carranza objected, pointing out that the landowners, clergy, and industrialists were stronger than Huerta's government. He maintained that the war would be shorter if there were only the illegal government to overcome. His decision prevailed, but the zealous youth exacted the assurance that, once Huerta was defeated, the government would formu-

17 González Ramírez, ed., *Planes políticos*, pp. 137–139.
18 See Herbert I. Priestley, *The Mexican Nation, a History*, p. 426; Kenneth J. Grieb, "The Causes of the Carranza Rebellion: A Reinterpretation," *The Americas* 25 (July 1968): 25–32; idem, *The United States and Huerta*, pp. 31–35.

late a social program. In a way it was a compromise. Carranza wrote the plan, leaving the wording of its innocuous preamble to the young men. Significantly, one of the signers was Francisco Múgica.[19]

Although the revolutionaries had an objective, a name for their cause, and a chieftain, they had little else. Leaders, mostly *norteños*, of small, scattered units were united only in their desire to unseat Huerta. There was no revolutionary program as yet. At a meeting of Constitutionalist chiefs from Sonora, Durango, Coahuila, and Chihuahua in Monclova on April 14, Carranza spoke of a need for municipal self-government and a divorce law; but he was unenthusiastic about strengthening labor unions in order to struggle more effectively against capital. He also spoke of the need for nationalizing subsoil rights which, as a heritage from the colonial period, had been alienated during the Díaz regime.[20]

Forced to abandon Coahuila to Huerta's forces, the First Chief and his small party made their way afoot, on horseback, and by train through Durango and Sinaloa to Sonora, finally arriving in Hermosillo, the state capital, on September 19. Except for the port of Guaymas, Sonora was in the hands of adherents to the Constitutionalist cause: Alvaro Obregón, Benjamín Hill, Salvador Alvarado, and Governor José María Maytorena. Here Carranza began the task of organizing a government. He also found it politic to make known his ideas on the philosophy of the Constitutionalist cause. Speaking at the city hall in Hermosillo on September 24, he proclaimed the need to assert "new social ideas" among the masses.[21] Specifically mentioning laws to favor the proletariat, Carranza declared that such measures would be promulgated by *campesinos* and workers, the ultimate winners of "this redeeming social struggle." Recognizing the yearning for justice and equality, he spoke of the need to write "a new consti-

[19] Alfredo Breceda, *México revolucionario, 1913–1917*, pp. 395–399; Juan de Dios Bojórquez [pseud. Djed Bórquez], *Crónica del constituyente*, pp. 42–53.

[20] Alfonso Taracena, *Venustiano Carranza*, p. 146. The problem of municipal autonomy is discussed in chap. 6; chap. 5 treats the matter of subsoil rights.

[21] "Discurso pronunciado por don Venustiano Carranza el día 24 de septiembre de 1913 en el salón de cabildos del municipio de Hermosillo," *Cincuentenario de las adiciones y reformas al Plan de Guadalupe, del 12 de diciembre de 1914*, pp. 23–26.

tution, which no one would be able to keep from exerting a beneficial influence upon the masses." This was Carranza's first known
public reference to the need for a new constitution. As for the statements on social reforms, the First Chief made them for the benefit
of the immediate listeners. He and his advisers were not radical reformers. When Gen. Lucio Blanco, one of the signers of the Plan
of Guadalupe, confiscated a large estate near Matamoros, Tamaulipas,
on August 25, 1913, and divided the land among the peons who
worked it, the general was summoned by the First Chief to Sonora for
disciplining. Subsequently, Blanco was reassigned to the forces of
Gen. Alvaro Obregón, where he could be watched. On his arrival in
Sonora, Obregón is reputed to have told Carranza that no agrarian
unrest existed in the state and that strikes were not tolerated. If the
workers got out of hand, Obregón was confident that Plutarco Elías
Calles, "the whip," would put them in their place. According to Obregón, he and others had taken up arms to avenge the death of Madero.[22] Social and economic reforms were clearly of secondary importance.

Strategy designed to defeat Huerta called for attacks against the
federal forces in the large northern cities located along the railroad
trunk lines leading to the capital.[23] Three columns from the north
(one from Sonora under General Obregón, one from Chihuahua
under Gen. Francisco Villa, and one from Nuevo León under Gen.
Pablo González) began the drive on Mexico City. Because Villa
and his Division of the North achieved greater immediate success
and because Villa's route was one of uninterrupted railroad track,
Carranza and his cabinet went to Chihuahua. Here the first difficulties developed with Villa. Nominally subordinate to the First Chief,
Villa soon demonstrated his unwillingness to follow orders. The two
men were each other's antithesis. Carranza, a product of the Porfirian
period, adhered to the principles of law and order; he was deliberate
in his actions, quiet, dignified, and antimilitaristic. Carranza had

[22] Taracena, *Carranza*, p. 195.
[23] For a succinct account of the major military and political events of the Constitutionalist movement through 1915, see Lyle C. Brown, "The Politics of Armed
Struggle in the Mexican Revolution, 1913–1915," in *Revolution in Mexico: Years
of Upheaval, 1910–1940*, ed. James W. Wilkie and Albert L. Michaels, pp. 60–72.

nothing in common with Villa, former peon and *vaquero*, semi-literate, impetuous, unwilling to submit to leadership, aflame with the fire of battle. Even before Huerta's defeat, the schism between the two widened.

With Villa's occupation of Zacatecas in June, 1914, the road to Mexico City lay open. The end of the usurpation rapidly approached, as Huerta's forces lost their will to fight. Far more serious to Carranza, however, was the threat from Villa. To save the Constitutionalist cause and to guarantee Carranza's supremacy, it was of the utmost importance that Obregón's army should occupy Mexico City. Fortunately for Carranza, Villa's locomotives lacked coal, and his troops had exhausted their supply of ammunition. Carranza, through his control of the coal fields of northern Coahuila and the port of Tampico, denied these needed supplies to Villa. Thus the forces of Obregón and González were able to reach Mexico City first.[24]

In an attempt to heal the breach between the First Chief and his insubordinate commander of the Division of the North, Gen. Pablo González suggested a meeting of revolutionary generals in Torreón in early July. Carranza neither acquiesced to nor placed obstacles in the way of sending representatives to the meeting. After six days of sessions, the delegates agreed on the Torreón Pact, which provided that Villa would continue to recognize Carranza, who, on assuming the office of provisional president, would call a convention to determine the form of government to be set up and the date for holding elections. Neither members of the Constitutionalist armies nor provisional officials of the movement would be eligible for public office. The conferees declared in Clause 8 that the revolution was a "struggle of the impecunious against the abuses of the powerful" and that the evils which beset Mexico sprang from "political militarism, plutocracy, and clericalism." They also agreed to work for the establishment of democratic institutions in Mexico; to "bring welfare to labor, financial emancipation to the peasant through an equitable apportionment of land and other means tending to solve the agrarian question; and to correct, chastise, and hold to their responsibilities

[24] Robert E. Quirk, *The Mexican Revolution, 1914–1915: The Convention of Aguascalientes*, pp. 33–34.

those members of the Roman Catholic clergy who materially or intellectually have aided the usurper, Victoriano Huerta."[25]

Villa accepted the agreement, but Carranza rejected it as an encroachment by the militarists on his executive authority. He even rejected Clause 8, insisting that the matter of reforms had nothing to do with the reason for calling the Torreón conference. Except for this statement of socioeconomic reform, which served to crystallize revolutionary objectives, the meeting was a failure. Carranza and Villa remained at odds.

Following Huerta's abdication in July, 1914, and Obregón's occupation of Mexico City on August 15, Carranza's authority weakened, as various generals wavered in their loyalty to him. The menace of Villa became more serious as each day passed. Another threat to the First Chief came from Emiliano Zapata, who quickly demonstrated that he had nothing in common with Carranza and the Constitutionalists. Since November, 1911, with the issuance of his Plan of Ayala, the agrarian leader from Morelos had opposed Madero as well as Huerta for their failure to return lands, woods, and waters taken illegally from the villages by "landlords, *científicos*, or bosses."[26]

When Carranza arrived in Mexico City on August 18, he did not assume the provisional presidency in accordance with the Plan of Guadalupe. He failed to do so because he wished to become the legally elected president, and acceptance of the interim position would have disqualified his candidacy. Carranza's failure to take this step infuriated Villa. On September 22 the ambitious general openly repudiated the First Chief. Generals of the Division of the North seconded their leader on September 30 with a manifesto justifying his action and castigating Carranza for failing to assume the title of provisional president and to hold elections.[27] Acting unconcerned, Carranza addressed a number of his loyal generals, together with some

25 Ejército Constitucionalista, División del Norte, *Manifiesto del C. Gral. Francisco Villa a la nación y documentos que justifican el desconocimiento del C. Venustiano Carranza como Primer Jefe de la Revolución*, pp. 121–125.

26 For an English translation of the Plan of Ayala, see Womack, *Zapata*, pp. 400–404.

27 Quirk, *The Mexican Revolution*, p. 83.

of his civilian advisers, on October 3. He deliberately exclusded *villistas* from the meeting and reiterated the objectives of the Constitutionalist movement: to call elections and to re-establish constitutional government. This implied government in accordance with the Constitution of 1857; but a few days later Luis Cabrera, one of Carranza's lawyers, spoke to the militarists of the need for a convention "to draw up a Constitution adequate to our needs."[28] Contrary to his earlier position on the Torreón meeting, Carranza now suggested various social, economic, and political reforms. He specifically proposed the establishment of municipal self-government; and he called for settlement of the agrarian problem by dividing the public domain, purchasing lands from large estates, and expropriating lands for "public utility." Furthermore, Carranza proposed weekly cash payments of wages to workers, limitations on working hours, nullification of unconstitutional contracts for concessions of public lands, banking reforms, and expropriation by villages of lands needed for schools and markets.[29] The generals, however, were in no mood to discuss reforms. Villa had challenged the leadership of the Constitutionalist cause. There would be no peace until the issue was settled. The future offered the specter of more bloodshed.

Opposing factions made one last effort to heal the breach. Meeting in the centrally located city of Aguascalientes on October 10, delegates from the camps of Carranza, Villa, and Zapata tried to resolve the problem of the leadership of the revolution, to determine its future course. Designating itself a "sovereign" entity, the Aguascalientes Convention deliberated until November 13. By that date most of the Constitutionalist delegates had withdrawn to support their leader in the impending struggle against Villa. Subsequently, the convention led a peripatetic existence, became a debating body of *villistas* and *zapatistas*, who could agree on little more than their opposition to Carranza. Although initial objectives were political, in April, 1915, the convention approved measures of socioeconomic reform.[30] Labor was granted the right to strike, to boycott, and to demand improved

---

28 *Cincuentenario de la ley de 6 de enero de 1915*, p. 41.
29 Frank Tannenbaum, *Peace by Revolution: Mexico after 1910*, pp. 157–158.
30 Quirk, *The Mexican Revolution*, pp. 236, 243–244.

working conditions. Payment of wages in anything but money was prohibited, and *tiendas de raya* were outlawed. In May the convention endorsed divorce in Mexico and approved secular education in primary and secondary schools, both private and public. These measures, however, had little influence on the course of the revolution. The Constitutionalists, who would ultimately triumph, decreed a more comprehensive program of socioeconomic reform and did so sooner. With Villa's eclipse and Zapata's unconcern about matters beyond the limits of Morelos, and with its authority resting on an unborn government, the Aguascalientes Convention ceased to exist after May, 1916. Its contribution to the solution of national problems was negligible.

In the fall of 1914, however, the convention was a definite reality, the only hope for peace in Mexico. In an atmosphere charged with jealousy and mistrust, it attempted to find a formula for peace but failed. Although Eulalio Gutiérrez, military governor of San Luis Potosí, was chosen president, he could not control the convention. Carranza refused to heed the request that he resign and thus give up the leadership of the Constitutionalist cause. Villa, itching for a battlefield showdown that would eliminate Carranza, moved his troop trains past Aguascalientes and prepared to march on Mexico City. He completely ignored Gutiérrez and the convention. Under these circumstances, the only alternative facing the various military commanders was to line up with Villa or Carranza. This they proceeded to do immediately. Fortunately for Carranza and the Mexican Revolution, Obregón elected to remain loyal to the Constitutionalist cause. As Villa approached Mexico City to make common cause with Zapata against the Constitutionalists, Carranza and his supporters retreated to Veracruz. Although the Aguascalientes Convention had failed, the issue was clear: Villa, the most purposeless and destructive force of the revolution, had to be destroyed. To do this the *antivillistas* grouped themselves about Carranza to hammer out a sensible program of social, economic, and political reform. According to one authority, "the program grew out of conflict and necessity rather than out of theory."[31]

31 Tannenbaum, *Peace by Revolution*, p. 160.

Carranza's political revolution against Huerta assumed a social and economic character only after Huerta's defeat, when the Constitutionalist movement was torn with dissension and Carranza was fighting against Villa and Zapata for the very survival of his cause. The First Chief had stressed repeatedly along the tortuous path from Guadalupe to Veracruz that his objective was to avenge Madero, unseat Huerta, and return the country to constitutional rule. By the end of 1914, however, the vindicating movement took a new direction. Emphasis shifted from purely political objectives to those embodying the major features of the revolutionary program: agrarianism, labor welfare, anticlericalism, and nationalism. In the dark days of late December, 1914, and of early 1915, defeat stared the *carrancistas* in the face. It became essential for them to formulate a program that would rally popular support. Their cause, almost crushed and confined geographically to small areas around the port cities of Veracruz and Tampico, needed all the support that it could wean from the masses. Consequently, promises of social reform began to be traded for popular support of the struggle against Villa and Zapata. With a clear definition of objectives, the *carrancistas* might persuade all those who saw the revolution as a means of obtaining social and economic betterment to give aid to the Constitutionalist cause.

Facing the task with determination and courage, Carranza began a phase in Mexican history that he chose to call the "preconstitutional" period. It lasted about two and one-half years. During this time he issued a series of executive decrees having the force of law. The first, issued on December 12, 1914, provided that the Plan of Guadalupe would continue in effect until the revolution was successful and that Carranza would remain as First Chief in Charge of the Executive Power of the Nation. In this capacity, he would issue and enforce "all the laws, provisions, and measures tending to satisfy the economic, social, and political needs of the country." His almost dictatorial powers included direction of the military campaign, expropriation of lands for distribution on the basis of public utility, and negotiation of loans. After his successful reinstatement in Mexico City and the holding of municipal elections in a majority of the states, the First Chief was to call for congressional elections. Once Congress was in session,

Carranza was to render an account of his custody of the government and of reforms decreed during the interim period which might be adopted "as constitutional precepts." While there was no mention of need for a new constitution, the following reforms were specifically enumerated: equality of Mexicans among themselves, agrarian laws to encourage the creation of small landholdings, the breaking up of the *latifundios*, and the return to the townships of lands unjustly taken from them.[32] Subsequent decrees in 1915 and 1916 shaped the revolutionary program later incorporated into the Constitution of 1917. But in the dark days of 1914 and 1915 it is doubtful if the transcendental nature of these decrees was realized. More pressing was the need to gain support in the struggle against Villa and Zapata, and for this Carranza was willing to make such promises as were necessary.

Agrarian reform, subject of the famous decree of January 6, 1915, had as a major objective the return of communal lands taken from the Indians during the Díaz regime. If villages could not show title to the lands of which they had been deprived, restitution would be on a basis of need. The decree established a National Agrarian Commission, with branches in each state, to administer the law. Pending organization of the commission, state governors and military chiefs in any district could return lands, although such restorations were provisional and subject to later confirmation.[33] Much confusion attended the initial stages of agrarian reform, but at least a start had been made. Because Carranza's movement ultimately triumphed, the decree of January 6, 1915, became the first legal measure of agrarian reform.

Of more immediate importance was a decree of January 29, by which labor legislation became the exclusive responsibility of the federal government.[34] As a result of this decree and within a month after its issuance, Carranza's secretary of *gobernación*, Lic. Rafael Zubaran Capmany, reached an important agreement with the Casa del Obrero

---

[32] "Decreto del 12 de diciembre de 1914," in *Codificación de los decretos del C. Venustiano Carranza*, pp. 136–138. For other governmental regulations issued by the Carranza administration during the preconstitutional period, see *Recopilación de los circulares, reglamentos y acuerdos expedidos por las Secretarías de Estado adscritas a la primera jefatura del Ejército Constitucionalista.*

[33] "Decreto del 6 de enero de 1915," in *Codificación*, pp. 154–157.

[34] "Decreto del 29 de enero de 1915," in *Codificación*, pp. 165–166.

Mundial. This labor union agreed that workers would defend the towns in possession of the Constitutionalist forces and fight at the front in specially organized "red" battalions.[35] In return for this service, the Casa del Obrero Mundial would receive the right to organize in territory captured from the enemy. While the importance of the pact in the outcome of the struggle has been minimized by some, there is evidence that at least five thousand artisans and other workers enlisted in the ranks of the Constitutionalist forces. With a foot in the door, the labor movement would be heard from more forcefully when the time came to constitutionalize social reforms.[36]

In addition to these significant agrarian and labor decrees, Carranza issued others with political, economic, and social objectives. A decree of December 25, 1914, declared that states should adopt a republican form of government, with the self-governing municipality as the basis of their political organization. The institution of the hated *jefe político* was abolished.[37] By a decree of December 29, 1914, Carranza legalized divorce after three years of marriage by mutual consent or for serious cause, and one month later an amendment to the civil code of the Federal District and the territories provided for divorce in those political divisions. Bidding for support of the anticlericals, Carranza announced on June 11, 1915, that the Laws of the Reform would be strictly observed and that church buildings would continue to be the property of the nation.[38]

The reform decrees turned Mexican sentiment to the First Chief and to his cause. With the Constitutionalist armed forces strengthened considerably, Obregón defeated Villa in the bloody battles of Celaya and León in April and June, 1915. Subsequently, Villa was forced to confine his operations to harassment and pillaging in the north, main-

[35] For the text of the agreement, see *Cincuentenario de las adiciones y reformas al Plan de Guadalupe*, pp. 61–62. For more detailed treatment of the Red Battalions, see Jean Meyer, "Los obreros en la Revolución mexicana: Los 'Batallones Rojos,' " *Historia mexicana* 21 (July–September 1971): 1–37.

[36] On the role of labor at this crucial time, see Rosendo Salazar and José G. Escobedo, *Las pugnas de la gleba, 1907–1922*, part 1, pp. 83–101, and Rosendo Salazar, *La Casa del Obrero Mundial*, pp. 124–144.

[37] "Decreto del 25 de diciembre de 1914," in *Cincuentenario de las adiciones y reformas al Plan de Guadalupe*, pp. 37–39.

[38] Mecham, *Church and State*, pp. 383–384.

ly Chihuahua. In the south, Zapata was unbeaten but at bay. Carranza's forces had definitely gained the upper hand. The First Chief announced that his government had control of over seven-eighths of the
national territory, was organizing public administration in twenty of
the twenty-seven states, and exercised authority over nine-tenths of
the population.[39] By mid-1915 the dark days of late 1914 had bright-
ened considerably. With the end of the revolution in sight, Carranza
reaffirmed his intention of bringing about a peace based on welfare
and justice for all. The task was staggering. In a country devastated
by a civil war that was still smoldering, with agriculture and business
at a standstill, the process of reconstruction could only be slow and
painful. Of real benefit was the de facto recognition accorded by the
United States and eight Latin American nations on October 19, 1915.
As the national economy gradually but definitely improved, it became
imperative to end the preconstitutional period and to return to
constitutional government.

On June 12, 1916, Carranza issued a call for elections to the municipal councils. In accordance with the decree of December 12, 1914,
the next step should have been a call for elections to Congress. Instead, on September 14, 1916, the First Chief issued a call for the
election of delegates to a constitutional convention to reform the Constitution of 1857. When did he decide to do this, and why? The title
of First Chief of the Constitutionalist Army, the legal argument invoked by Carranza as governor of Coahuila when he arose against
Huerta, and the very name Constitutionalist were all based on the
Constitution of 1857. Would the people accept this new proposition?
Carranza, it will be recalled, had spoken of a "new constitution" in his
Hermosillo address of September 24, 1913. But these words, addressed to a provincial audience, were all but forgotten during the
bloodshed and turmoil that followed. On February 3, 1915, however,
he had broached the idea formally: "When peace is established, I
shall convoke a Congress duly elected by all the people which shall
have the character of a *congreso constituyente* for raising to constitutional precepts the reforms dictated during the struggle."[40]

39 "Decreto del 11 de junio de 1915," in *Codificación*, p. 217.
40 *El Constitucionalista*, no. 7 (February 5, 1915): 1.

According to Ing. Félix F. Palavicini (Federal District), member of Carranza's civilian coterie, the First Chief made the decision in late December, 1914, or early January, 1915. When Palavicini suggested the advisability of a return to law and order based on a new document more in keeping with the spirit of the times, Carranza was, at first, opposed. Later, however, he agreed to permit Palavicini to undertake a press campaign to convince the adherents to the cause, especially the most important army generals, of the need to convoke a constitutional convention.[41]

In a series of articles published between January and April, 1915, in *El Pueblo*, official organ of the Constitutionalist cause, Palavicini explained why Mexico needed to replace the Constitution of 1857 with a new one. First, he argued that it would be necessary to incorporate the revolutionary reforms into the constitution if they were to receive deserved respect. He explained, in part, "We wish to legalize for the future what is a reality in the present . . . that there will be no Congress to take from the *ayuntamientos* the autonomy that señor Carranza has granted them; that there will be no future Congress capable of taking from the villages the *ejidos* that the people have already received and are now cultivating; that there will be no Congress of tomorrow with sufficient legality to nullify the new marriages of divorced spouses; that each future Congress will be powerless to destroy the new villages created by the Revolution; that there will be no legislature able to repeal our labor laws governing accidents at work, minimum wages, professional [*sic*] unions, and working hours."[42] When Congress met to legislate for the nation, Palavicini believed it could do so more effectively if reforms had already been written into the constitution.

Second, Palavicini pointed out that the Constitution of 1857 had led, in practice, to subordination of the executive to the legislative branch. In redressing the imbalance, the executive had resorted to dictatorship. Palavicini criticized the venerated document as progressive only in the sections dealing with individual rights, the federal

---

[41] Preface by Félix F. Palavicini to Alberto Trueba Urbina's *El artículo 123*, pp. 9–10.

[42] Félix F. Palavicini, *Historia de la Constitución de 1917*, I, 28.

judiciary, and the Laws of the Reform (which had been added in
1873). Furthermore, Palavicini asserted that the document was very
different in 1910 from the one promulgated in 1857. Of the original
128 articles, 49 had been amended by 1910 to suit political factions
and powerful interest groups. The rest, he argued, had been unob-
served or were out of date.

Having established the need to incorporate reforms into the constitution in order to make it a more relevant document, Palavicini explained the difficulty, if not the impossibility, of doing so through
the amending process.[43] A procedure that often occasioned considerable delay under peaceful conditions would, he reasoned, take even
longer with the country still unsettled and state and national governments not yet functioning smoothly. Finally, Palavicini pointed out
that not one reform, but many, had to be written into the constitution;
each of them would have to be submitted separately, thus causing an
even longer delay. With Mexico torn by dissension among *villistas*,
zapatistas, and *carrancistas*, the probability of rejection would be great.
The only logical solution was to call a constitutional convention to
write all the reforms into the supreme law at one time.

In justifying the need for a new constitution, Carranza, in his decree of September 14, stated that the Magna Carta of 1857 had led to
tyranny.[44] Either the chief executive had absorbed the other branches
of government, or they, especially the legislative, had blocked the
orderly process of public administration. This predicament had to be
avoided in the future; there had to be a true separation of powers. As
for socioeconomic reforms, Carranza believed that the enemies of the
revolution, whom he dubbed "the enemies of the nation," would attack them as coming from a government that was unrepresentative
of the national will. Only a constitutional convention, a popularly

43 Article 127: "The present Constitution may be added to or amended. No amendment or addition shall become part of the Constitution until agreed to by the Congress of the Union by a two-thirds vote of the members present and approved by
a majority of the State legislatures. The Congress shall count the votes of the legislatures and make the declaration that the amendments or additions have been
adopted."
44 For the text of the decree of September 14, 1916, see Bojórquez [pseud.
Bórquez], *Crónica del constituyente*, pp. 95–104.

elected body, could incorporate the desired reforms into fundamental law in a short time and in such a way that "no one would dare oppose them." Doubting that the reforms could be constitutionalized through the amending process provided for in the Constitution of 1857, Carranza maintained that the calling of a constitutional convention was a manifestation of the will of the people as stated in Article 39 of the Constitution of 1857.[45] Finally, he asserted that since there had never been any doubt about the legality of the Constitution of 1857, despite the fact that it had not been drawn up in accordance with the Constitution of 1824, there should not be, for the same reason, any doubt about "the legality of a new constitutional convention and the legitimacy of its work."

In the Constitutionalist camp little opposition to the idea developed, although some of the generals were not so easily convinced. But tradition was on Carranza's side. The "right of revolution" implied the right of the victorious faction to express its ideals in the national constitution. The First Chief believed Mexico needed a new fundamental law. As the leader of his side, he would have his way.

The decree of September 14 completed a cycle of events in Mexican history that made the calling of a constitutional convention inevitable. The Constitution of 1857 had been tried and found wanting, its principles of liberty and equality betrayed, its democratic process emasculated by dictatorship. To achieve national harmony following the War of the Reform and the struggle against the French, the Mexicans had yielded their liberties to Porfirio Díaz, who promised peace—and material progress. After thirty-five years of dictatorship and economic development had perverted justice, benefited the foreigner and the influential few at the expense of the many, and driven the labor force to misery and near starvation, there was a great cry for land and liberty, as the people demanded changes. Between 1910 and 1914, Madero's struggle for democracy, Huerta's counterrevolu-

[45] Article 39: "The national sovereignty is vested essentially and originally in the people. All public power emanates from the people, and is instituted for their benefit. The people have at all times the inalienable right to alter or modify the form of their government."

tion, and the Constitutionalists' triumph over the forces of the usurper were all carried on for political objectives. Social and economic reform received scant attention. But in 1915 the course of the revolution changed, as basic reforms became the means of attracting support for Carranza in his struggle against the Villa-Zapata alliance. When the Constitutionalists finally gained the upper hand, they sought a return to law and order based on a reformed Constitution of 1857, one more in keeping with the realities of the twentieth century. In contrast with the reformers of 1857, who first wrote a constitution and then defended its liberal principles on the battlefield, the early twentieth-century revolutionaries fought first and then wrote a new law of the land, the Constitution of 1917. In a real sense this document legalized the Mexican Revolution.

2. Elections, Delegates, and Preliminary Sessions

As a result of the tremendous upheaval produced by the Constitutionalist Revolution, the work of the delegates to the Convention of 1917 must forge in the life of the Mexican people a new path toward regeneration and progress.

Bruno Moreno (Jalisco)
Fernández Martínez Album

Among the great promises which the Revolution has been fulfilling one by one is that of having united us to give to our beloved people a Constitution adaptable to their present way of life, a Constitution which has been drawn up by true revolutionaries who have understood the needs and wretchedness of the people and who will protect them forever.

Alvaro L. Alcazar (Morelos)
Constituyentes—1917: Pastrana Jaimes Album

WITH APPROXIMATELY 80 PERCENT of Mexico under his control, but acting as though he were the undisputed master of the whole country, Venustiano Carranza boldly convoked a constitutional convention by a decree of September 14, 1916. It stipulated that principal and alternate delegates were to be chosen from each state, territory, and the Federal District on the basis of one for each sixty thousand inhabitants or fraction greater than twenty thousand, according to the census of 1910. Eligibility requirements remained the same as for election to Congress under the Constitution of 1857. Clearly determining the one-party character of the convention was the requirement that those who had served governments or factions hostile to the Constitutionalist cause, i.e., *huertistas*, *villistas*, and *zapatistas*, in a military or civilian capacity were barred from running. Once the convention was installed, the First Chief was to present the draft of a constitution embracing reforms of the preconstitutional period.[1] These would be discussed and approved or modified as necessary. Delegates were not to take up any matters other than those in Carranza's draft and were to finish their work in two months. Once the new constitution was promulgated, general elections would be held, and the First Chief would surrender his authority to a duly elected successor as soon as Congress was installed.

A second and more detailed decree followed on September 19.[2] It specified Sunday, October 22, 1916, as election day. With emphasis on loyalty to the First Chief, candidates were required to have demonstrated "with positive deeds their adherence to the Constitutionalist cause." Each delegate was to take an oath that he would do his duty to work for the re-establishment of constitutional order in accordance with the Plan of Guadalupe and its subsequent modifications. Those elected were to assemble in Querétaro for preliminary sessions on November 20, with the first formal session set for December 1. Freedom of expression would prevail during the sessions, and a simple majority could transact business. The convention was to decide questions of legality and contested elections. If a delegate missed three consecutive sessions without permission, or was absent five times within a fifteen-day period, his alternate was to be seated in his place. Each delegate was to receive sixty pesos per day as well as traveling ex-

---

[1] A committee of eight lawyers, all hand-picked by Carranza, had worked steadily and in semisecrecy from March through August, 1916, to prepare a preliminary draft of proposed reforms to the Constitution of 1857. Three members of this committee were later elected to the convention: Lic. Fernando M. Lizardi (Guanajuato), Lic. Francisco Espinosa (Federal District), and Fernando Moreno (México). This draft probably served as a point of departure for Lic. Luis Manuel Rojas (Jalisco) and Lic. José Natividad Macías, who are generally credited with the authorship of the draft Carranza later presented to the convention. For the text of the preliminary draft, see Libro de actas de la Comisión Legislativa.

[2] Juan de Dios Bojórquez [pseud. Djed Bórquez], *Crónica del constituyente*, p. 105. For the complete text of both decrees, see ibid., pp. 95–110.

penses to and from Querétaro. Although Mexico City would have offered better accommodations, many revolutionaries considered the national capital to be too conservative. Carranza chose Querétaro, the provincial city that had been the provisional capital since February, 1916, because its peace and quiet would be more conducive to the transaction of business. There the delegates would be relatively free from diversions, political intrigues, and pressure groups.

In spite of Palavicini's press campaign of 1915 and talk in Constitutionalist circles of a "new constitution," the decrees of September 14 and 19 took the people by surprise. However, they quickly recovered, as candidates announced from all over Mexico except in the areas controlled by Villa and Zapata. Aspirants either were backed by local political groups, some old and others hastily formed, or ran as independents. No national parties developed. In the Federal District the most successful group was the Opposition Constitutional party which had been established in 1912. Meeting on September 30, it designated eleven candidates, of whom eight were later elected. Seven other political clubs, including the Liberal Nationalist party, met in convention to resolve their differences and choose a slate. Calling themselves the United Political parties, they agreed on four candidates. Before the other eight could be designated, police appeared and dissolved the meeting because, it was alleged, candidates unacceptable to Don Venustiano had been nominated, and disrespectful remarks had been made about the First Chief and his servile association with the Díaz regime.[3] The majority of the delegates elected from the Federal District owed their nomination to the First Chief and were, therefore, indebted to him. In electoral districts outside the capital, interest was generally passive. A sole candidate limited the voters' choice in many. Juan de Dios Bojórquez (Sonora) said he had no opposition as an alternate. Professor Luis G. Monzón (Sonora) declared that he was a "spontaneous candidate." He repeatedly, almost boastfully, told

[3] Charles Parker, Mexico City, to Secretary of State, telegram, October 9, 1916, Records of the Department of State Relating to Internal Affairs of Mexico, 1910–1929, microcopy 274, roll 56, 812.00/19470; Parker, Mexico City, to Secretary of State, telegram, October 10, 1916, 812.00/19487. Carranza served in the senate as alternate senator from Coahuila from 1900 to 1902 and as principal senator almost continuously from 1904 to 1911.

the voters that, if elected, he would "be one more unit in the radical, red and advanced nucleus" that would "have to face the compromisers, the conformists . . . the conservatives and reactionaries who, masked as redeemers," would enter the assembly.[4]

In other districts, however, two or more candidates announced, and the campaign was hard fought. Lic. Francisco Ramírez Villarreal (Colima) won in a spirited contest against an opponent actively supported by the state government.[5] Ing. Adolfo Villaseñor Norman (Zacatecas), proposed as a substitute for his father, Lorenzo Villaseñor, a well known pharmacist who died shortly before the issuance of the decree convoking the convention, won against a single opponent in an animated contest.[6] Professor Jesús Romero Flores (Michoacán) was hard pressed to win against two opponents. The only delegate from Chihuahua, Manuel M. Prieto, had ten opponents but won with 1,747 votes out of 1,864 votes cast. His alternate had fifteen opponents.[7] A real free-for-all developed in one Puebla district, where astounded voters were offered choices among thirty-one candidates for the principal position and forty-four for the alternate![8] In Nuevo León, representatives of two splinter groups of local *carrancistas* met with the interim governor and the chief of military operations in the Laguna (the area around Torreón, Coahuila) to agree on "official" candidates. Telegrams were then sent to the nominees notifying them of their selection, and the ballots were printed and sent to the *presidentes municipales.* There was little or no opposition except in the fourth electoral district, where Col. Ramón Gámez won over an opposition candidate who polled a considerable number of votes.[9]

The elections held on October 22 were free, peaceful, and orderly. Two hundred and sixteen of the nation's 244 electoral districts chose

[4] *El Constituyente*, no. 4 (January 7, 1917).

[5] Francisco Ramírez Villarreal, interview, Cuernavaca, Morelos, May 31, 1965.

[6] Adolfo Villaseñor Norman, interview, Mexico City, March 3, 1965.

[7] Computa general de la votación recogida en el cuarto distrito electoral para la elección de diputados propietario y suplente al Congreso Constituyente que se reunirá en la Ciudad de Querétaro el 20 de noviembre próximo.

[8] Gabriel Ferrer Mendiolea, *Historia del Congreso Constituyente de 1916–1917*, p. 42.

[9] José P. Saldaña, interview, Monterrey, Nuevo León, January 25, 1967; *Diario de los debates del Congreso Constituyente, 1916–1917*, I, 129.

representatives. The Federal District and each state and territory, except Campeche and Quintana Roo, had at least one delegate at Querétaro. The highest representation came from Guanajuato (all 18 districts represented), Jalisco (19 out of 20), Veracruz (17 out of 19), Michoacán (16 out of 17), and Puebla (16 out of 18). Considering the unsettled conditions existing in many of the rural areas and the lack of time in which to campaign, voter interest and turnout were substantial. Two commentators claimed that the elections were held "without enthusiasm and without any interest, within the coldness of the tomb; as if we still found ourselves under the influence of the Porfirian terror, and as bitter proof that we are still far from having awakened ourselves to the democratic way . . ."[10] Another complained that "the *carrancista* mobs, and they alone, organized under the direction of their generals . . . manufactured the lists of representatives and obtained credentials for those in fraudulent elections, availing themselves of the public forces managed by the Secretaries of War, Foreign Affairs, and Gobernación, by the military commanders acting as governors of the states, and the heads of garrisons and military posts."[11] In at least one state, Morelos, this accusation carried a ring of truth. There Gen. Pablo González, fighting a life-and-death struggle against Zapata, permitted "elections" in which the Constitutionalist garrisons in the three most important municipalities chose headquarters officers to compose the state's three-man delegation.[12] State governors, who owed their position to the First Chief, undoubtedly exerted strong influence in selecting candidates partisan to Carranza. From the North came a group dubbed the "apostolate" by the more independently minded delegates. It included Dr. José María Rodríguez (Coahuila) and three from Nuevo León: Manuel Amaya, Dr. Lorenzo Sepúlveda, and Nicéforo Zambrano, all said to be "unconditionally devoted" to Don Venustiano.[13] Customarily the secretary of *gobernación*, Lic. Jesús Acuña, would have played a leading role in seeing that delegates faith-

[10] L. Melgarejo Randolf and J. Fernández Rojas, *El Congreso Constituyente de 1916 y 1917*, p. 136.
[11] Jorge Vera Estañol, *Carranza and His Bolshevik Regime*, pp. 21–22.
[12] John Womack, Jr., *Zapata and the Mexican Revolution*, p. 270.
[13] Bojórquez [pseud. Bórquez], *Crónica del constituyente*, p. 176.

ful to the First Chief and his views were chosen and elected. Acuña, however, involved in a developing power struggle between Carranza and his secretary of war, Obregón, actually worked against some candidates who were close to the First Chief, an error of judgment which resulted in his dismissal on November 29, two days before the inaugural session.[14] Lic. Andrés Molina Enríquez, who later served as adviser to the framers of Article 27, stated with justification that "if the same elections did not represent, as a whole, a triumph of effective suffrage, they represented the upset caused by the Revolution."[15] If there were qualms about whether the delegates were truly representative of the Mexico of 1916, ensuing deliberations in the convention would dispel these fears. Everything considered, it is doubtful that a more representative group could have assembled in Querétaro.

Carranza expected the Constitutional Convention, of which he was the spiritual father, to be a harmonious one-party gathering. After polite discussion, and perhaps minor modification, he anticipated ready approval of the proposed reforms to the Constitution of 1857 that he would present on December 1. This is evident from the fact that he allowed a period of only two months for the deliberations, a far cry from the conventions that had drawn up the constitutions of 1824 and 1857, each of which was in session for eleven months.[16]

---

[14] Félix F. Palavicini, *Historia de la Constitución de 1917*, I, 57–59; *Memoria de la Secretaría de Gobernación correspondiente al período revolucionario comprendido entre el 19 de febrero de 1913 y el 30 de noviembre de 1916*, pp. 389–392. Primarily a justification of the Constitutionalist movement, this is a collection of documents, revolutionary plans, diplomatic notes, and decrees issued during the preconstitutional period. Although prepared especially for the delegates, it was never distributed among them and would have been of little value if it had been.

[15] Andrés Molina Enríquez, *Esbozo de la historia de los primeros diez años de la revolución agraria de México*, V, 168.

[16] The *Diario de los debates* contains frequent references to the strain this limitation imposed on the delegates. By January 13 they were almost desperate. In secret session Gen. Salvador González Torres (Oaxaca) proposed that an extension be requested from Carranza. Considerable discussion followed. Supporters of the First Chief's draft naturally opposed any prolonging of the convention. In the end it was decided that a delegation composed of members of the two committees studying the Carranza draft should call on the First Chief to ask for the extension. On January 14 General Múgica reported on this meeting but asked that the press make no comment on the matter. Since the convention did not continue into February, it is

However, the Convention of 1916–1917 would prove to be neither a mere formality nor a harmonious gathering. Rather, it reflected the spirit of the times: conflict, unrest, and demand for social, economic, and political reform. Zapata was unconquered in Morelos. Villa, who had just recaptured Torreón, was once more on the warpath in the North. With the country emerging from the throes of economic chaos, strife, and famine, the delegates, uncertain of what was expected of them, began to assemble in Querétaro to write a new fundamental law.

For the next two months this picturesque colonial city would be their home. The presence of numerous government offices made lodging difficult to obtain. Delegates unable to find a room in a hotel, *pensión*, or with friends had to board in a private residence, as did Bojórquez. To him life in Querétaro during the sessions was boring, like that of the "cloister." The only "refuge" most of the delegates had, according to this young Sonoran, was El Puerto de Mazatlán (The Port of Mazatlán), a bar across from the convention hall.[17] Adolfo Villaseñor Norman complained that behind his residence was a house of women of the *vida alegre* where delegates of military rank were accustomed to go after the sessions. He found that music from the house, played by bands of the various military detachments in Querétaro, made sleeping difficult.[18]

In reality the delegates, under great pressure to finish their work before February 1, 1917, would have little time for other matters. Following inauguration of the convention on December 1, there would be sixty-six regular sessions before the permanent session of January 29–31. In general a single daily session was held from December 2 through January 13, although on several days there were both morning and afternoon sessions. Four days of inactivity followed the reading of Carranza's draft proposals on December 6. After the traumatic debate and vote on Article 3 (December 16) the delegates took a day of rest. Christmas was a work day, but there was a recess

---

assumed that Carranza's reply was negative (Congreso Constituyente, *Actas secretas, 1916–1917*, pp. 9–11).

[17] Bojórquez [pseud. Bórquez], *Crónica del constituyente*, p. 680.
[18] Villaseñor Norman, interview.

from December 30 through January 1. By January 8 it was apparent that only through night sessions could the work be finished on time. These commenced January 14. From then through the twenty-ninth there were both afternoon and evening sessions, the latter often lasting until the early morning hours. Approximately two-thirds of the delegates attended regularly.

Nevertheless, in spite of such an intensive schedule, the record of seventeen secret sessions reveals the time lost in discussing inconsequential matters. On December 22 there was much debate on whether to vote funds for the poor children of Querétaro, as proposed by Manuel Cepeda Medrano (Coahuila), or to alleviate the plight of the unemployed workers of Guanajuato as proposed by Dr. Jesús López Lira of that state. In the end no action was taken.[19] On January 4, four delegates sympathetic to labor proposed that a delegation call on the First Chief to obtain the freedom of certain workers held in the penitentiary of the Federal District since July 31, 1916. Again no action was taken.[20] Although no one objected to paying the government of the Federal District sixty pesos for the cost of a wreath to be placed in the name of the convention on the grave of the patriot, Morelos, on December 22, there was much discussion as to whether a delegation should be sent to Veracruz to place a wreath on the grave of Gen. Jesús Carranza on January 11. Carranza, a brother of the First Chief, had been captured during action against anti-Constitutionalists in Oaxaca in 1915 and summarily executed. Professor Alfonso Herrera (Federal District) even asked the suspension of sessions on that day. Fortunately, wiser counsel prevailed, and it was decided to let representatives in Veracruz lay the wreath.[21] Some delegates would even find time to edit and publish two small newspapers, which provided opportunities for the more effervescent to express in writing their opinions on issues and personalities of the convention. Rafael Vega Sánchez (Hidalgo), poet and song writer, and Gen. Heriberto Jara (Veracruz) edited *El Constituyente*, which expressed the radical point of view. Ten numbers appeared from December 20 to January 31.

19 Congreso Constituyente, Actas secretas, pp. 2–3.
20 Ibid., pp. 5–6.
21 Ibid., pp. 6–7.

The other, *El Zancudo*, edited by Col. Pedro A. Chapa (Tamaulipas) and Dr. Salvador R. Guzmán (Puebla), expressed a more moderate line. With fine irony it twitted the rabid anticlericals of the convention and their extremist opinions.[22]

Who were the men who suddenly and almost without warning found themselves entrusted with the responsibility of writing the third basic constitution since independence? The reforms that they wrote into Mexican constitutional law and the controversy attending implementation of these reforms have, through the years, overshadowed the framers themselves. Fifty-five years later Mexicans tend to revere the authors of the Constitution of 1857 more than they do those of the present constitution. This is evident from the postage stamps, schools, statues, busts, parks, etc., that bear the names of the framers of the former rather than the latter. Only recently have the authors of the 1917 document begun to receive recognition.

To understand what happened at Querétaro is to know the delegates, their backgrounds and idiosyncrasies, and what they understood the revolution to mean. Of the 220 delegates, including principals and alternates, Romero Flores breaks down the composition as follows: 62 lawyers, 22 military officers of senior rank, 19 farmers, 18 teachers, 16 engineers, 16 physicians, 14 journalists, 7 accountants, 5 labor leaders, 4 miners, 3 railroad workers, 2 pharmacists, 1 actor, and 31 from other occupations, including artisans, merchants, and employees.[23] At least 30 were not natives of the states they represented, further evidence of the upheaval brought on by the revolution. While some were members of masonic orders, more belonged to mutualist societies. A few were staunch Catholics; others were only nominally so. More had lost the faith and were only too ready to chastise the Church for its alleged sins of omission and commission. By race they were *criollos*, mestizos, and Indians. At least one, Juan Manuel Giffard (México), was a mulatto. Elected from the same state was light-hearted Rubén Martí, nephew of the great Cuban revolutionary. He annoyed many delegates with his flippancy and his habit of repeatedly asking for a point of order. Many would have agreed with

[22] Palavicini, *Historia de la Constitución de 1917*, II, 626.
[23] Jesús Romero Flores, *La Revolución como nosotros la vimos*, p. 153.

him when he said, "I have turned out to be more of an ass than my father would have wanted me to be."[24] On one occasion he irritated General Múgica, who accused Martí of having "mounted this rostrum to profane it and to profane his family name."[25] So strong was the opposition of the nationalistic Mexicans that Martí, born in Cuba but a Mexican citizen since 1910, was almost denied a seat.

Gen. Esteban B. Calderón (Jalisco) had been one of the leaders of the strike against the Cananea Consolidated Copper Company in 1906. For his efforts he had suffered confinement in the dungeons of San Juan de Ulúa. As a former collaborator of the Flores Magón brothers in the MLP, Jara had worked for the overthrow of the Díaz regime since 1902. He pointed with pride to the fact that he had been with "the Revolution and with the Chief in hours of trial, not like others who came when the magnificent Mother Treasury opened its arms!"[26] This blast was directed against the civilian coterie of Don Venustiano, especially those who had only recently jumped on the Constitutionalist bandwagon.

Young Luis Fernández Martínez innocently admitted, "I come from the sticks." No one doubted him. In fact, the great majority of the delegates were from the rural areas, provincial in their outlook. Lic. Luis Espinosa (Oaxaca), a native of Chiapas, quit his job as clerk in a store in San Cristóbal de las Casas at the age of fifteen to go to Mexico City. Desperately poor, he sold his few belongings to village friends for fifty pesos in order to obtain funds and borrowed a horse to ride to Arriaga, Chiapas, from whence he made his way to the

---

24 Album of Lic. Luis Fernández Martínez, partially published in *El Nacional*, February 5, 1937 (hereafter cited as Fernández Martínez Album).

25 *El Constituyente*, no. 4 (January 7, 1917). An enigmatic person, he once expressed this opinion: "Blessed be the day when all the bars, churches and gambling houses can be kept open day and night because no one enters and the doors of the schools kept closed because everyone is anxious to push them in so as to drink from the cradle of science the medicine that cures all ailments and kills all hatreds: philosophy" (Constituyentes—1917: Album de David Pastrana Jaimes [hereafter cited as Pastrana Jaimes Album]). On another occasion he reasoned that "the citizen who frees 100 countrymen from ignorance has done more for his native land than the general who has won a great battle" (Album del Congreso Constituyente de 1917, Querétaro, JPR [hereafter cited as Ruiz Album]).

26 *El Constituyente*, no. 2 (December 26, 1916).

capital. There he worked and studied law. In 1913 he attacked Huerta in newspaper articles. Forced to flee to the hills, pursued by *rurales*, he engaged in guerrilla activities until Carranza entered Mexico City in 1914. He then went to the capital to join the First Chief's forces.

Gilberto M. Navarro (Guanajuato) would soon be dubbed El Buen Campesino by his fellow delegates because he proudly admitted being the son and grandson of *campesinos*. He and his brothers had had the courage to claim the assassinated President Madero's body when no one else had dared to do so. Gerzayn Ugarte (Federal District) was the private secretary of Don Venustiano, a position which raised charges of conflict of interest. Héctor Victoria (Yucatán) had worked as a newspaperman. Referring to himself as a "revolutionary by atavism," he crowed that his "ancestors, the Mayas, were the ones incinerated during the Inquisition."[27] Dionisio Zavala (San Luis Potosí), a miner, had been commissioned by Carranza to organize workers in the North, especially the miners. To win their support he repeatedly stressed the social objectives of the Constitutionalist cause. Because he knew how to handle dynamite, he had also seen action by blowing up railroad bridges. López Lira was a strong believer in secular education. He also had an eye for the women, remarking once: "It seems incredible, gentlemen, but although we come from Guanajuato, we have become admirers of the plumpness of the women of Querétaro."[28] Col. José Alvarez y Alvarez (Michoacán), one of the firebrands of the convention, had a burning desire to cleanse the Mexican political, economic, and social structure once and for all. He said, with humor yet conviction: "The law of Moses was written on two tablets of rock and the Constitution of Mexico must be written on two bars of soap."[29]

During applause Cepeda Medrano showed his enthusiasm by shouting "Viva Coahuila" and pronouncing the name of his native state as its *campesinos* did: Kwa-whee-la. Professor Manuel Dávalos Ornelas (Jalisco), no longer in the classroom, applauded by stamping his feet, to the annoyance of those seated near him. Lic.

---

[27] Pastrana Jaimes Album.
[28] *El Constituyente*, no. 4 (January 7, 1917).
[29] Ibid., no. 9 (January 25, 1917).

David Pastrana Jaimes (Puebla) always had a toothpick in his mouth, even when speaking from the rostrum. At least two delegates, Jorge E. von Versen (Coahuila) and Gen. Emiliano Nafarrate (Tamaulipas), carried pistols in holsters. The latter, a genial son of Sinaloa, more courageous than cultured, would speak without rhyme or reason. Certainly no delegate was the butt of more laughter and snickering than he.

So much for the background and idiosyncrasies of a sampling of the delegates. Most were young men, in their thirties and forties. Bojórquez, under the legal age limit of twenty-five, was seated anyway. Of 138 delegates whose ages are known, 29 were in their twenties, 62 were in their thirties, 31 were in their forties, 14 were in their fifties, and 2 were in their sixties. They were generally lacking in governmental experience. Twenty-three had served in the last Congress, the twenty-sixth, and others had received administrative experience in provisional state governments or in Carranza's preconstitutional regime. Representatives of a cross section of Mexican society of the times, nearly all were products of the revolution, swept to the fore by its cataclysmic process.

With the exception of the lawyers, the heterogeneous group was almost completely unprepared for the great responsibility of drafting a new constitution. As far as Carranza was concerned, special preparation was unnecessary for a group of partisans whom he expected to ratify his draft of proposals with a minimum of debate. He did provide for the convention, "as an aid in preparing its work," a revised edition of Francisco Zarco's *Historia del Congreso Extraordinario de 1856 y 1857*, which omitted the views of Ponciano Arriaga, one of the more reform-minded delegates to that gathering, on the agrarian problem. Hoping to avoid radical solutions to controversial issues, Don Venustiano and his advisers sought a simple revision of the Constitution of 1857.[30]

While the delegates were most familiar with Mexican history, especially contemporary, discussions during the sessions indicate that they were also acquainted with the history of Rome, Christianity, and the

[30] Daniel Cosío Villegas, "The Mexican Revolution, Then and Now," in *Is the Mexican Revolution Dead?* ed. Stanley R. Ross, p. 118.

French Revolution and its principal figures. They referred to or quoted from the French novelists Victor Hugo, Tristan Bernard, and Emile Zola. The lawyers, of course, were well versed in Roman law, and several showed they had read Rousseau's *Social Contract*, Montesquieu's *Spirit of the Laws*, and Herbert Spencer's books. Lic. Hilario Medina (Guanajuato) was familiar with the works of the leading sociologists of the later nineteenth century. José Natividad Macías had read Karl Marx. The works of the Russian revolutionary, anarchist, and author, Peter Kropotkin, were also known. Not surprisingly, a number of delegates were familiar with American political history and the American constitution. Among them were Macías, Lic. Rafael Martínez de Escobar (Tabasco), Monzón, Lic. Paulino Machorro y Narváez (Jalisco), Lic. Zeferino Fajardo (Tamaulipas), and Palavicini. Nevertheless, most of the delegates did not have the necessary background or training. During the acrimonious debates on Article 3, Lic. Luis Manuel Rojas, the convention's presiding officer, lamented that "a good part of this assembly does not have sufficient juridical preparation . . . the majority . . . has not known or has not sufficiently understood what the section on individual rights [*garantías*] means."[31] Lic. Enrique Colunga (Guanajuato) complained that the majority of the convention members were *ignorantes*.[32] To the young radicals, overwhelmed with the frightful reality of contemporary Mexico, preparation was really unnecessary. As Bojórquez put it during the afternoon session of January 16, "I can say, and many of my fellow delegates will agree with me, that not only do we lack that preparation in economics but neither do we have it in constitutional law nor in any of the other fields of law; therefore . . . we decide these highly important matters after hearing the pros and cons because when we vote, it is our revolutionary instinct that guides us rather than our understanding."[33] Many Mexicans better qualified by training and experience in government or public administration were barred because they had been in different political camps.

The first meeting, held on November 20 in the Academy of Fine

---

[31] *Diario de los debates*, I, 652.
[32] Ibid., II, 73.
[33] Ibid., p. 507.

Arts, failed to produce a quorum. The next morning at 10:30 the first official preliminary session with an attendance of 140 persons chose Antonio Aguilar (México) provisional president because his name was first alphabetically. Before he could organize a permanent steering committee, a delegation of Queretaran residents, mostly textile workers accompanied by their families, interrupted the meeting to wish the convention success in its work. Their spokesman hailed the revolution for its goal of redeeming the native race, saying it had been received by all with "open arms, as a blessing from heaven, by all the unfortunate, by all those who carry on their foreheads the shame of not having enough to live like human beings and who must dwell in filthy hovels, all because of the greed of the evil Mexican capitalists."[34] A representative of the Liberal party of Querétaro followed. Praising Madero and the movement that he had begun, he railed against the "hydra of the priest, the *latifundista*, the *cacique*, and militarism" that had oppressed and exploited the people and "entombed the nation." In the days ahead, the delegates would heed these voices of protest, would act decisively to free Mexico from forces considered pernicious to the national welfare.

The task of organizing the convention, interrupted by the Queretarans, was quickly resumed. A provisional president, two vice-presidents, and four secretaries were elected by secret ballot. Although he had few qualifications to recommend him other than that of being a personal friend of Don Venustiano, the assembly chose affable Manuel Amaya, rancher and smoker of corn-shuck cigarettes, over General Calderón by a vote of 50 to 49. Amid applause the newly elected officers took their places, and the convention turned to the work of approving credentials. After some discussion it was decided that there should be an eighteen-member committee divided into two groups, one of three members to review the credentials of the other fifteen, who were in turn to review those of all the other delegates. Following the selection by secret ballot of these two committees, the president adjourned the session until November 25 to await the recommendations.

Ten preliminary sessions held from November 25–30 determined

[34] *Diario de los debates*, I, 29.

the character of the convention and foretold the conflicts that would lie ahead. Determination of eligibility for membership, a process requiring the investigation of revolutionary backgrounds, provoked heated debates and shattered the harmony of what many expected to be a rubber-stamp convention. Since the initiation of the Constitutionalist movement, differences of opinion had existed among the followers of the First Chief. Except for Villa's defection, these were not serious. In 1915 and 1916, however, a breach had developed between the civilian advisers of Carranza in his preconstitutional government and the military who had started the armed movement in 1913. Discussion of the credentials of the *renovadores* dramatically emphasized the differences within the convention.[35]

The *renovadores*, a bloc of the Twenty-sixth Congress, which served from September 2, 1912, until its dissolution by Huerta on October 10, 1913, had initiated various measures of socioeconomic reform and supported President Madero. Following his assassination, some had resigned their seats; others had remained in Congress and suffered imprisonment when it was dissolved. Upon their release the latter had joined the Constitutionalists, some becoming influential advisers to the First Chief and prominent in his administration. Those who had voted to accept the resignations of Madero and Pino Suárez and had not resigned their seats following the assassinations were looked upon with contempt by the Constitutionalist military. *Renovadores* elected as delegates to the convention were Rafael Nieto, Rafael Curiel, and Samuel M. de los Santos (San Luis Potosí); Enrique O'Farrill, Guillermo Ordorica, and José J. Reynoso (México); Marcelino Dávalos, Luis Manuel Rojas, and Carlos Villaseñor (Jalisco); José Macías and Manuel G. Aranda (Guanajuato); Félix Palavicini and Gerzayn Ugarte (Federal District); Carlos M. Ezquerro and Pedro Zavala (Sinaloa); Alfonso Cabrera and Luis T. Navarro (Puebla); Alfonso Cravioto (Hidalgo); José Silva Herrera (Michoacán); Crisóforo Rivera Cabrera (Oaxaca); Juan N. Frías (Querétaro); and Antonio Ancona Albertos (Yucatán). Heriberto Jara was a member of the Twenty-sixth Congress but not a *renovador*.

Determined to thwart any attempt to deny them their seats, Carran-

[35] Political alignments in the convention are summarized in chapter 7.

za telegraphed the convention on November 25 that he had specifically ordered the *renovadores* to remain in Congress, organize opposition to Huerta, and, if possible, force him to dissolve the body. When this had happened, some had openly offered their services to the Constitutionalists and, said Carranza, had served him faithfully.[36] Although the First Chief was trying to aid some of his close supporters, to many his telegram smacked of intervention and the sacrifice of a principle.

Following the reading of the controversial telegram, Doctor Rodríguez, chairman of the nominating subcommittee of the Committee on the Review of Credentials, presented a list of fifteen names for approval for membership on this committee, four of whom were *renovadores*: Ordorica, Rivera Cabrera, Cravioto, and Ancona Albertos. This raised a storm of protest; and, as the delegates lined up to speak for and against the list, the fight to seat the controversial group began.

Hot-blooded Martínez de Escobar led the attack. In a hard-hitting speech he condemned the *renovadores* for accepting the resignations of Madero and Pino Suárez and voting funds for Huerta to put down the now triumphant revolution. Believing that the group should be judged individually as well as collectively, he impugned them all but singled out Rojas as being much more acceptable than Palavicini, Macías, and Cravioto, whom he lumped together as not being "revolutionaries in ideas, . . . in sentiments . . . [nor] in action."[37]

In reply, Cravioto, nearly thirty-three, an intellectual, poet, journalist, and gifted orator, endowed with an extraordinary memory, spoke logically and convincingly. Prematurely deaf, he used a crude hearing aid, which became the butt of numerous jokes during the convention. Nevertheless, he commanded attention and respect. The *renovadores*, he said, had voted to accept the resignations of Madero and

[36] *Diario de los debates*, I, 49.

[37] Ibid., p. 59. In late January, 1917, Martínez de Escobar was still excoriating the *renovadores*, as seen in the following sentiments he expressed in the album of his fellow delegate, Fernández Martínez: "Jacobinism, when it is only a morbid product of epileptic and anarchic popular movements, provokes the reaction toward obscurantism and backwardness . . . but when it dwells in the mind as a vigorous and conscious ideal, as it is with the jacobins of the left wing of the Congress of 1916–1917, it is a battering ram which terrorizes the reactionaries and backward ones, known as '*renovadores*,' and then ennobles the human spirit and dignifies the national conscience" (Fernández Martínez Album).

Pino Suárez at the request of the Madero family. Had they not done so, the lives of both would have been endangered. At that time the assassinations could not have been foreseen. It was not treachery to the revolution, he argued, to have accepted the resignations which guaranteed their safe departures from Mexico. Alive and free, Madero would then have been able to lead a vindicating revolution to regain the presidency. Furthermore, Cravioto reasoned, a vote to accept the executives' resignations signified an attempt to avoid foreign intervention and war with the United States, both of which would have been likely, had the prevailing anarchy of Madero's last days in office continued. Reminding the assembly that he had served six months in prison for attacking the seventh re-election of President Díaz, he asked it to decide on bases of justice and morality who among the *renovadores* should or should not be seated. In conclusion, Cravioto made a fervent appeal for harmony, asking the delegates to work together as good Mexicans to the "glory of freedom."[38] Prolonged applause followed.

Answering Cravioto, General Múgica made it clear he believed that all *renovadores* should not be judged alike. Some, he said, had made significant contributions to the revolutionary cause. Identifying Palavicini and Macías as the most offensive ones, he asked the delegates to approve credentials with an open mind. They should not be influenced by the First Chief's telegram, for above it stood "our principles" and the Plan of Guadalupe. In the end, the seating of three of the *renovadores* (Ordorica, Cravioto, and Ancona Albertos) on the Committee of the Review of Credentials was approved by a vote of 148 to 3, an indication of light opposition. The fourth, Rivera Cabrera, had already removed any stigma from his name by proving that he had left Congress to join the campaign against Huerta.

In a report submitted on the afternoon of November 28, the committee impugned Palavicini's right to be seated on the grounds of

---

[38] *Diario de los debates,* I, 67. Cravioto expressed his concept of freedom in practical terms: "Man's freedom is in direct proportion to his cultural and economic status. For that reason we have come asking for land and schools for our people" (Album de Autógrafos y Retratos de los Constituyentes de 1917, coleccionado en Querétaro por José Alvarez y Alvarez, Constituyente Michoacano [hereafter cited as Alvarez Album]).

voting irregularities in his electoral district. Fernando M. Lizardi, who had served as chairman of the committee which canvassed the votes, promptly refuted the charges. Rising to the opportunity, Martínez de Escobar, whose credentials had been approved only that morning, again assailed Palavicini, his fellow *tabasqueño* but bitter enemy, as a slave of Porfirio Díaz and as one who had served Huerta for pay. He denied Palavicini's revolutionary spirit, accusing him of having abandoned Madero and of having enriched himself while serving as Carranza's secretary of public instruction. Urging the delegates to take political rather than legal criteria into account in evaluating credentials, Martínez de Escobar received applause when he asked the assembly to refuse to seat "impostors like señor Palavicini."[39]

For the rest of the afternoon and until adjournment at 10:50 P.M., Palavicini defended the legality of his credentials, his revolutionary background, and his right to a seat in the convention.[40] Thirty-six years old, of aquiline features and nervous temperament, he had received his title of *ingeniero* from the Juárez Institute of San Juan Bautista (now Villahermosa), Tabasco, in 1901. After working as a surveyor, he went to Mexico City in 1903 and taught manual arts in a school attached to the Normal School. There he revealed an aptitude for teaching, because of which the Ministry of Education sent him to Paris in 1906 on a government scholarship to study the organization and management of vocational schools. Returning to Mexico the following year, Palavicini was soon caught up in the quickening pace of political life. He founded a small newspaper and launched an attack on the *científicos*. This led to his election as one of the secretaries of the Centro Antirreeleccionista, a political club founded in Mexico City in May, 1909, to impress on Mexicans the need to practice democracy. The following month he undertook a successful speaking tour through four states with Madero, during which the speakers

[39] *Diario de los debates*, I, 214.
[40] In the Fernández Martínez Album he wrote: "In Mexico it is not men of talent who triumph but those who work; this is a country of laziness and sleep; those who work and stay awake are the ones who will dominate." For biographic data on Palavicini, See Félix F. Palavicini, *Mi vida revolucionaria*; *La Herencia del Constituyente*, no. 6 (February 5, 1964); and Marcos E. Becerra, *Palavicini: Desde allá abajo*.

stressed the need for political liberty. On his return to Mexico City in July, he became editor of *El Antirreeleccionista*, a newspaper openly critical of Díaz and the dictatorship, which the government soon suppressed. After Madero's election in 1911, Palavicini became director of the Industrial School for Orphans in Mexico City. In 1912 he was elected to the Twenty-sixth Congress from Tabasco and served until its dissolution by Huerta in October, 1913, after which he was imprisoned and not released until the following April. Until Huerta's forced exile in July, 1914, Palavicini remained in hiding. The following month he joined the Carranza administration as *oficial mayor* of the Ministry of Public Instruction and Fine Arts, becoming subsecretary and later secretary. In early 1915, as has been seen, he undertook the newspaper campaign to persuade the people of the need for a new constitution. Shortly before the Querétaro Convention, Palavicini founded *El Universal*, a Mexico City newspaper, which, during the convention's period of sessions, would see that his speeches and role in the assembly did not go unnoticed by the reading public.

Realizing that he was on trial before the assembled delegates, Palavicini ably defended himself. First, he ridiculed Martínez de Escobar as one who had joined the revolution "at the moment of triumph," as a "fifi," a friend of Jorge Huerta, son of the usurper, and as a tool of Jesús Acuña, former secretary of foreign affairs in Carranza's cabinet.[41] Furthermore, Palavicini stated, when Gen. Cándido Aguilar (Veracruz) took over the same ministry, he had to dismiss Martínez de Escobar for incompetence—a charge promptly confirmed by the general. Then Palavicini defended his own revolutionary activities. Recalling that he had attacked the Díaz dictatorship, had campaigned with Madero and suffered persecution and imprisonment as a consequence, and had never accepted the martyr's resignation, he avowed that he had strongly opposed Huerta in the Twenty-sixth Congress. If he was not a revolutionary, he said, it was strange that Carranza had accepted his services not for "one week, two weeks, one month, or two months, but for two years." Declaring that if the

[41] Although Acuña was secretary of *gobernación* from June 21, 1915, until November 29, 1916, Carranza had also placed him in charge of foreign affairs on June 22, 1915, and he served in this position until March 16, 1916.

delegates thought him unworthy of the work that lay ahead of them, they should reject him in order to maintain the honor of the assembly, he concluded by saying: "The charges that were made against the *renovadores* have been readily disproved. If Madero answered for my past during the *porfirismo*, Carranza has not only passed sentence on my political past, but can certify to my present status as well (Vigorous applause and *vivas*)."[42] So strong was the power of his oratory and the logic of his defense that Palavicini obtained his seat by a vote of 142 to 6; Martínez de Escobar, who had earlier left the salon in a huff, did not return for the voting. According to one delegate, however, the assembly was against Don Félix but seated him anyway because the delegates were exhausted from the debates and because of "threats" made by Cándido Aguilar of what might happen if they did not get down to business soon. He also admitted that it would have been unjust to have denied Palavicini a seat, since the idea of the convention was partly his own.[43]

Last of the *renovadores* to come under attack was José Natividad Macías (Guanajuato), fifty-nine, a well-known lawyer and coauthor of the proposed reforms to the Constitution of 1857 which Don Venustiano would submit to the convention on December 1. After graduating from the law school in Guanajuato in 1883, he had practiced in the state capital, served in the local legislature, and then gone to Mexico City, where he established a reputable practice. A contemporary of Carranza, he had been a friend of the First Chief since the time they had served together in the Porfirian Congress.[44] Elected to the Twenty-sixth Congress in 1912, Macías had suffered imprisonment following Huerta's dissolution of the body. When Carranza entered Mexico City in July, 1914, he appointed Macías director of the National School of Jurisprudence, a position he was forced to give up a few months later when the Constitutionalists retreated to Veracruz. There he played a prominent role as a member of the important Social Legislation Section of the Ministry of Public Instruction, which

---

[42] *Diario de los debates*, I, 232.

[43] Bojórquez [pseud. Bórquez], *Crónica del constituyente*, p. 121.

[44] Scoffed José Alvarez y Alvarez, "José de Natividad Macías was the representative in Congress for seventeen years from Apatzingán, Michoacán, a district he does not even know" (*El Constituyente*, no. 2 [December 26, 1916]).

drafted decrees and regulations of the preconstitutional period. Well-to-do, spectacled, mustachioed, usually dressed in an outmoded Prince Albert coat, and dubbed "Monseñor" by the anticlericals because he was supposedly a practicing Catholic, Macías had one of the best legal minds of the convention.[45] He was also one of its longest-winded speakers. While his credentials were in order, he was assailed for having been a *renovador* and for having accused President Madero of the theft of some land planted in guayule, a plant which yields a rubbery substance of commercial value. Although Macías was absent on the morning of November 30 because of illness, Cravioto and Palavicini ably defended the committee report recommending approval of his credentials. Not only did they refute charges against him, but they testified to his service to the Constitutionalist cause. Cravioto pointed out that Macías was really an exceptional person, "an honorable *porfirista* who changed into a *maderista* no less honorable."[46] Even the impetuous Martínez de Escobar was drawn into the debate, although he renewed his attack on Palavicini, accusing him of responsibility for ministerial crises when Carranza and his government were bottled up in Veracruz and of being a "vulgar intriguer."[47] He hinted that General Aguilar, former secretary of foreign affairs, was a party to Palavicini's intrigues. This drew from the general the retort that General Obregón and Jesús Acuña were really Palavicini's enemies, that the former had told him "that Palavicini is giving a lot of trouble; but you will see, he will not get to the convention."[48] Appealing to the delegates' sense of unity, Aguilar asked them to put aside the "petty passions" of Obregón and Acuña and work patriotically toward

[45] Macías expressed his political philosophy in these terms: "In order to establish democratic institutions in Mexico, it is necessary for her children to practice them; liberty depends on the will of the people to be free" (Alvarez Album). Macías also had a sense of humor. During a debate, Col. Antonio de la Barrera (Puebla) contemptuously referred to Macías as a *zapatero*. Later Macías said from the floor, "Ever since the day Señor de la Barrera told me I was a shoemaker, I am no longer a lawyer; I am a shoemaker" (*El Constituyente*, no. 4 [January 7, 1917]). For biographic data on Macías, see *La Herencia del Constituyente*, no. 2 (October 5, 1963), and no. 14 (October 5, 1964).
[46] *Diario de los debates*, I, 336.
[47] Ibid., p. 339.
[48] Ibid., p. 341.

writing the constitution. Confusion and disorder followed, as various speakers rushed to the platform, one saying to Martínez de Escobar, "I want to shut you up forever." As the president rang the bell for order, the secretary called for a vote on Macías, who had been almost forgotten in the commotion. By a standing vote, he was seated. The issue of the *renovadores*, however, was far from settled. They had come under strong attack for solely political reasons. Opposition to them, especially to the more prominent members of the group, would continue until the end of the convention.

The racial and nationalistic bent of the Mexican Revolution clearly revealed itself in the contest between rival candidates from the ninth district of Puebla. *Zapatistas* had been in control of that part of the state and had only recently been expelled. Due to the confused situation at the time of the election, two delegates came to the convention bearing credentials: Maj. Federico Jiménez O'Farrill, a creole of Spanish blood, and Col. Epigmenio A. Martínez, of pure Indian blood. Each candidate spoke several times in his own behalf, seeking to defend the legality of his election. Colonel Martínez appealed to the sympathies of the delegates, saying: "Here you have the Indian blood . . . which is unafraid in the face of danger . . . which . . . is always fighting for one ideal which is justice. I am not going to hurl insults at my opponent because he is a more intelligent person, because I recognize this . . . but I ought to warn you that the Mexican Indian, the native Indian who possesses all the virtues of the oriental race . . . is stamped on me and such an imprint never lies."[49] With the matter sufficiently discussed, the assembly approved the credentials of Martínez, the Indian, by a vote of 129 to 15, whereupon O'Farrill went to the front of the chamber and, congratulating his opponent, shook hands with him. This prompted Múgica to exclaim that the show of good will proved that the Mexican people could govern themselves. If this feeling of euphoria was exaggerated, the vote clearly indicated what might be expected from the convention. To the delegates, the pure-blooded creole was symbolic of foreign oppression. The Indian symbolized the indigenous, the oppressed masses. At least they would receive sympathetic consideration.

49 Ibid., p. 284.

Discussion of credentials continued through the afternoon of the last day of the preliminary sessions, November 30, with all aware of the pending election of permanent officers before adjournment. Although the credentials of only 180 delegates had been approved, leaving some 50 yet to be discussed, it became increasingly clear as the evening wore on that further discussion would be impossible, that the restless delegates would break the quorum. Consequently, Amaya proposed immediate election of officers. The delegates approved and were granted a ten-minute recess for the selection of candidates.

Lic. Manuel Aguirre Berlanga (Coahuila) had been favored for election as permanent president, but at the last minute his appointment by Don Venustiano as secretary of *gobernación* had forced his withdrawal. Manuel Amaya, presiding officer during the preliminary sessions, received little or no consideration for this all-important position. Undiplomatic and not versed in parliamentary procedure, he had offended some of the delegates during the preliminary sessions by telling them to "shut up" or "sit down." Nor had he won any friends by enforcing the no-smoking rule.[50] On the morning of November 29, Don Manuel had even been attacked as an enemy of the revolution. Shrugging off this charge with the only words that brought him any repute during the convention, "agua pasada no mueve molino" (water past the mill no longer turns it), he asserted that after the battle of Tierra Blanca, Chihuahua, against the *huertistas*, when ammunition was running low, he had mortgaged his properties for U.S. $25,000 to buy 300,000 cartridges for the *carrancistas*. Although these statements won the sympathy of the delegates, they never considered Amaya for the important position of permanent president. This office required greater talents.

By secret ballot, seven permanent officers were elected: president, Lic. Luis Manuel Rojas, forty-six, a journalist, a *renovador* who voted

---

[50] Amaya was adamant on this point, even though an inveterate smoker himself. Nor would he allow the delegates to leave for a smoke, for fear of breaking the quorum. On one occasion, after two hours of continuous debate, he left the hall for a few moments. The delegates thought he had gone out for a few quick puffs, but Amaya, on returning, promptly announced from the presiding officer's chair, "No salgo para fumar, sino para mear [I did not go out to smoke but to urinate]" (Palavicini, *Historia de la Constitución de 1917*, II, 619).

against accepting the resignations of Madero and Pino Suárez, former director of the National Library, coauthor with Macías of Carranza's constitutional draft, and a leading mason; first vice-president, Cándido Aguilar, thirty-seven, participant in the Madero uprising against Díaz in 1910 (which almost cost him his life), Constitutionalist general, former interim governor of Veracruz, former secretary of foreign affairs in Carranza's cabinet, and soon to marry the First Chief's daughter, Virginia; second vice-president, Gen. Salvador González Torres, native of Michoacán and former Madero supporter; first secretary, Fernando Lizardi, thirty-three, lawyer and intellectual, member of the Legislative Commission formed by Carranza in March, 1916, to draft constitutional reforms; second secretary, Ernesto Meade Fierro (Coahuila), twenty-nine, a journalist, secretary to the generals of the Division of the Northeast during their meeting with the *villista* generals in Torreón in July, 1914;[51] third secretary, Lic. José María Truchuelo (Querétaro), thirty-six, a lawyer, former holder of various positions in the revolutionary state government of Querétaro, and strong advocate of judicial reform, affectionately described by his fellow delegates as having a mouth like a *rebanada de melón*;[52] and fourth secretary, Antonio Ancona Albertos, thirty-three, former private secretary to Pino Suárez, journalist, and *renovador*.[53] In addition, Dr. Jesús López Lira, Fernando Castaños (Durango), Juan de Dios Bojórquez, and Flavio A. Bórquez (Sonora) were elected assistant secretaries. Amidst applause, the officers took their seats and were

51 A confirmed nationalist and libertarian, Meade Fierro expressed his faith as follows: "The men of the present century should have only one religion, their native country; and within that religion, worship only one god, liberty" (Pastrana Jaimes Album).

52 At the end of the convention, Truchuelo wrote with pride of his "determined efforts to base the judicial power on free and direct elections by the people so that it will not be a simple tribunal subject to the intrigues of persons with influence but will be the true interpreter of national justice" (Pastrana Jaimes Album). For biographic data on Truchuelo, see *La Herencia del Constituyente*, no. 9 (May 5, 1964).

53 Another strong nationalist, he expressed his blind faith in Mexico as follows: "I believe in my country as the ancients believed in God. I do not discuss it nor do I permit it to be discussed. Likewise I believe that the present upheavals in Mexico are opening the way to the future Hispanic American civilization" (Fernández Martínez Album).

sworn in, whereupon President Rojas solemnly declared, "The Constitutional Convention of the United Mexican States, convoked by the First Chief of the Constitutionalist Army entrusted with the Executive Power of the Union, is today legitimately constituted in accordance with the decree of the 19th of September."[54]

Inspired by the occasion, several delegates expressed their sentiments. Alfonso Cravioto reminded everyone of his great responsibility before history, "because from here will come the new Constitution that will rule the destiny of the Mexican people." Asking the delegates to forget their personal resentments, he urged all to work together "for the greater stability of our political institutions, for a more splendid *patria*, and for the glory of the Revolution."[55] The ominous warning of Múgica on this occasion has already been noted (chapter 1). General Aguilar, like Cravioto, asked the delegates to forget personal attacks that had occurred in the preliminary sessions. He urged that "as of tomorrow" they should dedicate themselves to the real task of writing the constitutional reforms. But however much Cravioto and Aguilar might plead for harmony, to achieve it would be another matter. Discord resulting from discussion of credentials and injuries stemming from personal attacks were too deep to be erased. They would persist throughout the convention, sometimes aggravated, sometimes latent, but always there.

Although the first three preliminary sessions had been held in the Academy of Fine Arts, the seat of all subsequent meetings was the Iturbide Theater. In this historic place, known today as the Theater of the Republic, Congress had met in 1847 to decide on whether to continue the war with the United States. Twenty years later the Council of War that condemned Maximilian to death had met there. Now it was to be the seat of an even more historic meeting. With sufficient space on the main floor for the delegates and for the press and with boxes and galleries reserved for visitors, the theater served the purpose well. Here at 3:50 P.M. on Friday, December 1, with 151 delegates present, President Rojas gaveled the inaugural session to order. Shortly thereafter, to the strains of the national anthem and the ap-

[54] *Diario de los debates*, I, 376.
[55] Ibid.

plause and *vivas* of spectators and delegates alike, Carranza entered
the hall to address the delegates. The First Chief, who had made the
trip from Mexico City to Querétaro—a distance of approximately 130
miles—on horseback for the occasion, was in fine fettle.

For the next hour Carranza enumerated shortcomings of the Constitution of 1857 and commented on the changes he proposed in his
draft of reforms in order to make it a more workable national charter.[56] Admitting that the constitution contained high ideals, he declared that they were abstract, always out of reach of the Mexican
people. Individual rights had been trampled underfoot by governments since 1857. Abuse of the writ of *amparo*, far from providing
intended safeguards, had made protection by judicial action almost
impossible. Other fundamental principles of the Magna Carta of 1857
had suffered likewise. National sovereignty, supposedly resting in the
people, had never been a reality. Separation of powers, guaranteed
under the constitution, was a joke, because all the public power became vested in the hands of one man. The states had never had either
the "republican, representative, and popular government" or the
"freedom in their internal affairs" promised by the constitution, for
they had always been dominated by the national government, the state
authorities being mere instruments in the hands of the national executive. Declaring that he wished to preserve intact the liberal spirit and
form of government established in the Constitution of 1857, Carranza
affirmed that his proposals would take from the constitution what had
been inapplicable; they would make some provisions more easily
understood; they would cleanse it of all features that had served no
other purpose than to enhance dictatorship.

Although he denounced the economic power of the Church and
asked for reinstatement of the Laws of Reform, Carranza's speech, in
general, emphasized the need for political changes. He wanted to reform the judicial system and provide for the complete independence
of the judiciary, to overhaul the administration of justice and im-
prove criminal judicial procedure, to remove restrictions on the exercise of the suffrage and make it more effective, and to limit the
powers of the legislative branch so that it would not interfere

[56] For the complete text of Carranza's speech, see ibid., pp. 385–399.

with or hinder the work of the president. He also asked for popular election of the president, instead of election by a "fraudulent electoral college"; no re-election; reduction of the presidential term of office to four years; elimination of the office of vice-president; and, as the basis of free government, establishment of the independent *municipio*, "one of the greatest accomplishments of the Revolution."[57] He asked that the lower house of Congress be stripped of the power to judge the president and other high officials, a power which, when exercised during dictatorships in the past, had resulted in the presence in the house of servile members, easily controlled by the executive branch.

In case some delegates might be thinking of changing the form of government, Carranza thought it necessary to expound the advantages of the presidential over the parliamentary type. Alexis de Tocqueville, he observed, had noted, in regard to American people of Spanish origin, that they will "go to anarchy when they tire of obeying, and to dictatorship when they tire of destroying." These people, Carranza believed, needed a strong president. Under the parliamentary system, Congress might exercise the powers of the president, and then where would the strength of the government be? It would be in the parliament, which is inept in administering the laws, a mere deliberative body, always struggling in the dark, fearful at each instant of being censured by the people. Why, he asked, should Mexico adopt a weak form of government, when strengthening the presidential type established under the Constitution of 1857 would be a simple matter?[58] As further justification, he pointed to its successful application in the United States, where the parliamentary type was considered to be impractical. In conclusion, Carranza assured his

[57] For discussion of the *municipio*, see chap. 6.

[58] Carranza was obviously influenced by Emilio Rabasa's *La constitución y la dictadura: Estudio sobre la organización política de México*. Rabasa was a defender of the Díaz dictatorship. A bitter critic of the Constitution of 1857, he proposed to reduce the powers it granted the legislative branch and increase the power of the executive branch. Daniel Cosío Villegas credits Rabasa's criticism of the Constitution of 1857 as influential in causing the delegates to the Querétaro Convention to have fewer scruples in departing from the philosophy of the 1857 document ("The Mexican Revolution, Then and Now," pp. 118–119). For commentary on Rabasa's views, see Cosío Villegas, *La Constitución de 1857 y sus críticos*, pp. 61–62, 167–193.

listeners that his proposed reforms would provide for liberty under the rule of law as well as guarantee the people's rights under a system of justice "administered by upright and competent men."

According to the *Diario de los debates*, the First Chief received "loud and prolonged" applause as he finished his speech and handed his draft proposals to President Rojas. To celebrate the occasion, quite a few delegates went to the Port of Mazatlán to drink tequila and *mezcal*. The speech, however, had displeased many. According to one, it "was not entirely satisfactory; a few minutes later I could tell that the majority of the delegates were not satisfied either."[59] If Carranza believed his draft constitution would be accepted with little or no change, he had underestimated the spirit of reform-minded delegates.

A cursory comparison of Carranza's proposals with the Constitution of 1917 reveals that the distinctive articles of the latter are lacking entirely in the First Chief's draft or drawn up on a greatly reduced scale. A surprising number of his proposals, however, were actually adopted, wholly or in part, and the 1917 document resembles Carranza's draft more closely than it does the Constitution of 1857.[60] Nevertheless, characteristic features of the Constitution of 1917, articles which have made it famous as an instrument of socioeconomic reform, did not come from Carranza.[61] His proposed Article 27 contains no basis for the attack on vested interests and redefinition of property rights found in the corresponding article in the Constitution of 1917. Agrarian reform in Carranza's draft is found in a simple provision that the *ejidos* taken subsequent to the Ley de Desamortización would be returned to the people and held by them in common.[62]

[59] Romero Flores, *La Revolución como nosotros la vimos*, p. 156.

[60] For a comparison of the three documents, see *Diario de los debates*, I, 503–532, for the Carranza draft, and H. N. Branch, "The Mexican Constitution of 1917 Compared with the Constitution of 1857," Supplement to the *Annals of the American Academy of Political and Social Science* 71 (May 1917). I have largely used the Branch translation in preparing appendices A, C, and E.

[61] Charles C. Cumberland estimates that the convention cost 150,000 man-hours and two million pesos. He rightly concludes that, had the new constitution been largely a repetition of the provisions of Carranza's draft, "without significant additions," it probably would not have been worth the effort and money expended (*Mexican Revolution: The Constitutionalist Years*, p. 341).

[62] The Ley de Desamortización is another name for the Ley Lerdo. For a sum-

Article 123 of the 1917 document is missing entirely. In his speech to the convention, Carranza referred to benefits for labor and the responsibility of employers to their employees, but his draft simply provided that Congress should legislate on labor matters, a simple constitutional provision to be implemented later through legislation. Finally, the anticlericalism of the Constitution of 1917 is missing from Carranza's recommendations, although his Article 129, containing a few mild anticlerical provisions, apparently served as the point of departure for the delegates in drafting the severe Article 130 that came out of the convention.

If Carranza did not understand the need for more than just political reforms to the constitution, visionary reformers among the delegates did. Having participated in the overthrow of Díaz, having suffered the frustrations of the Madero period, having defeated the counterrevolution of Huerta, and having withstood the challenge of Villa, they would not settle for mere political revisions and innocuous statements of socioeconomic reform. Considering Carranza's draft lacking in the bases for national reconstruction, they would now set out to write a constitution with teeth in it. In doing so they would produce their own upheaval, the revolution at Querétaro.

---

mary of the provisions and the unfortunate effects of the law on rural inhabitants, see Helen Phipps, *Some Aspects of the Agrarian Question in Mexico: A Historical Study*, pp. 77–81.

3. The Apogee of Anticlericalism

> The Republic will be saved when the Mexican people learn to
> read before they learn to pray, know the road to the workshop
> before the one to the saloon, and get used to the plow before
> the censer.
>
> Salvador R. Guzmán
> Pastrana Jaimes Album

> The Mexican people will know how to defend their liberties
> stated in the Constitution of 1917 when they learn civics in
> secular schools.
>
> Juan de Dios Palma (Veracruz)
> Pastrana Jaimes Album

S HARP DEBATE OVER CREDENTIALS during the preliminary sessions
indicated the political cleavage between self-styled "true revolutionaries" and those more conservative in their outlook. At no time would
this division be more pronounced than in the discussion of the role of
the Church in the new social, economic, and political order.[1] Charged
with tension and emotion, with logic and illogic, these debates shook
the convention profoundly. Coming at the beginning of the regular
sessions, they divided the delegates into two irreconcilable camps and

[1] In this discussion, Church refers to the Roman Catholic church. In 1910, 99.2
percent of the 15,160,000 Mexicans were Catholic. There were 4,461 priests, or one
for each 3,398 inhabitants. For additional statistics on Catholicism in Mexico and an
analysis of the impact of the revolution on the Church, see James W. Wilkie, "Statistical Indicators of the Impact of National Revolution on the Catholic Church in
Mexico, 1910–1967," *Journal of Church and State* 12, no. 1 (Winter 1970): 89–
106.

earned for the extreme leftists the title of "jacobins of Querétaro." As Luis Espinosa remarked during the heated discussion of Article 3, "the Revolution in these solemn moments is this Constitutional Convention. The armed struggle was not nor has it been more than a means of arriving at its realization . . . here is the war of ideas."[2]

Church-State relations during the period 1857 to 1876, with attending anticlericalism, and through the *porfiriato*, when the Church recovered much of its economic, educational, and clerical strength, have been recounted. Upon the outbreak of the Revolution of 1910, the Church showed little sympathy for Madero; a Catholic party denounced him. Hoping that Huerta would restore peace and order, many elements of the clergy supported the usurper, thereby closely identifying the Church with him and his regime. The Church generally opposed the Constitutionalist movement and the program of social and economic reform. It could, therefore, expect little sympathy from the delegates to the Querétaro Convention.

Debates on the religious issue manifested an antireligious and atheistic bias, which added to the anticlerical theme that had woven its way through Mexican history since independence. Furthermore, since the majority of the delegates looked on the Church as a foreign body, a "state within a state," they singled it out for special attack in an exuberant spirit of nationalism. Close followers of Carranza, liberals in thinking although well to the right, saw the clergy as closely allied with the conservative elements of society. To destroy this bond they urged reinstatement of the Laws of the Reform, which the First Chief asked for in his speech before the convention on December 1. However, the anticlerical features of Carranza's draft proposals were, with one exception, not too severe. He asked for secular education in the public schools (Article 3); the prohibition of religious ceremonies outside the churches, which were to be maintained under governmental supervision (Article 27, paragraph 2); and a series of provisions (Article 129) granting the federal government the right to intervene in the regulation of religious worship (as in Article 123, Constitution of 1857), affirming the separation of Church and

---

[2] *Diario de los debates del Congreso Constituyente, 1916–1917*, I, 770.

State, preventing Congress from establishing or prohibiting any religion, and declaring matrimony to be a civil contract. Paragraph 3 of his Article 27, a drastic measure, forbade charitable and educational institutions to be under the patronage or administration of religious corporations or the ministers of the different denominations.

Not content with merely revitalizing the Laws of the Reform, the jacobins, while accepting some of Carranza's recommendations, seized the opportunity to write into the new constitution measures clearly aimed at eliminating the political, economic, and social influence of the Church. Its power would henceforth be confined to the field of religion.[3] Considering the jacobins' vengeful spirit and radical proposals, the Church was fortunate at Querétaro to have escaped restrictions that would have made its position in Mexico completely untenable.

ARTICLE 3

Unlike the pressing agrarian and labor problems, which were not resolved until the final days of the convention, the religious question erupted early and was settled by mid-December. In the sensational and bitter debates on Article 3, concerning the role of the Church in education, the radical leftists utilized the pretext of removing the Catholic church from its historical position in this field to launch an attack on the Church in general.

Whereas Article 3 of the Constitution of 1857 simply stated that "education is free," Carranza's draft article went further and declared, "There will be complete freedom of instruction; but that given in official educational institutions will be secular, and in the elementary and superior primary levels of the same institutions it will be free."[4] Although the secular requirement contradicted the right of freedom in teaching, the First Chief and Luis Manuel Rojas, who claimed to be the author of Article 3, were apparently unconcerned. What did concern them, however, was Article 3 as reported out by

---

[3] J. Lloyd Mecham, *Church and State in Latin America*, p. 389.

[4] *Diario de los debates*, I, 503. Primary instruction comprised the first six years of formal education. Grades 1–4 were the "elementary" level; 5–6, the "superior" level.

the Committee on the Constitution on December 11. Boldly rejecting the Carranza draft, the committee proposed the following as a substitute:

There shall be freedom of instruction but that given in official educational institutions shall be secular, the same as in the elementary and superior primary levels of private institutions. No religious organization, minister of any creed or person belonging to any similar association can establish or direct schools of primary instruction, nor teach personally in any *colegio*. The private primary schools can only be established subject to governmental supervision. Primary education will be obligatory for all Mexicans and in official institutions it will be free.[5]

Here it is necessary to identify the all-important Committee on the Constitution, which would report favorably or unfavorably on each article of Carranza's draft. The need for a friendly majority on the five-man committee was only too apparent to President Rojas and other close followers of the First Chief, who hoped to steer his draft through the convention with little change. Control of the committee would be the key to control of the convention. On December 5, Rojas proposed Macías, Ordorica, Ugarte, Colunga, and Enrique Recio (Yucatán) for membership. The first three were of unquestioned loyalty to Carranza. Reaction from the floor was instantly negative to the trio, especially to Macías. Speaking for a considerable number of delegates, Hilario Medina and Esteban Calderón impugned Macías. Although they respected him as a prominent lawyer, they believed that he could never judge impartially a constitution of which he was coauthor. Stunned at this reversal, Rojas withdrew the names, only to propose the same slate again the following day. The opposition, however, was adamant, Calderón saying, "If the chair keeps on making proposals, now the assembly . . . will keep on rejecting them and we will never reach an agreement."[6] The arguments that Macías provided a direct link with the First Chief and that the committee should represent the whole assembly and not factions did not prevail. By secret ballot the convention then chose Colunga, Recio, Dr. Alberto Román (Veracruz), Monzón, and Múgica, all pronounced

[5] Ibid., p. 543.
[6] Ibid., p. 499.

leftists. This sign of opposition to the Carranza leadership in the convention indicated that the First Chief's proposals would receive careful scrutiny as to their revolutionary nature.

Enrique Colunga, thirty-nine, born in the desert town of Matamoros, Coahuila, moved at an early age to Guanajuato, where he received his education, studied law, and was admitted to the bar in 1898. Prior to his election, he practiced in Celaya, Guanajuato; although not a man of great learning, he was considered well prepared in his field. Colunga spoke for rural Mexico and was a firm believer in states' rights.[7] He served as secretary of the committee.

Enrique Recio, thirty-two, native of Halachó, Yucatán, studied law but dropped out during the political ferment of the revolution without receiving his license to practice. Like other visionaries of the period, he wrote for radical newspapers and was a founding member of the Socialist party of the Southeast. Recio described himself simply as a "revolutionary in the field of ideas," but Palavicini, irritated at his election to such an important committee, described Recio as a "Yucatecan worker, perfectly ignorant and hot-headedly anticlerical; naturally his understanding of the great responsibility that was entrusted to him amounted to nothing."[8]

Alberto Román, a physician from Huatusco, Veracruz, was probably competent in his profession, although he possessed no background in the social sciences that would qualify him for the drafting of a constitution. His outlook on life was provincial. His voting record would prove his leftist ideas.

Luis Monzón, forty-four, a primary schoolteacher of decidedly leftist ideas, was expelled from his native state, San Luis Potosí, in 1899 for seditious activities and fled to Sonora. There he read Kropot-

7 He expressed this concept as follows: "Among the aspirations that we share, the one I have most in common with you [Pastrana Jaimes] is to defend the interests of the *provincia*. We are convinced that it has vitality, intellectual strength, and a splendid moral health. This conviction is the basis of our strong desire for federalism" (Pastrana Jaimes Album). For additional biographic data on Colunga, see *La Herencia del Constituyente*, no. 15 (November 5, 1964), and Alberto Morales Jiménez, *Hombres de la Revolución mexicana: 50 semblanzas biográficas*, pp. 267–270.

8 Félix F. Palavicini, *Historia de la Constitución de 1917*, I, 163.

kin and Bakunin, turned to anarchism, and in the early 1900's became an active *magonista* and contributor to the Flores Magón brothers' newspaper, *Regeneración*. For these activities he is said to have been jailed in Agua Prieta, Sonora. Considered dangerous in Sonora because of his outspoken opposition to the Díaz dictatorship and his espousal of radical ideas, he found difficulty in obtaining employment except in remote areas of the state. As he was no friend of the Church or the clergy, his wife had to suggest to him from time to time to "take a little trip" so that she could have various of their eleven children baptized. Forced to leave Sonora in 1908, he returned to San Luis Potosí; but the start of the revolution brought him back to Sonora. In 1912 and 1913 he served as state inspector of education, was imprisoned by the *huertistas* in 1913, and on his release held various positions in the Constitutionalist movement. One of his more important achievements was the establishment of the normal school in Sonora in 1915. A firm believer in class struggle, he wrote these prophetic words while in prison in 1913: "The regeneration of Mexico will be achieved, but only at the cost of tears, at the cost of blood, at the cost of unmentionable sacrifices . . ."[9] Monzón usually spoke slowly, with a smile on his lips; he was not very convincing, but firm in his convictions. He later became one of the first Mexican Communists.

By far the outstanding member of the committee was its president, Francisco Múgica. At thirty-two, he possessed the preparation and intellectual stature lacking in most of the delegates. Son of a Michoacán teacher, he had enrolled in the preparatory school of the seminary in Zamora, where his father held a minor governmental position in order to supplement his modest salary. There Múgica studied Latin, the classics, chemistry, physics, history, and philosophy. He also developed a strong aversion for theology and a rabid anticlericalism. Suspended from his religion class, he was permitted to continue in the seminary only with the special permission of the

---

[9] Juan de Dios Bojórquez, *Monzón: Semblanza de un revolucionario*, p. 13. A believer in unrestricted suffrage for the masses, Monzón said, "To restrict the vote among our people because of their ignorance would be like cutting off the ears of a deaf person because he cannot hear" (*El Constituyente*, no. 10 [January 31, 1917]).

Bishop of Zamora. A natural rebel, he soon left the seminary and
began writing for various Michoacán newspapers. He attacked the
authoritarian Díaz system and strongly advocated social and economic
reform. In 1906 Múgica became associated with Jesús and Ricardo
Flores Magón. Embracing wholeheartedly their anarchistic ideas and
the platform of the Mexican Liberal party, he became the Michoacán
correspondent for *Regeneración*. As the Díaz regime drew to a close,
Múgica, like other liberals, showed some sympathy for Bernardo
Reyes as the most likely to overthrow the old dictator. With Reyes's
exile in 1909, Múgica threw his support to Madero. Unable to find
employment in the Madero administration, he obtained from Governor Venustiano Carranza in 1912 the position of director of statistics
for the state of Coahuila. When Carranza began his movement against
Huerta, Múgica signed the Plan of Guadalupe and followed the First
Chief. From 1913 to 1916 he held various civilian and military positions in the Constitutionalist government. While engaged in the military campaign in the Northeast, he participated in the first agrarian
reform at Matamoros, Tamaulipas, in 1913; served as port director at
Tampico, where he organized the customs, port works, railways, and
postal service; and served as administrator of the Port of Veracruz.
Promoted to brigadier general in January, 1915, he headed the Supreme Court of Military Justice and then served a year as governor
and military commander of Tabasco, where he achieved distinction as
a reformer and administrator. An able speaker, logical and methodical
in his delivery, Múgica seethed with determination to create a new
social and economic order, no matter how necessary it might be to
break with tradition.[10] In the convention he served as floor leader and
spokesman for the radical reformers.

The members of the Committee on the Constitution (hereafter referred to as the First Committee to distinguish it from a second committee established in early January) shared the common belief that
the Church had to be stripped of its primacy in the field of education.

[10] For additional biographic data on Múgica, see *La Herencia del Constituyente*,
no. 8 (April 5, 1964), no. 9 (May 5, 1964), and no. 10 (June 5, 1964). Two
biographies are Armando de María y Campos's *Múgica: Crónica biográfica (aportación a la historia de la Revolución Mexicana)* and Magdalena Mondragón's *Cuando
la Revolución se cortó las alas*, neither of which is a critical study.

To understand the deep aversion of Múgica and his fellow committee members to the clergy, one only has to read the report accompanying Article 3, excerpts of which are quoted as follows:[11]

In the history of our country, studied impartially, the clergy is revealed as the cruelest and most tenacious enemy of our liberties; its principle has been and is: the interests of the Church before the interests of the country. Rendered powerless as a result of the Laws of the Reform, the clergy had the opportunity later, under the tolerance of the dictatorship, of patiently working toward the re-establishment of its power above that of the civil authority . . . Well known are the means that it has used to take possession again of the conscience; to absorb education; to declare itself to be the propagator of scientific principles in order to better inhibit their diffusion.

The committee believed that the State must restrain the exercise of a natural right, the right to an education, when the free exercise of that right had a bad effect on society or obstructed its development. Because religious education taught ideas the youthful mind could not grasp, ideas that later developed into a blind fanaticism, the committee believed that the State, in the best interests of Mexican society, had to outlaw religious education in all public or private primary schools. To accomplish this objective, the committee demanded that the ministers of the sects be prohibited from all association with primary education. Furthermore, the attempt of the clergy to control education was viewed as "nothing but a step preparatory to usurping the powers of the State," a situation to be prevented at all costs.

What did the committee understand secular education to mean? To them it meant education "devoid of all religious belief, . . . which presents the truth and frees from error, that which is motivated by a strictly scientific judgment." One member of the committee went even further. In a minority report, Monzón proposed that the word "rational" be substituted for "secular" as more in keeping with educational trends of the twentieth century. Rational education, he believed, would "destroy the lie, the error, and the absurd wherever they are found."

In the presence of the First Chief himself, who had informed the

---

[11] *Diario de los debates,* I, 541–543.

convention that he would like to attend the debates on this important article, discussion commenced on the afternoon of December 13 with 167 delegates present. For the next three days the impassioned debates on the Church's role in education were the decisive ones of the convention. To Carranza, who suffered the discomfort of hearing the rejection of his Article 3 in exchange for a more radical text, this rejection signified a vote of no confidence, a demonstration that he did not control the convention. His followers had hoped that his presence might exert a restraining influence on the radicals, but they were mistaken. This was evident even to the First Chief. To avoid further embarrassment, he attended no subsequent debates on this or any other article.

Opponents of Article 3 as reported out by the First Committee charged that limitations and restrictions on individual freedom were out of place in that section of the constitution, on personal rights, and that the article contained provisions contrary to the rights of the Mexican people. Close followers of the First Chief utilized these arguments time and again in trying to defeat the committee report.

Realizing the seriousness of the matter, Rojas stepped down from the presidential chair to speak against the radical report. Referring to the personal rights, he said, "If the section on individual rights concerns only the limitations on authority, it is entirely improper and out of place to bring up there the matter of obligatory education . . ."[12] Furthermore, he believed—although here he was stretching a point—that prohibiting the clergy from teaching was unnecessary, since Article 27 of Carranza's draft (see appendix D) provided for this in substance. Arguing that Carranza's draft, as well as that of the committee, provided for secular education in the public schools, Rojas thought that the statement outlawing religious education would be more acceptable if less harshly worded. He concluded by asking the convention to postpone discussion of Article 3 in order for the committee to reword it, but a standing vote defeated his motion.

Silver-tongued Cravioto, next to speak against Article 3, declared that the "jacobin proposal of the Committee" did not crush the priests

---

[12] Ibid., p. 652.

in general but suppressed fundamental rights of the Mexican people. Freedom of instruction, he said, was derived directly from freedom of opinion, "the most transcendental of all of man's liberties." If man had the right to think and believe what he wished, he also had the right to tell others his thoughts and beliefs. Freedom of instruction, he believed, was an unquestionable right, and the secular requirement, as well as the denial to clerics of the right to establish or direct primary schools or teach in secondary schools, directly violated this freedom. To him an attack on one individual right was an attack on all and would provide just cause for rebellion, not of the reactionaries but of the liberals. Ending his long speech with a request for the rejection of the committee report, Cravioto took his seat amidst great applause and *vivas*.[13]

Palavicini continued the argument by stating that the real question was whether the individual rights of the constitution were going to be preserved or not. Urging the assembly not to abandon the liberal creed "that has been our flag," he said it would be a shocking change to deny an individual, simply because she was a nun, the right to teach French or English in the schools. Chiding the jacobins for forgetting that all revolutionary doctrines emphasize human freedom, he urged them to remove their radical restrictions on individual liberties and to adopt a policy of prudence, simplicity, and moderation without vain egotism.[14]

Although the rightists placed individual freedom above all, it must not be inferred that they were proclerical. On the contrary, several boldly expressed their anticlerical views, even citing activists of the French Revolution. Cravioto made clear his stand when he quoted, "If we need ropes to hang tyrants, my hands will braid them with the intestines of the priests."[15] These words, coming from a former official of the Ministry of Education, indicated no fondness for the clergy. Admitting that clericalism was an enemy, he considered that "jacobinism" was too, that it was useless to exchange one error for another. Since Church and State were separate, Cravioto believed gov-

13 Ibid., pp. 658–665.
14 Ibid., p. 707.
15 Ibid., p. 658.

ernment could not require secular education in the private schools directed by the clergy. Palavicini added, "I want to confess that we all . . . want to fight the clergy in all their strongholds in a practical, precise, and energetic way; but this must be done skillfully because if it is done clumsily, we will not be combatting anyone nor will our work have a lasting effect."[16] Later he went so far as to promise, "I will praise from my seat each one here who insults the priests."[17]

In a long-drawn-out historical analysis of the role of the Church in education, Macías concluded that the Church had always held a firm grip on the human mind. Each attempt to escape from this domination had failed. He accused the clergy of being invariably linked to dictatorships, never to liberty and progress. The clergy, he said, constantly schemed to oppress the people. Recalling that they had supported Huerta, he said that it would be worthwhile to abolish the clergy, but that freedom of conscience should never disappear. Macías also minimized the number of clergymen in the educational field and the influence they exerted. In doing so he too displayed his contempt for the priest, charging that "the clergyman is naturally lazy. He enjoys the comforts of life. He enjoys talking with overpious women, sipping chocolate at a convenient time, and having them bring him nutritious broths in order to be better able to endure human wretchedness; the clergyman does not work; the clergyman has someone to work for him; the Catholic schools have been under the direction of teachers paid for by them . . ."[18]

Supporters of Carranza's draft, the rightists or moderate liberals of the convention, generally agreed on the need for secular education in the public schools. The committee had simply carried this requirement over to the field of private education, largely sponsored by the Church. Although most of the rightists supported this restriction, they divided over where it should be placed in the constitution. Palavicini believed that the committee should accept Carranza's draft of Article 3 with the additional requirement that education be secular in private schools. He thought this would be acceptable to the delegates, but he

16 Ibid., p. 702.
17 Ibid., p. 710.
18 Ibid., p. 682.

hoped they would reject other limitations found in Article 3, if necessary placing them elsewhere in the constitution. In his opinion, Carranza's Article 3 and the feature of his Article 27 prohibiting religious corporations or their ministers from directing and administering schools should satisfy the jacobins. Not realizing the radical changes Article 27 would later undergo, he asked that these two articles be voted on together.

Lizardi thought that the secular requirement should be placed in Article 3 but that other limitations on the Church and the clergy should be placed in Article 129 on Church-State relations. Colonel Chapa affirmed his support of the secular requirement for primary schools but attacked the committee's denial to religious organizations of the right to establish and direct private schools and to the ministers of the different faiths of the right to teach in them. Quoting Count Mirabeau of French Revolution fame to the effect that "every man has the right to teach what he knows and to learn what he does not know," he classified these restrictions as infamous blows to freedom of education. As a compromise, he suggested that the government offer free, secular, and obligatory primary education for children from six to twelve years of age.[19] This proposal, however, received no consideration.

In debating such a controversial subject, the nationalistic spirit of the delegates manifested itself in an old and successful theme: anti-Americanism. Speaking on December 13, Palavicini pointed out that no matter how much one impugned the Catholic church and its influence, to crush this influence would be to give an open invitation to American Protestantism to step up its proselytizing of the Mexican people. He warned against exchanging "a national religion for one of a powerful and dominating neighbor." Palavicini believed that the committee meant well but that it had overlooked the danger "of the Yankee conquest. (Voices: No! No! Hisses)." Ridiculing Protestant efforts, he said:

The Protestant minister has organized sport clubs which have all the English terminology, he has organized the Young Men's Christian Association where there is music, where bad verse is recited, where the "one step"

[19] Ibid., p. 694.

is danced, and where from time to time the epistles of Saint Paul are read; but the Protestant minister does not stop there . . . he infiltrates in all the official establishments masked as a radical revolutionary . . . he collects with the right hand the salary of a lay teacher, while with his left hand he receives money from the Protestant missions of the North American Republic. This is the price of the evangelization of the Mexican Republic and is an aspect of conquest . . . it is not the Mexican people who maintain the Protestant faith; I assure you that the Protestant faith in the republic is supported with Yankee money. (Applause).[20]

Palavicini saw little choice between Protestant and Catholic fanaticism, since one was as tenacious as the other. But he thought that Mexico had made progress in rejecting both. As proof, he pointed out that delegates to the Constitutional Convention of 1857 had gone reverently to mass before beginning their sessions, but he was sure that two-thirds of the present convention had not even visited the monument to Santa Rosa in Querétaro! In citing the Protestant missionary movement as an example of foreign intervention and in arguing that Article 3 in its present form was detrimental to Catholicism, hence favorable to the spread of Protestantism, Palavicini hoped to arouse the nationalistic sentiment of the delegates to the point that they would reject the article. This was a clever ruse but it was not successful.

The adroit opposition offered other arguments. Cravioto introduced data showing that the menace of church schools was exaggerated. In 1907, he said, there were 9,620 public schools with an enrollment of 666,723 students. At the same time there were only 586 church schools, with an enrollment of 43,720.[21] Certainly this was nothing to be alarmed about. Likewise, Macías pointed out that the clergy carried out very little religious educational work, since no more than 10 percent of Catholic schools were actually under clerical control. In his opinion Mexicans received their religious education at home. Instead of outlawing religious instruction in the schools, he believed that the convention should fight it on its own ground by increasing the number of public schools. He warned that it would be better for

20 Ibid., pp. 705–706.
21 Ibid., p. 661.

the liberals to win a victory over religious education in this manner than to impose excessive restrictions, which would only produce a disastrous reaction.

Speaking again on the afternoon of December 16, Rojas unsuccessfully called attention to the effect of the committee report on the public. In Mexico City, he said, the effect "had been terrible," especially that of Monzón's report, which had been interpreted as sanctioning anarchism in education. Furthermore, he announced the receipt of a telegram from the United States asking confirmation of a report that Carranza had been assassinated during one of the sessions of the convention! Stating that the work of a constitutional convention gets wide publicity, he accused Múgica and his fellow committeemen of being novices in politics, of not taking into consideration the effect of their work on the people. They would have to learn, he said with irony, that they could not talk at a convention the same way they could "at a party or in school." Earlier Macías had warned that any persecution of the Catholic faith might bring on American intervention. This could be prevented only if the assembly left the basic freedom of the people intact.

It is clear from the foregoing that the opponents of Article 3 based their case on the need to maintain human freedom. Although some were not against imposing secular instruction in the private schools, they did oppose other restrictions, including compulsory education, either in substance or on the grounds that such limitations on the freedom of education were out of place in the constitutional chapter on individual rights. In attempting to defeat the committee report, they resorted to other arguments, such as the danger of American imperialism veiled as Protestantism, the minimal influence of the small number of church schools and the clergy which operated them, and the adverse effect of the report and discussion at home and abroad.

Supporters of Article 3 argued that secular education was necessary for the welfare and development of Mexican society, no matter how much this and other restrictions might infringe on individual freedoms. Herein lies the basic difference between the moderate rightists (or classical liberals) of the convention and the leftists: whereas the former placed the rights of the individual before those of society, the latter placed the rights of society before those of the individual. The rightists considered the chapter on individual rights as the most sacred part of the constitution; the leftists believed it necessary to modify these rights in the interests of society. Considering Mexican life to be jeopardized by the social and political influence of the Church and its clergy, the jacobins were determined to destroy this influence as completely as possible. Their thinking reflected antireligious as well as anticlerical views.

Múgica, the intellectual father of Article 3, delivered the keynote address in the attack on the Church on December 13. Declaring this to be the most solemn moment of the revolution, when the future of the country and of the youth of Mexico was at stake, he attacked religious education as causing a moral and physical degeneration of the individual. Excoriating the clergy as the "saddest and most perverse enemy of the country," he declared that they taught children, workers, and country people "the most absurd ideas, the most tremendous hatred for democratic institutions, the strongest hatred for those principles of justice, equality, and fraternity preached by the greatest apostle . . . of our times, who was called Jesus Christ." Múgica left no doubt about his intentions when he warned, "If we allow absolute freedom of education so that the clergy can participate in it with their antiquated and backward ideas, we will not create new generations of thinking, sensible people; rather our posterity will receive from us the inheritance of fanaticism, of insane principles."[22] This, of course, is what so aroused the opposition of the rightists: limitations and restrictions on the grant of freedom of education contradicted the very right that had been granted.

José Alvarez y Alvarez, a youthful colonel in the Constitutionalist forces and, like Múgica, a drop-out from the Zamora seminary, had no love for the clergy. To him Article 3 was not strong enough. Speaking on December 16 in support of Monzón's proposal for rational education, Alvarez y Alvarez asked that instruction be "scientifically based on the truth." He also took advantage of the opportunity to deliver some caustic blows against the rightists who demanded un-

[22] Ibid., p. 643.

limited freedom of education. What had happened, he asked, when this condition existed under Madero? After a few months in Zamora, "a town enveloped in the perfumery of incense, the peal of church bells, and the sermons of the friars, the principal bishops of the Republic and the best known conservatives met to plot the fall of Madero." Alvarez y Alvarez feared that Carranza's government would leave the door open again so that the clergy and the conservatives could strike another blow against the State.[23]

Clearly, the radicals launched an attack on religious education as a means toward an end. In order to reconstruct Mexican society it was necessary to destroy the regressive influence of the clergy and the means by which this influence was exerted: the education of the individual. Unconcerned about the logic of their arguments, the leftists vehemently denounced religious education as well as the clergy in general.

Doctor López Lira declared on December 13 that the school should be the "light of the world, the torch of civilization," but that this was impossible when instruction was in the hands of those who could not separate reason from dogma. How could the religious teach science, when all they were used to teaching was religion? He believed that the church schools were established not to educate, but to hold the faithful and to serve as bases for the dissemination of religious propaganda. He stressed the need to protect the conscience of the young from all "humbug, or at least from all doubtful or questionable matter."[24] Múgica stressed the same theme again on December 14, contending that Carranza's Article 3 was dangerous because it "did not have all the radicalism that was necessary to save the country," because it handed to the clergy something that was sacred, something that should always be defended: "the conscience of the child, the defenseless conscience of the adolescent."[25]

Supporting Monzón's report on rational education, González Torres affirmed that the sole intention of the leftists was to safeguard child-

[23] Ibid., p. 763.
[24] Ibid., p. 667. López Lira believed that "the diffusion of education, especially secular, will mold the strong spirit of the race and with the economic betterment of the Mexicans, their devotion to the country will be strengthened" (Ruiz Album).
[25] *Diario de los debates*, I, 712.

hood education. He opposed church schools, saying "we are all convinced that religions are perfectly corrupt and that they have been converted into a plot of stories and legends and aberrations with which they [the clergy] attempt to surround the intelligence and the heart of the children for the purpose of taking them over in the future and afterwards being able to manipulate them as they please, always with bastard purposes."[26] Finding specific fault with religious education, Doctor Román, speaking for the committee report, asserted:

The act of associating religion with education is to associate error with truth. . . . The child is given a general idea of the essence of creation, the necessity of reproduction, and then he is told there is a being [i.e., Christ] who has been born outside these biological laws. . . . If the State, then, has the duty of protecting children, it is certain that it has the obligation of avoiding . . . a system [of education] that is completely detrimental. The political problem of Mexico is of even greater importance; no one will deny that the Catholic schools have simply been the means of turning the future generations against the liberal creed.[27]

In a harangue against the clergy, Celestino Pérez (Oaxaca), a young lawyer, attacked religious instruction on the primary level as contrary to the moral development of society. He too thought that the State must prescribe secular education until the child was old enough to distinguish between right and wrong. Then he could go to a church school if he chose to. The child, he insisted, could not be left in the hands of individuals "who are not going to do anything else but confuse his conscience and teach him to lie."[28] Luis Espinosa, one of the staunchest defenders of the committee report, saw nothing contradictory in granting "freedom of education" and then imposing restrictions upon it. Refuting Macías's contention that Article 3 destroyed freedom to teach and to learn, he asked, "From whom does it take the right to learn what one wants to or to teach what one knows, whether it be good or bad . . . fantastic or absurd?"[29] The child, he said, could learn at home; the priest could teach outside of school or use the news-

[26] Ibid., p. 760.
[27] Ibid., p. 657.
[28] Ibid., p. 699.
[29] Ibid., p. 773.

paper or the book. Furthermore, he could even teach from the pulpit. Attacking the contention that restrictions on freedom of education were out of place in the chapter on individual rights and should be placed elsewhere, i.e., in Article 129 on Church-State relations, Espinosa declared that Article 3 concerned education and that restrictions and limitations on it should be placed in the same provision, whether rights were violated or not. Alvarez y Alvarez used the same argument but with a different twist. He asked: "Does not the Indian deserve guarantees? Is he not an individual? Are we going to tell that neglected race . . . that it was not possible to grant them rights because that would bother the friars?"[30] To Alvarez y Alvarez and his fellow leftists, the individual rights signified more than protection of the individual against the arbitrary acts of the government. They should also protect the underprivileged against the abuse of a privileged minority, i.e., the clergy.

After two days of heated debate, Múgica asked permission to withdraw the report and present it in modified form. He interpreted the sentiment of the delegates as favoring secular education in public and private schools but opposing the restriction which forbade the clergy to teach "in any school." When presented again on December 16, Article 3 read as follows: "Instruction is free; but that given in official educational institutions shall be secular, the same as the elementary and superior primary instruction imparted in private institutions. No religious organization nor minister of any sect shall be permitted to establish or direct schools of primary education. Private primary schools shall only be established subject to official supervision. Primary instruction in public schools will be free."[31] In a brief defense of the revision, Múgica said that the committee had taken into account the opinions of Palavicini and others, but that it was not disposed to remove the "so-called limitations," for if the constitution was to have the proper ideology, it must be expressed in Article 3.

The new draft revealed that concessions had been made. The prohibition on teaching by ministers of the sects and the stipulation that primary education was obligatory had been eliminated. Realizing the

[30] Ibid., p. 763.
[31] Ibid., p. 732.

contradiction of saying "there will be freedom of education" and then restricting this right, the committee had watered down the first line to read "education is free," a reversion to the wording of Article 3 of the Constitution of 1857. Even though the report was now somewhat more acceptable to the rightists, they still objected to placing limitations on any authority other than that of the government in the chapter on individual rights. Palavicini, lamenting that he and his colleagues had worn themselves out trying to explain this to the leftists, accused them of having circulated the new draft the day before to secure enough favorable votes to assure passage.[32] Múgica himself had mentioned a "private" meeting the previous evening in the School of Fine Arts to discuss Article 3. Although further manifestations of faith by the leftists were unnecessary, Dr. Miguel Alonzo Romero (Yucatán) declared that he would support the article "with the same faith of the girondists, singing as they mounted the guillotine."

After three days of continuous and heated debate, which had cast the legal-minded rightists against the reform-minded leftists, it was obvious that little more could be said pro or con. The vote on Article 3 came at the end of a five-hour session which began at 3:40 P.M., Saturday, December 16, one punctuated by frequent requests from the secretary, as the evening wore on, to end the discussion. By roll-call vote the committee report on Article 3 was approved, 99 to 58. The result was greeted with prolonged applause and shouts of "Long live the Revolution! Long live the First Chief! The *patria* has been saved!"

The vote on Article 3, the most significant of the convention, showed that the Carranza draft was wide open to attack, that the delegates would decide the great issues according to their own convictions and not according to loyalty to any particular revolutionary chieftain or interest group. Cándido Aguilar had joined the radicals in voting against his future father-in-law's draft. On the other hand, Jorge von Versen, leftist labor leader and journalist, had voted against the measure. Later he explained, "When we discussed Article 3, *señores*, I was trembling, not exactly because we were going to strip the power from clericalism, I hate clericalism to death, I would have

[32] Palavicini, *Historia de la Constitución de 1917*, I, 265.

advocated complete castration of that party, but, *señores*, I trembled from the fear that thousands of children would go without knowing the alphabet, without that torch which illuminates the dark road of life for them."[33] Undoubtedly others had equally good reasons for voting as they did.

It has been said that soldiers wrote the Constitution of 1917 and that on the important issues the lawyers voted against the majority. Yet at least eighteen of those who voted for Article 3 were lawyers, while only ten or eleven from the same profession cast negative votes. The vote revealed that a bloc of radical leftists considered religious instruction injurious to Mexican society and especially detrimental to the tender minds of the young. They were determined to strip the Church of its dominant role in education. It was also clear that they were in the majority or sufficiently persuasive to get majority support for their views. Rightists could take little satisfaction from the fact that Luis Monzón's request for "rational" education had received no consideration. The presence of the First Chief, the insinuation that a rejection of Carranza's Article 3 would be an affront to him, the dual threats of American intervention and increasing Protestant influence, and the logical argument that limitations and restrictions on the right to education were out of place in the chapter of the constitution on individual rights had not deterred the jacobins. Basic to their thinking was the belief that rights must be restricted for the benefit of society as a whole, regardless of whether this violated the customary norms of written constitutions. Having tasted blood, the radicals would henceforth be difficult to pacify. Subsequent debates on articles concerning the Church were bound to be heated. Colonel Chapa could justifiably say, "If each article of the Constitution is approved with the spirit, the partiality, and the intent of Article 3 proposed by the Committee, we will have made a Constitution of rabid jacobinism."[34]

ARTICLE 24

Following the adoption of Article 3, the anticlerical issue lapsed

---

[33] *Diario de los debates*, I, 984.
[34] Ibid., p. 692.

into the background until January 27, 1917, when discussion of
Article 24, on the religious practice of the faithful and its regulation
by the government, rekindled old sentiments and prejudices. Although the article was first read on January 4, discussion did not take
place until the twenty-seventh. The majority report of the First Committee, signed by four of its members, read as follows: "Everyone is
free to embrace the religion of his choice and to practice all ceremonies, devotions or observances of his respective creed, either in
places of public worship or at home, as long as they do not constitute
a crime or misdemeanor punishable by law. Every religious act of public
worship shall be performed strictly within the places of public worship, which shall be at all times under governmental supervision."[35]
The Constitution of 1857 contained no similar provision. Both paragraphs were drawn largely from the Laws of the Reform of December
14, 1874.[36] The wording, almost identical to the correspondingly
numbered article in Carranza's draft, would probably have been approved with little or no debate had not Enrique Recio submitted a
minority report asking for two additions: (*a*) that the minister of any
creed be prohibited from hearing oral confession and (*b*) that exercise of the ministry be limited to native-born Mexican citizens, who
should be civilly married if they were less than fifty years old! This
attracted immediate attention and presaged another struggle, which
did not take place until the end of the month, when the delegates,
hurrying to finish their work, were less disposed to argue the matter.

In his reasons for proposing such harsh and discriminatory measures, Recio revealed his anticlerical and nationalistic bias. The oral
confession, he charged, strongly bound the conscience and placed the
private life of the family under the censorship of the priest. Furthermore, the priest used the oral confession to gain power and wealth for
the Church. On the pretext of exercising the priesthood, foreigners
had come to Mexico to administer the sacraments "without any affection for our country and its republican institutions." Not only should
this be forbidden, but priests carrying out their duties should be required to marry, because "the laws of nature cannot be broken." To

[35] Ibid., II, 84.
[36] Mecham, *Church and State*, p. 386.

expect the priests to live in perpetual chastity was ridiculous, since they constantly violated this vow, "bringing, as a result, disgrace and grief to the home." The requirement of marriage would assure the sanctity of the home and at the same time would "give a certain degree of respectability to the priests."[37]

When debate commenced on the night of January 27 with a quorum of 131 delegates, young Doctor Alonzo Romero strongly supported Recio's proposal. Claiming to be a "revolutionary by temperament," he asserted that the private confession had replaced the public confession in the fifth century because the honor of a high prelate had been compromised by a woman who mentioned during the public confession her intimate relations with him. The hotheaded Yucatecan considered the private confession to be immoral because it forced women to pour out their intimate sentiments into the "dissolute ears" of the priests. He reminded his listeners that the private confession had furnished the information that furthered the political ends of the Inquisition. As for celibacy, Alonzo Romero attacked it for resulting in an unnatural suppression of human desires. The priest, a human being of flesh and blood, who had a nervous as well as a reproductive system, could not and did not keep his vow of chastity. He warned that if the assembly did not take steps "to prevent those insults to morality," it would never successfully achieve its objective but "would provide the opportunity for each home to be wrecked, for each woman to be an adulteress, . . . each priest to be a free satyr in the bosom of society. (Abundant applause)."[38]

Lic. Alberto Terrones Benítez (Durango), thirty, was the next speaker to support Recio's minority report. When Don Venustiano swept into Mexico City in September, 1914, young Terrones Benítez obtained a job in the Ministry of Foreign Relations, probably because of his fluency in English, acquired while working for British and American mining companies in his native Durango before the revolu-

[37] *Diario de los debates*, II, 1029.
[38] Ibid., p. 1032. At the end Alonzo Romero thoroughly approved the convention's anticlerical stand, saying that "the jacobins of the Chamber who knew how to obtain through their impulsiveness the happiness of the Mexican people have done well" (Ruiz Album).

tion. To him, great national upheavals were just one of various indi-
cations of humanity's march toward perfection. He considered religion
of any kind as injurious. Like a cancer that was slowly destroying
society, it prevented the individual from thinking for himself. Instead
of offering scientific explanation, religion encircled the individual in
obscurantism. When one sought the cause of certain phenomena, one
was told that they were the work of the supernatural or some supreme
power. Religion, he insisted, was an obstacle that man must overcome.
If man were not bound by such superstitious beliefs, he could progress.
Otherwise, he would regress. As Terrones Benítez saw the problem,
the solution was simple: "We ought to definitely assert here that religions are the greatest and sublimest lies." Then, turning from a sacri-
legious to an anticlerical theme, the young *duranguense* added that it
was time to put a stop to the abuses which disparaged "the command-
ments of the Church as the great jacobin Christ defined it." He urged
freedom, not for the Church, not for the clergy, but for the people.
The convention had to take steps to "emancipate them from the clerical yoke to which they are submitted from the moment they are born.
(Voices: Vote! Vote!)."[39]

In the discussion of the Recio proposals, the logic of the opposition
matched the fervor of the leftists. Two who spoke against were Fernando Lizardi and Hilario Medina. Probably no other state sent as
distinguished a delegation to Querétaro as Guanajuato, and among
this group these two men were outstanding.

Lizardi, thirty-three and a native of the city of Guanajuato, or-
phaned at the age of eleven, managed to get his early education in
Celaya and Guanajuato, finally obtaining his law degree in Mexico
City in 1906. For a while he was a law partner of Enrique Colunga,
the only lawyer on the First Committee. An active supporter of Madero, Lizardi held judicial positions in his native state during the
Madero administration. Persecuted by *huertistas*, he fled and joined
the Constitutionalists, serving in various civil positions, including that
of lieutenant governor (*secretario general de gobierno*) of the state of
Hidalgo. After recuperating from typhus in Mexico City in 1915, he
taught banking at the Superior School of Business Administration

[39] *Diario de los debates*, II, 1036.

and gave a course at the School of Jurisprudence. He was a man of great intellectual depth and perspicuity. A conciliator, in the most heated discussions he would inject wit or relate an anecdote that immediately relieved the tension. Although he was a rightist, those of the left considered him to be "a sincere Bohemian, an invigorating companion, and a noble friend."[40]

First, Lizardi cautioned against attacking the confession as an act of religious worship. Catholics considered it a moral act, and, although "we who are nonbelievers think it is an immoral act," it should not be prohibited by law, because, if it were, a great many other immoral acts would have to be prohibited too. "We would have to say . . . that masturbation was also prohibited (Laughter), which is as immoral as the confession, but it would be absurd to put it in a Constitution. (Applause)." In Lizardi's opinion, the immoral feature of the private confession lay in its abuse. Any person with a difficult problem might seek the counsel of a priest. To forbid a person to relate personal matters to another and to seek that person's advice would be "extremely difficult." If confession to a priest might result in an act of adultery, could not a relation of domestic affairs to a layman result in adultery also? To him the blame lay not with the priests to whom confessions were made, but with the heads of families who permitted their wives and daughters to confess.

Next, Lizardi attacked the marriage requirement as contrary to the freedom of the individual. He doubted it would produce the desired results. Although the marriage requirement was supposed to have a moralizing effect, he reminded the assembly that the revolution had also brought a liberal divorce law. The priests, he thought, would take advantage of this and marry and divorce as often as they pleased! Furthermore, with complete separation of Church and State, it would be inconsistent to impose obligations upon the clergy. If the delegates wanted to do something "more practical," why not propose a national religion based on logic? With fine irony, he said, "Let us look for a pretty, young girl and declare her to be the goddess of reason and ap-

[40] Bojórquez [pseud. Bórquez], *Crónica del constituyente*, p. 696. For additional biographic data on Lizardi, see *La Herencia del Constituyente*, no. 15 (November 5, 1964).

point Citizen Recio high priest and Citizen Alonzo Romero as first acolyte. That will make it complete." In conclusion, Lizardi reminded the assembly that more than fourteen million of Mexico's fifteen million people were Catholics. To keep them from going to confession would require so many police that the law could never be enforced.[41]

Medina delivered a more reasonable attack. Twenty-five years old and a native of León, Guanajuato, he had received his education in the schools of the state capital. He too had graduated from the School of Jurisprudence and had been a revolutionary since the Madero period. Medina thought the additions proposed by Recio violated freedom of conscience, "the highest principle of modern intellectuality," granted in Article 24. The private confession, he said, had a historical as well as a moral significance, and evidence of the former was overwhelming. With one line in the constitution prohibiting it, the delegates would destroy the work of forty centuries, something which "humanity will probably not be able to do in even another forty (Applause)." If the historical evidence was not enough, however, acts of religious faith could certainly be justified on a moral basis. All governments and societies sought organization and discipline in order to assure progress. Religions furnished, he believed, that sense of public morality necessary to achieve this objective. As for the requirement that priests marry if they were under fifty, Medina reminded his listeners that a similar proposal had come before the French Revolutionary Convention of 1793, but its sponsors had been forced to withdraw it. To those comparing the Mexican Revolution to the French Revolution, he warned that Robespierre, convinced of the need for marriage and civil regulations governing the priests, had died under the guillotine for his radical views.[42]

In rebuttal, Recio said that Lizardi, as head of his household, might prevent his wife and daughters from going to confession; but "we did not come here to legislate for those who can take precautions; we came to legislate for the Mexican people who are eighty-five percent illiterate . . . the oral confession . . . is one of the great immoralities . . . and we ought to ask vigorously and once and for all

41 *Diario de los debates*, II, 1033–1034.
42 Ibid., pp. 1038–1040.

. . . that it be completely abolished." As for the marriage requirement, Recio asked, "How much longer are we going to permit, *señores*, the ministers of the faith in the Republic of Mexico to be subjected to the authority of the sovereign of Rome?" Priests would like to marry, he contended, but had not done so because they lacked ecclesiastical permission. If the constitution authorized marriage for priests under fifty as a requisite for the performance of services, then papal control over the clergy in this regard would cease.[43]

In the end the views of Lizardi and Medina prevailed. On Saturday evening, January 27, by a vote of 93 to 63, the convention approved Article 24 as reported out, thereby rejecting the amendments proposed by Recio. If a vote against Article 24 indicated disapproval because it was not strong enough, i.e., a vote for Recio's proposals, it is interesting to note that forty-six delegates identified as voting against had voted for the committee report on Article 3. These forty-six were the rabid anticlericals of the convention. On the other hand, thirty-seven of those who voted against Article 3 had joined with twenty-nine who had voted in favor of the same article to give the necessary majority approval of Article 24. These were the moderates of the convention. Among those who voted for both Article 3 and Article 24 was the *come fraile*, Múgica, who explained that he thought it his duty to respect the spirit of the section on individual rights and not try to write restrictive measures into Article 24—a far cry from his position on Article 3!

Recio's proposals had been too discriminatory for the majority to swallow. Abolition of the oral confession would have been a serious blow to Catholic worship. The marriage requirement for priests under fifty, a provision compelling the violation of the vow of celibacy, was clearly aimed at driving the Catholic clergy out of the country. Although Recio had lost, this did not mean that the convention had heard the last of him. The discussion of Article 129 shows repeated attempts to outlaw the oral confession and require priests to marry.

ARTICLE 129 (LATER 130)

Coming the same night, right after the vote on Article 24, with

[43] Ibid., pp. 1040–1041.

the delegates already agitated over the religious issue, the discussion of Article 129, which became Article 130 in the final constitution (see appendix A), kept the pot of anticlericalism at the boiling point. Even the first reading on the previous day had been greeted with applause and cries of "Vote, Vote!" This article contained a potpourri of provisions on marriage as a civil contract, the juridical personality of "religious institutions known as churches," restrictions and limitations on the clergy and their participation in nonreligious activities, and government control of church buildings. With no separate discussion of the article's provisions, the convention voted on them as a whole, accepting each one without change.

Article 123 of the Constitution of 1857 had simply stated that "the federal authorities shall have power to exercise in matters of religious worship and outward ecclesiastical forms such intervention as by law authorized." Carranza's draft added three innocuous paragraphs, one of which provided for the civil nature of the marriage contract. None was really anticlerical. However, the Second Committee of Reforms added twelve paragraphs that gave Article 130 the distinction of containing the most severely anticlerical provisions in Mexican constitutional history. Why and how did this come about? At least part of the answer lies in the composition of the Second Committee.

This committee was established on December 23, when it became apparent to all that the First Committee would be unable to report on each article of Carranza's draft within the time remaining. As in the case of the First Committee, President Rojas tried to dictate the membership. Again the assembly overruled him. Those finally approved were Machorro y Narváez, Medina, Jara, Dr. Agustín Garza González (Nuevo León), and Dr. Arturo Méndez (San Luis Potosí).

The chairman, Machorro y Narváez, thirty-nine and a native of Durango, obtained his law degree in Guadalajara. Before the revolution he served with the Ministerio Público in Jalisco and as a judge in Aguascalientes. Active in municipal politics in Guadalajara in 1913, he was appointed director of the preparatory school in that city by the Constitutionalist military governor of Jalisco in 1914, only to have to flee when the *villistas* took over the state in early 1915. Making his way to Veracruz, where he held a position in the Ministry of Gobernación, he is said to have written radical articles in the labor organ *Vanguardia de Orizaba*. When elected to the convention, he was serving as attorney general (*procurador de justicia*) of the Federal District and territories.[44]

Hilario Medina has been briefly described as a participant in the debate on Article 24.

Heriberto Jara, thirty-six, heavy set, with tousled hair, ably combining humor with seriousness during debate, was an old *magonista*, labor sympathizer, and revolutionary. He participated in the Río Blanco strike of 1907, supported Madero, and served in the Twenty-sixth Congress. Joining the Constitutionalist movement, he experienced considerable combat and rose to the rank of general. Although he had little or no preparation in constitutional law, he did know the needs of the people. He considered himself as fighting for the "vindication of the proletariat" and fortunate to "represent the working class in this Constitutional Convention." He voted for Article 3 and against Article 24. Jara, the only confirmed activist and anticlerical on the committee, undoubtedly played a leading role in the deliberations.

Doctor Garza González, almost forty-four, was mayor of Monterrey in 1912. Like many others opposed to Huerta, he fled to San Antonio, Texas, in 1913 to join the Constitutionalist junta there. Serving later as Mexican consul in Brownsville, he returned to Monterrey in 1914 as director of a clinic. In March, 1915, Carranza named him director of customs in Nuevo Laredo, a post he held until his election as delegate to the convention. Unfortunately, Doctor Garza González suffered gastrointestinal problems in Querétaro and missed many sessions. His name does not appear as a signer of the report on Article 129.

Dr. Arturo Méndez, almost forty-nine, a native of Nuevo León, studied medicine in Mexico City and received his degree when only twenty-one years old. Later he had taught at the medical school in San Luis Potosí and served as *presidente municipal* of the state capital in

[44] For biographic data on Machorro y Narváez, see *La Herencia del Constituyente*, no. 7 (March 5, 1964); on Jara, see Bojórquez [pseud. Bórquez], *Crónica del constituyente*, pp. 692–694; on Garza González, see *La Herencia del Constituyente*, no. 16 (December 5, 1964).

1911 and 1912. Working for the Constitutionalist cause in varying positions as medical doctor, he fled to Veracruz with Carranza in 1914 and subsequently became responsible for providing all the *carrancista* forces with medical supplies, hospital equipment, etc. From this post he asked leave to attend the convention.

The Second Committee clearly had two objectives in mind when it drafted Article 129. First, instead of reasserting the principle of separation of Church and State, it stressed the necessity of establishing the supremacy of the State over the Church. Furthermore, the committee recommended denial of the legal personality of the Church and religious bodies, which even the Laws of the Reform had not attempted. Consequently, with the clergy now considered as private citizens, the State could impose on them the regulations and restrictions it considered necessary.[45]

Second, the committee sought to end once and for all the clergy's influence in the political life of the country by prohibitions and restrictions "on the expression of ideas, by ballot and other means such as periodical religious publications, . . . and the formation of political parties from religious orders."[46] Perhaps the most disturbing provision of the article was the last, which denied trial by jury for the violation of any of the article's preceding provisions. "The reason for this was obvious," said the committee: the majority of the jury would probably be of the same belief as the minister being judged, hence not inclined to apply the law. Not only was this a denial of rights under Article 20; it was also frank recognition by the drafters of Article 129 that their reforms might not be very popular.[47]

As soon as debate commenced on Article 129, Pastrana Jaimes and twelve fellow delegates proposed an amendment and an addition. The former asked that matrimony be declared a "dissoluble" civil contract, whereas the committee had simply referred to a civil contract. The latter, manifesting strong nationalism and aimed squarely at the Catholic church, read as follows: "The churches which have been allotted to or will be allotted to the religious denominations and which

---

[45] *Diario de los debates*, II, 973.
[46] Ibid.
[47] Mecham, *Church and State*, p. 388.

are the property of the nation, shall not be given in lease, use, operation, administration, assignment or in any other way, direct or indirect,
to ministers of any religious cult or sect who recognize authority, jurisdiction, or dependence on any sovereign or foreign power."[48] Of the
thirteen signers, twelve were rabidly anticlerical, nine having voted
against Article 24, probably in protest against the exclusion of Recio's
proposals. The only name out of place on the list was that of Lizardi,
one of the most distinguished of the rightists. Was this a display of
his bohemian nature?

During the two hours and fifteen minutes of debate that followed,
little opposition developed to Article 129. In demanding even stricter
curbs upon the clergy, the speakers manifested the strongest spirit of
nationalism yet displayed in the debates on any of the religious features of the constitution. They assailed not only the Church but also its
teachings and its clergy. Modesto González Galindo (Tlaxcala) vehemently expressed complete contempt for the Christian religion:

I come to speak here without fear of censures, without fear of excommunication, without fear of hell, without fear of eternal damnation. (Applause.
Laughter.) . . . Unfortunately, not all are like many of the delegates.
There are some who call themselves liberals, but these gentlemen, to be
sure, wear a scapulary, they hear mass, they cross themselves, they bless
themselves when they go to bed, they have their fountain of holy water.
(Laughter. Applause. Hisses. Voices: Anything else?). . . . It has been
agreed that religions have developed through an evolutionary process, even
arriving at Christianity which is supposed to be more perfect. Theologians
say it is the most truthful; I call it a farce, a string of lies, of fabulous
stories. (Laughter. Applause). . . . The Christian Bible asserts in one
of its first chapters . . . a very stupid legend: it says that Adam and Eve
had children. (Laughter. Applause. Hisses. Bell). Good; I ask for a little
more silence. They had Cain and Abel, the first human pair, and from them
all humanity descends; well then Cain killed Abel and only three remained;
afterwards, Abel [*sic*] goes away to Lot's country. (Laughter. Applause).
Listen to me, *señores diputados*. There he found his mate, and that mate
was not a daughter of Adam and Eve. (Voices: Shut up, man! Laughter.
Hisses) That is the first nonsense, the first absurdity of the Christian religion. If you would permit me to relate all the absurdities that there are . . .

[48] *Diario de los debates*, II, 1043.

(Voices: No! No! No!) you would see that they have no explanation . . . the Catholic religion brings us a dogma which is of the purity of Mary. I am going to show you, *señores* . . . (Whistles. Laughter.) If it is true, gentlemen, that the Virgin Mary is pure, then . . . (Laughter. Whistles. Disorder. Bell).[49]

With the delegates now thoroughly aroused, González Galindo got to the point: the need to abolish the oral confession, which of course had nothing to do with Article 129. Defeated by the vote on Article 24, he and his ultraradical cohorts were trying again. Declaring that the oral confession was utilized by the clergy as an instrument of political control, he asserted that its abolition would have no effect on the liberals or the Protestants. As the convention had "snatched the children from clericalism by the vote on Article 3," González Galindo now exhorted his colleagues to snatch "the woman from the confessional," since women were the instrument by which the Church achieved its political objectives and the clergy "stripped the home of its honor."[50]

Speaking for Article 129, Alvarez y Alvarez lambasted the clergy right and left. Declaring that his race had been exploited by the "white and chubby hand of the Catholic priest," he went on to say, that he did not believe a religious problem existed in Mexico. He saw the question as a political one, since the clergy, Catholic or Protestant, were interested not in propagating the faith but in obtaining a hold on the minds of the people in order to control national politics. Characterizing the clergy as an institution "noxious to society as well as a political enemy of the government," he asserted that the State had to be strong enough to regulate them. Alvarez y Alvarez thanked the committee for having accepted his suggestion that legal recognition be denied religious institutions, going on to say that this would facilitate control of the clergy. They would now be considered as members of a profession, hence susceptible to regulation through the provision allowing state legislatures the right to limit the number of priests in each *población*. Alvarez y Alvarez considered this measure as absolutely necessary because of the "scandalous number" in some states who

49 Ibid., pp. 1044–1045.
50 Ibid., pp. 1045–1046.

did "absolutely nothing" but go through the streets and parks "saying mass" for want of a place to carry out religious services.[51]

The predominant theme in the debate on Article 129 was nationalism. Whether he spoke against the papacy as the symbol of foreign religious domination, against Protestant influence, against United States imperialism, or against the number of non-Mexicans who were Catholic priests, nearly every speaker exploited this theme in attacking or defending the committee report. Denying that Christianity had ever penetrated the conscience of the Mexican people, "who are not religious but fanatic," Pastrana Jaimes gave a résumé of the history of the Catholic church in Mexico, which, he said, "teaches us very bitter truths." For four hundred years the papacy had worked against the best interests of Mexico: it had authorized the "great plunder" of the country committed by the godless conquistadors, had been reluctant to recognize independence or the liberal principles of the Constitution of 1824, had issued an encyclical to the bishops authorizing them to support the return of Mexico to Spain, and had opposed the Constitution of 1857 as well as the Laws of the Reform. Now less danger existed from the papacy than from the alliance between the Mexican clergy and those of other nations, particularly the United States. Consequently, it was necessary to deny the use of churches to any denomination responsible to foreign authority. Then Pastrana Jaimes proposed the establishment of a national church, an expression of the sovereignty of the Mexican people. He thought the action of the Philippine clergy, who disavowed the Pope in 1898, set an example. They had set up an independent church, and the Filipinos in matters of religion were much better off. To free the Mexican clergy from allegiance to the Pope would lead them on the road to obtaining their independence and their autonomy. Surely, he said, there must be among the Mexican priests some Hidalgo, some Morelos, some Matamoros who would risk excommunication (Voices: "El Padre Cortés! Laughter. That one is a *gachupín*").[52]

[51] Ibid., pp. 1047–1051.

[52] Ibid., pp. 1046–1047. The Philippine Independent church was founded in 1902 by a Catholic priest, Gregorio Aglipay. Appealing to Philippine nationalism, he led a schismatic group out of the Catholic church upon the refusal of the Vatican to recognize Filipino clergy of the first Philippine republic.

No one at Querétaro exploited the nationalistic sentiments of the delegates more successfully than Palavicini. He believed elements from "the other side of the Bravo" had stirred up the religious problem. President Wilson, a great statesman who understood the spirit of the Mexican Revolution, believed the Mexicans alone should settle their own problems. Unfortunately, Secretary of State Robert Lansing, lacking the idealism of Wilson, saw things only from the legal standpoint. Worse still, Wilson's private secretary, Joseph P. Tumulty, whom Palavicini branded as a fanatical Roman Catholic, exerted a doleful influence on the president and Lansing and was the one responsible "for all the intrigue spun around Woodrow Wilson by those who exploit the religious problem of Mexico," i.e., those demanding intervention in Mexico to save Catholicism. Directing his remarks to Pastrana Jaimes, Palavicini criticized his support of the Philippine Independent church, saying this church was "a shame and a disgrace," tantamount to the Filipinos' rejection of their religious faith. Applauding the delegates' determination "to overcome the danger of the priests," he nevertheless warned that the Mexican people had to defend the essential characteristics of their nationality: their religion, language, and hybridized Latin race. To combat clericalism in a sensible manner would avoid subjecting the "soul of the Mexican people to a still worse instrument of domination, . . . the American evangelist, because it would be handing us over to a foreign domination." Undermining the Catholic faith as an element of nationality could not be permitted.

Having vented his wrath against the neighbors to the north, Palavicini then got around to criticizing Article 129. First, he found fault with the provision that only a Mexican by birth could be a minister of any religious denomination. He suggested the wording, "In Mexico in order to be a minister of the Catholic or Protestant faiths, it is necessary to be a Mexican by birth," a change of little importance. Palavicini also thought the framers of Article 129 erred in not requiring those in charge of church buildings to be Mexicans by birth, because, he said, "the foreign priests are the ones who have robbed our churches and have taken away . . . all the works of art, the pictures and the sculptures. (Applause.)" Palavicini also attacked the provision giving state legislatures the power to regulate the number of priests according to the needs of each locality. How could this be done? Would it not be as absurd as trying to limit the number of doctors, lawyers, or engineers, who were also members of professions? Furthermore, since State and Church were separate, what right did state governments have to determine the number of priests in a certain locality? How could a legislature, especially one supposedly composed of liberals, apportion religion to the people?[53] Knowing he had little chance of swaying the vote on Article 129, Palavicini attempted to appeal to the spirit of nationalism, to the absurdity of writing illiberal restrictions into the constitution.

Last to speak, the indefatigable Múgica affirmed that the Mexican people were not as fanatically Catholic as one might believe. Speaking of anticlerical outbursts during the revolution, he said he had seen the people "delirious and joyful in Michoacán, in Tamaulipas, and along the northern border" as they watched the burning of the images that they had previously worshipped on the altars. "That, gentlemen," said Múgica, "is consoling: that goes to show that the religious problem does not really exist in Mexico but exists there on the other side of the Bravo."[54] If President Wilson knew what was really happening in Mexico, that the heads of priests were not paraded around, that nuns had not been violated, then he should also know what immoral acts the clergy had committed. To substantiate the charges against them, Múgica read six documents taken by revolutionary forces from episcopal archives that proved, he said, that the Mexican people had acted justly in persecuting the clergy, who were really "thieves, outlaws, and swindlers." Piqued by the hisses he had received on voting *sí* during the roll call on Article 24, Múgica asserted his intention of demonstrating anew his jacobin spirit. Article 129, he said, was all right, but it needed an addition outlawing the oral confession.

The belated support of Múgica for such radical proposals was, however, of no avail. Unperturbed by the jacobins clamoring for a vote on the additions proposed by Pastrana Jaimes and his fellow radicals,

[53] *Diario de los debates*, II, 1051–1055.
[54] Ibid., p. 1058.

President Rojas simply announced that Article 129 would be voted on as presented. The *Diario de los debates* records unanimous approval, the voting taking place about 2 A.M., January 28. Anticlericalism in the convention had reached its zenith. Most of the discussion had centered around proposed additions rather than the actual provisions. The only delegate to criticize any of these was Palavicini, and his proposals received no consideration. Interestingly enough, persistent advocates of the abolition of the oral confession made a final, desperate attempt during the permanent session of January 29–31 to obtain its approval. Then, by a majority vote, it was decided not to discuss the matter but to continue with the business at hand. This finally ended the attempt to write the abolition of the oral confession into the constitution.

ARTICLE 27 AND CHURCH PROPERTY

Although Article 27 will be discussed more completely in a subsequent chapter, its various provisions relating to the right of religious organizations to hold and administer real property must be dealt with here as a continuation of the efforts of the delegates to the Querétaro Convention to subject the Church to the strict control of the State.[55] The time had come to strip from the Church the properties it had clandestinely acquired during the *porfiriato*.[56] The delegates believed it necessary to reaffirm and amplify the Laws of the Reform.

With reference to property held by religious bodies, Carranza proposed substantially the same provisions as those contained in Article 27 of the Constitution of 1857. There were, however, two additional features, one radical in itself. He asked that charitable and educational institutions be prohibited from acquiring real property other than that required for their immediate use. Furthermore, he proposed that under no circumstances should these institutions be under the patronage, direction, or administration of religious corporations or their ministers. The latter stipulation was indeed serious in a country where religious bodies traditionally operated hospitals, asylums, and orphanages.

[55] For the texts of these provisions, see appendix E.
[56] Mecham, *Church and State*, pp. 376–377.

The First Committee's report on Article 27, presented on January 29, included provisions on church property harsher and more restrictive than those of Carranza's draft. Now churches were forbidden to acquire, hold, or administer real property or loans made on the same. Places of public worship, seminaries, and convents were to be nationalized and used exclusively for the public services of state and federal governments. Furthermore, churches constructed later were to become the property of the nation if paid for by "public subscription," but, if constructed from private funds, they were to be subject to the laws governing private property. As for charitable institutions, the committee accepted Carranza's proposals, although wording them in slightly different form.

Applause greeted the reading of paragraph 7, clause II, concerning church property. However, several provisions were immediately criticized. Medina asked that all churches erected in the future be placed under governmental control regardless of the means by which their construction was financed. Samuel de los Santos even declared that he and some other delegates opposed the building of more churches, because the clergy got private persons to do this, regardless of the funding. But no one paid any attention to him. General Múgica, however, in the name of the committee, did answer Medina. He said that there were many private chapels in Mexico over which the committee did not think the government should have jurisdiction. Furthermore, a colony of Russian Jews had requested permission to establish a colony and build their own "churches," which the committee thought they should be allowed to do. In granting this specific right to a religious minority, Múgica expressed his implicit intention of discriminating against the Catholic church. However, he indicated that the committee would not oppose Medina's proposed amendment.

Further criticism came from Lizardi, who thought churches should be prohibited from owning movable as well as real property. History had shown, he said, that it was customary to convert real property into movable property through shares payable to the bearer. In this way the clergy, denied the ownership of real property, could acquire stock in corporations and be on the way to taking over the ownership of all the industrial concerns of the country. This had happened in the past to agricultural property. Now the Church must be prevented from taking over industry in the same way. This proposal drew the support of Doctor Garza González, who said that a document seized from the episcopal archives in Monterrey revealed the plan of a Catholic engineer to take over all the city's industries; Froylán C. Manjarrez (Puebla) also backed it for the sole reason that it revealed the assembly's willingness to "increase radicalism rather than decrease it." Lizardi's proposal, however, was attacked by his fellow *guanajuatense*, Medina, on the grounds that it would be impossible to determine the nonreal property of the clergy. If they were to invest this in stock to be held by intermediaries, nothing less than inquisitorial proceedings, he believed, could be used to determine the amount.

Alvarez y Alvarez complained that the committee had seriously erred in asserting that the Church would "not be able to obtain lands or other properties." Actually, the clause did not read that way, but Alvarez y Alvarez thought it did. He reasoned that Article 129 denied juridical personality to the Church, and now Article 27 was taking certain rights from the Church, thereby implying that the Church could acquire other properties, hence conceding juridical personality.

When Múgica announced the committee was withdrawing clause II in order to incorporate the changes asked by Medina, Alvarez y Alvarez, and Lizardi, the delegates expected it to be modified accordingly. When it was presented again within a few minutes, there were two changes. In the opening line, the phrase "religious associations known as churches" was substituted for "the Church," and the last line now read: "All places of public worship which shall later be erected shall be the property of the nation." Medina had won his point. As for Lizardi's fear, Múgica declared it was "completely exaggerated, his proposal impossible to put into practice." Nothing was said about Alvarez y Alvarez's proposal, and the clause was then reserved for voting.

In regard to clause III, concerning the right of charitable institutions to hold or administer loans on real estate, Medina asked the committee to strike out the provision limiting these loans to a maximum period of ten years. If retained, he believed that this provision would permit the property to remain under the "dead hand" of the clergy. Speaking for the committee, Macías allayed Medina's fears, saying that a period of ten years was not unreasonable, although a longer one would only favor the clergy, because of the manner in which these loans were customarily handled in Mexico. The assembly sustained Macías; clause III underwent no change. The provision barring religious corporations or ministers of denominations from administering or supervising charitable institutions was not even questioned. One can only wonder whether the delegates realized the consequences of their action. In their haste and anxiety to impose restrictions on the ownership of property by religious institutions, or to finish the constitution, they were apparently willing to jeopardize the welfare of all who were cared for by private charitable institutions.

OTHER ARTICLES CONCERNING THE CHURCH OR THE CLERGY

Although the articles discussed above are the principle ones concerning the Church and the clergy, others deserve at least passing attention. Article 5, better known as the forerunner of Article 123, on labor, contained two provisions regarding the clergy when reported out by the First Committee on December 12. One, worded similarly to Article 5 of the Constitution of 1857 as well as to Carranza's draft of the same article, outlawed religious vows resulting in the loss of freedom to the vower. The other, taken from the Laws of the Reform, forbade the establishment of monastic orders. Carranza's draft simply said that "the law . . . does not recognize monastic orders." No one spoke in opposition. Supporting both measures, Monzón took advantage of the opportunity to scourge the Church as well as the clergy, saying that all the churches in Sonora were closed and the friars were all "on the other side of the line [i.e., in the United States]. (Applause)." Classifying churches as "real holes of corruption because there is where the girls lose their virginity and the honor of the married women is perverted," he denounced the friars as "the most uncompromising enemies of civilization and of the libertarian revolutions." Monzón said he wished all the towns of the republic were like his, Cumpas, where most of the inhabitants were not baptized. "My children are not either," he affirmed, "they do not even have Christian names; Señor Bojórquez knows how my children are

named. (Voices: How?) They are numbered. (Laughter)."[57] In the
end the convention accepted the religious provisions with the rest of
the article on the night of January 23 by the affirmative votes of 163
delegates.

Article 13 prohibited trial by private laws or special tribunals.
Worded like the corresponding article in Carranza's draft, it was
basically the same as Article 13 of the Constitution of 1857. All discussion concerned its application to military tribunals. Without ques-
tioning the prohibition on clerical courts, the old *fuero* of the clergy,
the article was approved on January 10 by a vote of 122 to 61.

Article 33, concerning aliens, was reported out by the First Committee with the provision of Carranza's draft giving the president the
exclusive right to expel any foreigner whose presence he deemed undesirable. A similar provision in the Constitution of 1857 had given
the government the right to expel the "pernicious foreigner." However, to the report of the First Committee, Múgica and Román issued
a minority report listing in detail eight classes of foreigners whom the
president might expel. Included in this list were "those who represent
the illegal wealth of the clergy" and "clergymen who are not Mexicans." The minority believed this would provide effective protection
to useful foreigners, "freeing them from any abuse on the part of the
executive power," yet leaving the president the right to act against
foreigners who deserved expulsion. Unconvinced of the need for such
biased stipulations, the delegates rejected the minority report during
the permanent session by a vote of 93 to 57.[58]

As the convention drew to a close, a significant amendment was
proposed to Article 37. Originally reported out on January 23 and
approved on the twenty-sixth, the article provided that a citizen could
be deprived of his citizenship for receiving titles or decorations from
another country or government without first obtaining permission
from the Mexican Congress. The amendment, signed by ten delegates,
four of whom were confirmed anticlericals, provided that Mexicans
could lose their citizenship "by compromising themselves in any way before ministers of any denomination or before any other person not

[57] *Diario de los debates*, I, 1030.
[58] Ibid., II, 1136.

to observe the present Constitution nor the laws arising thereunder."[59] Perhaps they remembered the attempt of the archbishop of Mexico and other prelates of the Catholic church to intimidate the faithful into rejecting the Constitution of 1857 after its promulgation. If so, the threat of loss of citizenship would deter any who might be influenced by similar clerical action with reference to the new constitution. On January 30, during the confusion of the permanent session, with much business still unfinished, the assembly accepted this addition without question.

Articles 55, 59, and 82 also showed signs of anticlericalism. Article 55, clause 6, denied eligibility for election to the House of Representatives to the "minister of any religious denomination." This was taken directly from Carranza's draft, the Constitution of 1857 having stated that anyone elected to the unicameral Congress could not be a member of the "ecclesiastical state." Of the six requirements for eligibility, clause 6 was the only one approved without debate and by the unanimous vote of the 171 delegates present. The same provision, also approved without objection, is found in eligibility for election to the Senate (Article 59). The convention was determined that no clergyman should ever sit in Congress. It manifested the same sentiment in regard to the requisites for election to the presidency. Whereas the Constitution of 1857 stated that no candidate could belong to the "ecclesiastical state," Article 82, clause 4, of the new constitution declared that "he shall not belong to the ecclesiastical state nor be a minister of any religious creed," the same wording used in Carranza's draft. It too was approved without discussion. In reality these provisions were unnecessary, for Article 129 affirmed that the clergy "shall have no vote, nor be eligible to office, nor shall they be entitled to assemble for political purposes."

If Catholic writers impugned the Constitution of 1857 for its failure to grant exclusive recognition to the Catholic religion, they were undoubtedly appalled that the Constitution of 1917 went far beyond this omission to impose on the Church and its clergy the harshest restrictions in Mexican constitutional history. Although much of the debate on the religious issue evoked the mouthings of blatant

[59] Ibid., p. 1143.

prejudice, the majority of the delegates sought to destroy, or definitely limit, the economic power of the Church and the social and political influence of its clergy. By denying the Church a legal standing, forbidding it to own property, drastically reducing its influence in education, and imposing numerous additional restrictions, the delegates believed they were accomplishing their objectives. The dividing line between anticlericalism and antireligion, between sincere reformer and unreasonable nonbeliever, can be a thin one. So it was at Querétaro, as the jacobins, convinced of the fanaticism of Catholic religious practices, went to the extreme of attacking dogma or requesting the inclusion in the constitution of provisions that would have impaired the continued practice of the faith in Mexico. With a grudge against the Church and the clergy that blinded them to the spiritual and charitable services the latter might render, the delegates could see only evil. It made little difference, despite the pleas of learned lawyers to the contrary, that the grants of rights in the constitution to individuals in matters of faith and worship were negated by stipulations contravening these very rights. Discussions in support of these restrictions show that the delegates were not attacking the Church for the benefit of any interest group; rather they were attacking the Church and its clergy for the benefit of Mexican society. It must be stated again that, although this assault was ostensibly directed against the Roman Catholic church, there is very little to indicate that the delegates favored Protestantism. The majority seemed to believe that Catholicism and Protestantism, Catholic and Protestant clergy alike, were undesirable influences on the people. Because the overwhelming majority of Mexicans were Catholic, however, it was this denomination that bore the brunt of the onslaught. Here a nationalistic bias manifested itself openly and strongly. Unafraid to speak out, delegates to the Querétaro Convention formulated during the course of the debates a new politico-ecclesiastic relationship for Mexico. No longer was the Church to be free and independent of the State. For the future the relationship was, in theory, to be one of complete subordination of the Church to the will of the State.

4. The Evolution of
a Labor Program

The laws of the Constitutional Convention of 1917 are not made to show off knowledge that is merely modern and theoretical but to cure the sores of an afflicted people.

Juan de Dios Robledo (Jalisco)
Fernández Martínez Album

The Constitution of 1917 is forged with workers' blood. Cursed be the people who violate it!

Dionisio Zavala
Ruiz Album

TEN DAYS AFTER the convention resolved the issue of religious education with the vote on Article 3, deliberation began on the role of labor in the new socioeconomic order. Almost by accident, the discussion of Article 5 led to the drafting of Article 123, "Labor and Social Welfare," the only article to merit an entire section of the constitution. It granted rights and privileges only partially expressed in the legislation of highly industrialized nations, rights that organized labor had been striving to obtain since the advent of the Industrial Revolution. That these were achieved in predominantly agricultural Mexico, where industry was only beginning to be of importance, is incredible.

Within the convention the formulation of Article 123 followed much the same procedure as that of the more famous Article 27. Both were originally drafted by extralegal committees. Both went far beyond Carranza's recommendations on labor and agrarian reform. Both were only briefly discussed on the floor of the convention and hastily accepted. Both broke with the tradition of the Constitution of 1857 by incorporating lengthy, detailed provisions into constitutional law. However, there was this difference. Whereas agrarian reform received no attention before Article 27 was presented and steamrollered through the convention during its final hours, Article 123 resulted from demands for labor reform heard during the first sessions. These demands reveal how seriously the delegates endeavored to provide for the welfare of labor in the new constitution.

Carranza's constitutional draft contained only four articles concerning labor, none of which was important. Article 4 provided that no person could be prevented from engaging in any lawful profession, industry, trade, or occupation. Article 5 stipulated that no one could be obligated to furnish personal services without just return and his own consent, that the State could not permit any contract impairing the liberty of man, and that a labor contract could not exceed a year or endanger the civil or political rights of the individual. Article 9 permitted peaceful assembly for any lawful purpose, presumably including a labor meeting, although numerous restrictions limited this right. However, Article 73, paragraph 10, was all important. It gave the federal Congress power to legislate on labor matters throughout the country. Unwilling to write details into the constitution, Carranza believed that a broad grant of power to the Congress was sufficient. In his speech of December 1 to the convention, he cited the need to legislate for the working class, specifically mentioning such items as limitations on hours of work and kinds of labor, adequate time for rest and recreation, compensation for accidents on the job, sickness and old-age insurance, a minimum salary, and other benefits.[1]

Prior to December 26, when debate commenced on Article 5, the convention discussed Articles 4 and 9. Article 4, on the right to engage in a lawful profession or occupation, was approved December 18 by a vote of 145 to 7. It was worded much like the corresponding article in Carranza's draft, but the First Committee had inserted an additional line stating that "no one shall be deprived of the fruits of his

[1] *Diario de los debates del Congreso Constituyente, 1916–1917,* I, 392.

labor except by judicial resolution." A proposal, undoubtedly inspired by Múgica, prohibiting the sale of intoxicating liquor and the operation of gambling houses was rejected by the committee as out of place in Article 4. However, the prohibitionists would be heard from again.[2]

Article 9, providing for freedom of peaceful assembly for lawful purposes, was reported out on December 22. In Carranza's draft, the same article listed five situations under which an assembly would not be considered peaceful and hence would be legally dissolvable. The First Committee, believing that the interpretation of these situations could furnish pretexts for authorities to arbitrarily dissolve meetings, had eliminated them from its draft, returning instead to the simple wording of the Constitution of 1857.[3] To Jorge von Versen, fiery labor leader and journalist from Monclova, Coahuila, any restriction on the right of assembly was onerous, because the only guarantee that the workers had was "the right to get together in order to demonstrate their strength before the powerful." Consequently, he urged the delegates to vote for the committee report. However, Nicolás Cano (Guanajuato), a miner with trade-union experience, was not so sure. He was concerned with the protection of workers on strike. Protesting the shooting by the police of striking workers in Mexico City in mid-1916, he believed Article 9 should positively state that strikers must not be considered as disturbers of public peace and order. They should receive the full protection of the law. After a poignant description of the miserable condition of labor in Guanajuato, he concluded with the plea that workers be put on an equal footing with capitalists. If the latter could not be forced to work, then gatherings of workers on strike should not be dissolved.[4]

Answering Cano, Múgica said his request could not be placed in Article 9, which related simply to gatherings with a lawful purpose. This did not include the strike, which was a "natural defense of

[2] See chapter 6.
[3] Article 9, Constitution of 1857: "The right of anyone to assemble or associate peaceably for any lawful purpose cannot be limited; but only citizens of the Republic may do so in order to take part in the political affairs of the country. No armed meeting has the right to deliberate."
[4] *Diario de los debates*, I, 877–878.

labor against capital." Jara, however, said he considered the right to be "understood" in its second paragraph: "No meeting or assembly shall be considered illegal, nor may it be dissolved, which shall have for its purpose the petitioning of any authority or the presentation of any protest against any act, provided the said authority is not insulted, nor violence resorted to, nor threats used to intimidate or to compel the said authority to render a favorable decision."[5] This, he believed, was sufficient to guarantee workers the right of assembly. In the end, Cano did not press his point, and Article 9 was approved as reported out by the committee by a vote of 127 to 26.

The brief debates on Articles 4 and 9 were but prologues to a spontaneous demand for the redemption of the Mexican proletariat, an outburst that found poignant expression in debates on Article 5. It was read for the first time on December 12, but discussion did not commence until the afternoon of the twenty-sixth, with 140 delegates present. As reported out by the First Committee, the article read as follows:

No one shall be obliged to render personal services without just compensation and without his full consent, except labor imposed as punishment by judicial authority. The law shall punish vagrancy and determine those who violate it.

In regard to public services, only the following shall be obligatory, subject to the terms established by law: military service; service in the judicial branch for all the lawyers of the Republic; jury service; offices filled by popular election; and service in connection with elections which shall be gratuitous and obligatory.

The State cannot permit any contract, pact, or agreement to be carried into effect which has as its purpose the impairment, loss, or irrevocable sacrifice of the liberty of man, whether for work, education, or religious vows. The law, therefore, does not permit the existence of monastic orders, whatever the denomination may be or for whatever purpose they may be founded. Nor can it permit an agreement in which man agrees to his own exile or in which he renounces provisionally or permanently the right to exercise his chosen profession, or industrial or commercial pursuit.

The labor contract shall only be binding to render the services agreed

[5] Ibid., p. 865.

upon for a period not exceeding one year and shall not cover in any case the renunciation, loss, or impairment of any political or civil right.

The maximum working day for obligatory labor shall not exceed eight hours, even if imposed by judicial sentence. Night work in industry for women and children is prohibited. The weekly day of rest is established as obligatory.[6]

Coming from a committee of known leftists, this wording was far from radical. Except for obligatory service for lawyers, the eight-hour day, the prohibition of night work for women and children, and the weekly day of rest, it closely resembled Article 5 of Carranza's draft and was not unlike the one in the Constitution of 1857. The First Committee, considering additional prolabor measures out of place in the section on individual rights, had decided against their inclusion in Article 5, although they had conveniently overlooked this restriction in drafting Article 3. On December 9, however, three delegates from Veracruz sympathetic to labor, General Aguilar, Jara, and Victorio E. Góngora, had petitioned the committee to include provisions on equal pay for equal work by both sexes, workmen's compensation in certain industrial jobs, the settlement of conflicts between capital and labor by committees of conciliation and arbitration, and the right to strike.[7] The First Committee turned down the petition, stating that legislation on such matters was more appropriately the concern of Congress.

Interest in the labor issue may be seen from the fact that fourteen delegates immediately registered to speak on Article 5. The first, the perceptive Lizardi, spoke against. The statement on vagrancy, he said, was completely out of place in Article 5, which "should not be concerned with legislating on crimes but with guaranteeing a right." Although a lawyer, he argued that the provision obligating lawyers to serve in the judicial branch of the government would only make the administration of justice much worse than it was! Furthermore, he asked, "Why not say that service is obligatory for doctors in the hospitals, for engineers in constructing highways and public build-

---

[6] Ibid., p. 970.

[7] Alberto Trueba Urbina, *El artículo 123*, pp. 84–85. For biographic data on Góngora, see *La Herencia del Constituyente*, no. 5 (January 5, 1964).

ings, and for pharmacists . . . in drugstores?" Finally, Lizardi struck out against the limitation of the working day to eight hours. Article 4 guaranteed the right to work, and Article 5 limited that right to an eight-hour day: Lizardi said this was as contradictory as giving "a brace of pistols to a blessed Christ." Such a limitation, he believed, should be placed in Article 4. Better still, let Congress decide the length of the work day, as the First Chief proposed in his draft.

First to support the committee report was Dr. Cayetano Andrade (Michoacán), twenty-six, poet and journalist, equally at home with the muses and with medicine. A native of Guanajuato, he finished his medical studies at the University of San Nicolás in Morelia, Michoacán, in 1914. He won election to the convention with the support of organized labor. Speaking for the eight-hour day and the prohibition of night work for women and children, he said that these measures were urgently needed to save the race from certain degeneration. No liberty, not even the right to work, he pointed out, was absolute. Workers had made possible the Constitutionalist victory; they were the ones whose needs had to be met.[8]

Stuttering as he spoke for the eight-hour day and the prohibition of night work for women and children, Jara won applause for the forceful manner in which he expressed himself. The eight-hour day, he said, was not proposed as an afterthought. It guaranteed the very life of the Mexican workers, who "have been no more than the meat of exploitation." Those defending the right to work were only leaving the worker to the mercy of the employer, who would work him for twelve, fourteen, or sixteen hours a day. If permitted to continue, this practice could only result in the degeneration of the race. Criticizing the doctrine that detailed provisions, like that limiting the length of the working day, were out of place in a constitution, he called it a sacrifice of individual rights merely to satisfy those who wished to preserve the terseness of the traditional constitution. If the lawyers objected to obligatory service, he urged that Article 5 be voted on by paragraphs; but he pleaded, "Remember those unhappy beings, those unfortunate ones who, limping and miserable, drag their misery

[8] For biographic data on Andrade, see *La Herencia del Constituyente*, no. 11 (July 5, 1964), and no. 12 (August 5, 1964).

across the floor with their eyes fixed on you for their salvation. (Applause)."[9]

Two workers, Héctor Victoria and Dionisio Zavala, both familiar with the problems of the laboring class, spoke next. Although they took opposite sides in the debate on this article, both showed strong concern for improving working conditions.

Victoria, thirty years of age, obtained his *bachillerato* at the State Literary Institute in Mérida. Later he worked as a mechanic at the railroad shops in Mérida and lost an eye in an accident. This did not deter him, however, for in 1911 he led the first strike of railroad workers in Yucatán; and, as a result, became first secretary of the Railway Workers' Union. In 1915 he served on the Mérida city council. Elected as a delegate to the convention, he was determined to see that labor got a square deal at Querétaro.

To Victoria, the First Committee report was as unacceptable as Carranza's draft of Article 5; neither treated the problem of the working class with due consideration. Furthermore, he thought it a mistake to grant the national Congress power to legislate on labor problems, which differed so greatly throughout the country. Showing typical Yucatecan distrust of central authority, he declared that the sovereignty of the states must be recognized and preserved. In his opinion the workers of Yucatán were probably better off, thanks to the Constitutionalist revolution, than any others in the country. Determined that their gains should not be lost, Victoria urged that the power to legislate on labor matters to be left to the states. He asserted, however, that Article 5 should contain bases for legislating on hours of work; a weekly day of rest; healthful working conditions in factories, mills, and mines; courts of conciliation and arbitration; prohibition of night work by women and children; accident insurance; and worker's compensation. In asking for these benefits, Victoria was merely trying to protect rights decreed for Yucatán in December, 1915, by Governor Salvador Alvarado.[10]

Speaking for Article 5, Zavala, an ex-miner, urged the convention to accept it because "the workers are the ones who have made the

[9] *Diario de los debates*, I, 978.
[10] Marjorie R. Clark, *Organized Labor in Mexico*, p. 202.

Revolution." Who had ever seen rich people engage in the fighting? Who had ever seen *la brigada de intelectuales?* No, the workers had been the cannon fodder, had done the dirty work; and they deserved recognition. Zavala also asked that Article 5 be voted on by sections in order to prevent the lawyers opposed to the provision on compulsory judicial service from voting against the entire article.

Jorge von Versen disapproved of the labor contract for a definite period of time. Owners of textile mills, he said, would enter into a contract with their employees for one year at low wages and then raise the price of their goods so that the workers would not even be able to buy a meter of coarse cloth "to cover their nakedness." Vehemently opposed to voting on the article by parts, he asked that it be rejected entirely and presented anew in a much stronger form, saying "give Christ leggings, pistols, and a .30-.30 so that he can save our humble class, our class that represents . . . our national greatness. (Applause)."[11]

Following von Versen came the first speaker to suggest a separate part of the constitution dedicated exclusively to labor and labor welfare. Whereas previous speakers had mainly proposed additions to or modifications of Article 5, Froylán Manjarrez made this significant proposal on December 26. Only twenty-five years old, he brought to Querétaro one suit of clothes and a great assortment of loud ties, of which he wore a different one to each session. He looked so youthful that few believed he could be a delegate. Yet he spoke with fervor and deep conviction:

I think our Magna Carta ought to be more explicit on this point . . . who will guarantee us that the new Congress will be composed of revolutionaries? Who will guarantee us that . . . the government, as señor Jara said, will not tend toward conservatism? Who will guarantee us that the General Congress must expedite [laws] . . . in accordance with our ideas? . . . what is important is that we pay due attention to . . . those men who fought in the armed struggle and who are the ones who most merit our efforts to bring about their well-being; and we should not be afraid if the Constitution, owing to errors in form, appears a little worse from the structural standpoint . . . let us introduce all the reforms that

11 *Diario de los debates,* I, 984.

are necessary for labor; let us give them the salaries that they need, let us attend to their each and every need . . . because there are many points that have to be discussed concerning the labor question, we do not want all this to be placed in Article 5, for that is impossible . . . if it is necessary to ask the Committee to bring us a draft in which all is included in . . . one part of the Constitution, . . . we will have performed our mission as revolutionaries. (Applause).[12]

The last speaker on December 26, Pastrana Jaimes, a lawyer, attacked the provision compelling members of his profession to serve in the judicial branch. He also wanted to know why the section on individual rights contained a provision obligating workers to labor for a year. Then he presented an addition to Article 5 which he had drawn up jointly with Porfirio del Castillo (Puebla). To them the only significant demands of labor in Mexico had been for higher wages, not for an eight-hour day, or for a court to resolve labor conflicts, or for an end to night work for women and children. In their opinion, the most important labor provision in the constitution should be a guarantee to the worker of a decent and humane wage. Upon this basis, each state legislature would then be expected to enact a law.

With the conclusion of Pastrana Jaimes's speech, the session adjourned. The first day of debate on Article 5 had clearly indicated the prolabor attitude of the delegates, for whom the First Committee's report did not go far enough. Although Article 5 would be debated for another two days before the convention accepted Manjarrez's proposal, he had convinced many delegates that the chapter on individual rights was no place for a detailed labor code. The only logical alternative was to set it up as a separate section of the constitution. The drive toward Article 123 was underway.

When discussion of Article 5 resumed on the afternoon of December 27, with 163 delegates present, Josafat Márquez (Veracruz) spoke for the committee report. He strongly supported the provision on vagrancy, believing that this would be an effective way of compelling the lazy to work. He wanted to be able to say to the whole

---

[12] Ibid., p. 986. For additional biographic data on Manjarrez, see Alberto Morales Jiménez, *Hombres de la Revolución mexicana: 50 semblanzas biográficas*, pp. 287–291.

world: "In my country everybody works; all the workers are fully protected." Porfirio del Castillo followed Márquez with a passionate plea for justice for the workers, especially the Indians. Self-conscious about his lack of education, unceremonial, yet proud of his Indian background, del Castillo spoke with deep sincerity. Refuting Márquez's contention that Mexicans were lazy and must be made to work, he launched a vigorous attack on capitalism and its exploitation of labor. The principal target of his attack was the obligatory labor contract, which he deplored as the means by which shrewd lawyers employed by management would force conditions on workers who were too ignorant to know what they were signing. Quoting Ignacio Ramírez, delegate to the Constitutional Convention of 1856–1857, he said that "to speak of contracts between employer and worker is to speak of a way of affirming slavery." Furthermore, in court action involving a contract, the workers received no justice. This went to the rich, because "the judges are their servants." Why, he asked, should workers be forced to sign a contract to work in factories where hours were so long and working conditions so vile, where the exhausted worker developed tuberculosis and promptly passed it on to his children? Supporting the eight-hour day and a decent salary, del Castillo concluded by asking for protection for the Indian, not only for his freedom and his rights but also for "something more positive, something more practical: a piece of bread for the thankful worker to share with his children, blessing the memory of the delegates to the Querétaro Convention. (Applause).[13]

Del Castillo's attack on the labor contract so influenced the youthful Luis Fernández Martínez that he arose to ask that all contracts of a specified length of time be declared illegal. Replying to Lizardi's contention that the constitution would be like a "Christ with pistols" if all the proposed additions were incorporated in it, he said: "Well, *señores*, if Christ had worn a pistol when they took him away to Calvary, *señores*, Christ would not have been assassinated. (Applause and laughter)." With a pronounced revolutionary spirit, he urged his fellow delegates to make the constitution a red flag and a Marseillaise

[13] *Diario de los debates*, I, 1008.

to be sung by all the common people and to be "defended by them and by us."[14]

If Fernández Martínez was ready to lead street fighters in defense of the rights of labor, the next speaker, Carlos L. Gracidas (Veracruz), was more practical. One of the few delegates to the convention who had trade-union experience, Gracidas, twenty-nine, a native of the state of México, began work as a typesetter when he was barely seven. In 1906 at the age of eighteen he went to Mexico City and learned to operate a linotype, one of the first in the capital. A founding member of the Union of Linotypists of the Mexican Republic, he also served the labor movement in the early days of the Casa del Obrero Mundial. Consequently, Gracidas brought to the convention considerable union experience. The last speaker of December 27, he criticized the committee report for not having defined "just compensation" and "full consent." To him, other benefits were of secondary importance if the constitution did not define these terms. Although he offered no definition of "full consent," he did interpret "just compensation" as the right of the worker to receive, in addition to his wages, a share of the profits, without being responsible for the losses. This, he argued, should be stated in Article 5. If some delegates wished to write "secondary" guarantees into the constitution, then let them be placed in a separate chapter on the rights of labor. In urging a clear definition of "just compensation," Gracidas was really pressing the demand for a decent and humane wage made the day before by Pastrana Jaimes and del Castillo. As finally approved, Article 5 contained no definition of "just compensation" or "full consent"; but Article 123 did define a minimum wage. Of more significance, paragraphs 6 and 9 of the same article provided for profit sharing, the revolutionary idea Gracidas had injected into the melting pot that later crystallized into the constitutional labor code.[15]

Up until that point the moderates of the convention, the so-called rightists, had not participated in the debate. The afternoon of Decem-

[14] Ibid., pp. 1008–1009.
[15] See appendix C (to show the derivation of Article 123 from the Rouaix draft, the two documents are compared paragraph by paragraph). For biographic data on Gracidas, see *La herencia del constituyente*, no. 13 (September 5, 1964), and Morales Jiménez, *Hombres de la Revolución mexicana*, pp. 293–295.

ber 28, however, was to be theirs. In a long but eloquent speech, Cravioto revealed his strong background in history and economics. He supported placing all the labor provisions in one article "as a stronger guarantee of the rights that we are trying to establish and for the greater security of our workers." His main purpose, it seems, was to prove that the *renovadores* too had always supported the demands of labor. Denying they were conservatives or even moderates, he asserted they were progressive liberals influenced by socialism, that they had always struggled against peonage, large landholdings, monopolies, privileged capitalism, clericalism, and militarism. On May 1, 1913, he said, a large delegation of workers had asked the *renovadores* to draft suitable labor legislation. But before this could be done, the Twenty-sixth Congress had been dissolved. Later in Veracruz under Carranza "the reactionary Señor Macías, the *porfirista* Señor Macías, Monseigneur Macías" had drafted a labor code that was now ready to be issued.[16]

Rojas had collaborated with Macías in writing the code, which did not form part of Carranza's constitutional draft, he said, because it was considered purely legislative in character. Announcing that Macías would later take the floor to explain it, Cravioto praised the proposals, saying that they contained features unthought of by the labor representatives or the most radical of the delegates. He asked the First Committee to withdraw the labor features of Article 5 for presentation later in a special article. However, if the committee insisted on leaving the labor provisions in Article 5, "although it is against my judgment and that of my friends because we also want the technical perfection" of the constitution, then he and the other *renovadores* would vote for them anyway. Cravioto had startled the convention, but the shock from Macías, soon to mount the rostrum, would be even greater.

Meanwhile, two radicals enlightened the convention on what they believed should or should not be in Article 5. First, Monzón defended Article 5, stating that if the tenor of the convention was to be radical, it was only right that the First Committee should be too. But the committee's radicalism was mild indeed compared to that of the

16 *Diario de los debates*, I, 1027.

Sonora government. In Sonora, he said, there was freedom to work, no vagrancy, and decent pay; the eight-hour day was in effect, and night work for women and children was "an unknown phenomenon"; furthermore, the weekly day of rest was enjoyed, as in California, Arizona, and New Mexico. If these benefits prevailed in far-off Sonora, he asked, why not in the heart of the republic? Refuting contentions that these provisions were more properly legislative matters or should be placed in the section of the constitution concerning the states, Monzón, speaking for the First Committee, said, "We believe that these fundamental precepts fit precisely in the section on the individual rights, and since in this section Article 5 is the one cut out for the liberation of the worker, we believe that is their place."[17] As for wages, indemnification, and committees of arbitration, he thought these too could be placed in Article 5, or in a special article in the section on the states. Most of the workers, he reminded the delegates, were still sunk in slavery. It was the duty of the convention to save them. This could best be done by approving Article 5 in its present form, but if the majority voted against in the belief that it should be more radical, then he was in accord.

Following Monzón, González Galindo announced that he would not defend the doctrines of the famous European socialists and that he was not acquainted with "those wise men of Russia who have written something about socialism." His concern was for a provision in Article 5 empowering each state to legislate on labor matters within its confines. He opposed the labor contract, but said that, if the convention accepted it, then it should only be for those who knew how to read and write "since they will be a little more responsible for their actions." As for the weekly day of rest, González Galindo considered it unnecessary because there were already so many religious holidays. He would accept Sunday as a day of rest, however, if the number of religious holidays were reduced accordingly.

The climax of the debate on Article 5 came with the speech by Macías early on the evening of December 28. Branded by the radicals as a "reactionary, *porfirista*, and monseigneur," this loyal follower and confidant of Carranza now presented in the name of the First Chief

[17] Ibid., p. 1031.

an advanced labor code embodying all the benefits expressed so far
with the exception of the profit-sharing idea of Gracidas. In a speech
covering twelve pages in the *Diario de los debates*, the venerable
Macías expounded his views on labor welfare and gave a brief history
of the labor code he had prepared.[18] It all began in late 1914, he said,
when the Constitutionalists vitally needed labor support. Carranza
had commissioned him and Luis Manuel Rojas to study the problem
and prepare bases for legislation. Their work completed and printed
by January, 1915, Carranza had then sent Macías to the United States
to observe working conditions there. He traveled to Chicago, Balti-
more, Philadelphia, and New York, where he visited factories, inter-
viewed labor leaders and managerial officials, and collected "all the
labor legislation of the United States." He also studied laws of
England, France, and Belgium.

Continuing, Macías commented on the major provisions of the
labor code. He considered the collective labor contract necessary to
assure employers that workers would fulfill their obligations as well
as to provide security for the employees. If workers contracted for
their labor individually, Macías believed that would be their ruin.
Citing Marx on the just return to labor, capital, and the inventor,
Macías stated that boards of conciliation and arbitration in the more advanced countries decided how much labor should receive by fixing
a minimum wage. Unemployment insurance would be of some benefit to the striker and his family if a strike were prolonged due to the
failure of the boards to reach agreement, but Macías advocated a new
concept of labor-management relations when he said that "the government has to be prejudiced in helping to better the situation of the
worker" and to arm him in his struggle against capital. Although
the boards proposed by Macías were to be composed of equal numbers of representatives of capital and labor, the next step would
logically be to add a representative of the government, a measure
bitterly denounced by a prominent conservative Mexican of the period,
who said, "When we consider that in the conflicts between capital
and labor, the deciding vote is cast by a salaried representative of the
government, the results will always be against capital because those

[18] Ibid., pp. 1035–1047.

who constitute the government at present are the armed proletariat, openly hostile to capital."[19]

Macías's statement recognizing the right to strike drew thunderous applause. Other features of his code included workmen's compensation for industrial accidents, hygienic working conditions, labor unions, and old-age benefits. Flattering the First Chief before the assembled delegates, Macías said it was Carranza's work—that all he, Macías, had done was to gather the necessary information and that Carranza had "resolved all the important questions one by one."

Why were these laws, known collectively as the Proyecto de Ley sobre Contrato de Trabajo, not issued? Macías believed it necessary to answer this question before it was asked. In 1915, he said, Mexico was torn by revolution, the laws unenforced. Had the labor laws been promulgated under such conditions, the workers would have felt betrayed; they would have lost faith in the Carranza government to fulfill its pledges. Furthermore, when Macías returned to Mexico, he found that the then secretary of *gobernación*, Lic. Rafael Zubaran Capmany, had advised Carranza to decree an amendment to Article 72 of the Constitution of 1857 giving Congress the power to legislate on labor matters throughout the country. Macías disapproved of such a sweeping grant of power, believing that working conditions varied so throughout Mexico that labor legislation was more appropriately a matter of state than of federal concern. Finally, since it would be ridiculous to revoke an amendment once decreed, he and Carranza had agreed to let the Constitutional Convention, although it would not meet for nearly two years, decide whether labor legislation should be within the powers granted to the states or to the federal government. Why had not Carranza placed this labor code in his draft of a new constitution? In Macías's own words: "Carranza did not put it in the Constitution because he believed it was a secondary matter."[20] But now the situation had changed. What the moderates and lawyer friends of the First Chief had excluded from the draft for the sake of brevity and conciseness must now be included, although in its proper

[19] Jorge Vera Estañol, *Carranza and His Bolshevik Regime*, p. 61.
[20] "El Señor Carranza no lo puso en la Constitución porque creyó que era cosa secundaria," *Diario de los debates*, I, 1045.

place. Asking the convention to reject Article 5 because its few provisions on labor were "the equivalent of giving a drop of water to a
dying person to quench his thirst," Macías said that the draft proposals, "a work of the Citizen First Chief which he has permitted me
to make known," were available for the convention to use. He then
suggested that all delegates interested in preparing the constitutional
bases for labor legislation should gather around Ing. Pastor Rouaix
(Puebla), a member of Carranza's cabinet with leave to attend the
convention. Although Macías had no authorization from the assembly
to make this proposal, he probably did so with the tacit approval of
President Rojas.

Macías's long address killed further debate on Article 5. He had
made the First Committee and all preceding speakers on the subject
look like amateurs and himself like the skilled draftsman, labor's
spokesman in the convention. Why did Macías present his project at
this time, three days after debate had begun on Article 5? It is safe to
say that Carranza and his small group of intimates in the convention,
knowing that the leftists were in control and working toward the
inclusion of a detailed labor code in the constitution, saw the opportunity to present their plan before the leftists could get one together
and thus receive the credit. This draft, with modifications and additions originating in the convention, eventually became Article 123.[21]

The remainder of the evening of December 28 was but the denoue-
ment of a memorable session. With the prestige of the First Committee at stake, Chairman Múgica defended the report on Article 5. With
fine irony, he prefaced his remarks by saying that the radicals were glad

<hr>

[21] Mario de la Cueva, *Derecho mexicano del trabajo*, I, 113, 116–117; Frank
Tannenbaum, *Mexico: The Struggle for Peace and Bread*, p. 117; Félix F. Palavicini,
Historia de la Constitución de 1917, I, 143–144; "Proyecto de Ley sobre Contrato
de Trabajo," *El Constitucionalista*, nos. 23–34 (April 20–May 28, 1915). The draft
Macías presented was never promulgated by Carranza. It was prepared by Macías,
Cravioto, Rojas, Juan N. Frías, and Manuel Andrade Prieto—the first four of whom
were delegates to the convention. Important because it is the source of many of the
foreign ideas which found their way into Article 123, the draft features labor
legislation of the United States, England, Germany, France, Holland, Belgium, Spain,
and Italy as well as the liberal ideas of statesmen and labor leaders of the times.
Since most of this information was acquired by Macías on his trip to the United
States, the draft reflects his influence on the provisions and wording of Article 123.

to learn that the First Chief "is as radical and as jacobin as we are." Obviously stung by Macías's charge that the committee had been satisfied with so little for labor, he asserted that the proposals were placed in Article 5 to safeguard the "natural rights of man." Let all subsequent proposals be placed elsewhere. Considering the economic diversity of the different regions of the country, the committee had found it very difficult to write into Article 5 any meaningful definition of the minimum wage. It had been just as hard, he said, to define "just compensation" and "full consent"; so the words of Article 5 of the Constitution of 1857 were used. However, Múgica stressed the need for an eight-hour day to keep the worker from working an excessively long day as well as overtime just to make more money. Science had determined how long a man could work each day without ruining his health, he said, and this limit should not be exceeded. The government had to keep the race healthy, not only to ensure reproduction but also to defend the country in time of war. For these reasons the committee had limited the right to work. As for the prohibition of night work for women and children, this would "save the race," would protect the weak from their greatest exploiters, rapacious mill and factory owners. The weekly day of rest also had to be raised to constitutional status. Furthermore, said Múgica, placing these measures in the constitution would provide the necessary support for state labor laws issued during the preconstitutional period. In conclusion, he asked the delegates to approve Article 5 as presented. However, if they wished to place the various proposals in another section, it mattered little where they were placed "as long as they are put in the Constitution."

Following Múgica, Gerzayn Ugarte mounted the rostrum to propose that the constitutional bases for labor legislation be placed in Article 72,[22] under which Congress would legislate on all labor matters in the Federal District and territories, leaving the state legislatures to pass laws on these bases as long as they were not contravened. If it was acceptable to the assembly, he proposed that the First Committee substitute Carranza's draft of Article 5 for its report. As a further re-

---

[22] Ugarte confused Article 72, on the passage of bills through Congress, with Article 73, on the powers of Congress.

buff to the leftist-dominated First Committee, he seconded Macías's suggestion of an ad hoc committee headed by Pastor Rouaix to assist in preparing the constitutional bases of labor legislation. No one paid any attention. Even a proposal by Froylán Manjarrez formalizing his suggestion of December 26 (on a separate chapter devoted to labor) went unheeded in the closing minutes of the session. Manjarrez thought that it should be titled Del Trabajo and that a committee of five persons, not necessarily delegates, should be named to study the proposals made during the debates for incorporating them into this chapter.

By now many delegates were in a quandary. Obviously there would be a chapter on labor, but what should be done with Article 5? Some of its provisions would surely have to be retained. At this time Rafael Ochoa (Jalisco), Rafael de los Ríos (Federal District), and Dr. José María Rodríguez presented a motion asking that Article 5 not be voted on until the labor chapter was approved. This satisfied the delegates. Realizing that further debate was futile, Múgica, on behalf of the committee, asked the assembly's permission to withdraw Article 5. This was granted, but not before Macías had read into the Ochoa–de los Ríos–Rodríguez motion something that certainly was not there originally: a proposal that interested delegates gather around Rouaix to prepare the labor chapter. There being no objection to this addition, the session ended at 8:30 P.M. A giant leap had been taken toward the formation of Article 123.

Now the scene of the action shifts from the convention hall to the former residence of the bishop of Querétaro, where those determined to hammer out a draft project grouped themselves around Rouaix. Because of his role in drafting Articles 27 and 123, Rouaix was one of the greatest of the founding fathers of the new constitution. A native of Tehuacán, Puebla, forty-two years old, he had in his youth seen the Spanish merchants exploit the indigenous population of the region; this had left a lasting impression on him. Graduating from the National School of Engineering in Mexico City, he went north to Durango, where he remained for some sixteen years, working as a surveyor and topographer. Again he witnessed the exploitation of the rural population by the *latifundistas,* observed their miserable living conditions, and became convinced that change could only come by revolution. At the beginning of the Maderist period he served as *jefe político* and as state legislator. As acting governor of Durango from July, 1913, to August, 1914, he decreed one of the first agrarian laws of the revolution, on October 3, 1913, and, on June 29, 1914, the expropriation of the rural and urban property of the Durango clergy, who were attempting to retain real estate under anonymous title. In August, 1914, Carranza called Rouaix to fill the position of chief clerk in charge of the Ministry of Fomento, Colonización, e Industria. In Veracruz, and following the return of the Constitutionalists to Mexico, Rouaix worked hard, preparing studies and making reports that served as bases for many reform decrees issued during the preconstitutional period. Promoted to secretary of *fomento,* he brought to Querétaro invaluable experience and knowledge. Deeply loyal to Carranza, for whom he had great respect, Rouaix also had the confidence of the radicals, probably because of his proven revolutionary actions in Durango. Although not adept at public speaking, he was a great organizer and one of the most modest of all the delegates.[23]

According to Rouaix, the preliminary draft of Article 123 was prepared by Macías; Rafael de los Ríos, Rouaix's secretary in Fomento; Gen. José Inocente Lugo, chief of the Office of Labor in Fomento, whom Rouaix had asked to come immediately to Querétaro and bring all available studies and data on labor; and Rouaix himself. They used the main features of Macías's research on labor legislation and the various points brought out in the debates on Article 5. Their draft was then presented to the delegates interested in discussing the matter, who met each morning in the chapel of the bishop's residence. They spent the first ten days of January, 1917, on the labor code and then took up Article 5. There was no organization, and unfortunately no record was kept of the proceedings. Debate was unin-

---

[23] Biographic data on Rouaix are found in his *Génesis de los artículos 27 y 123 de la constitución política de 1917,* pp. 52–57, 64–65. See also *La Herencia del Constituyente,* no. 4 (December 5, 1963), and Morales Jiménez, *Hombres de la revolución mexicana,* pp. 251–255.

hibited; but Rouaix, acting as a moderator, was always there to guide it. In the evening hours, he, Macías, de los Ríos, and Lugo reworked each paragraph, putting the ideas and opinions expressed during the morning into suitable form for discussion and final approval the following morning. By January 13 the work was completed.[24]

Macías wrote most of the introduction. A justification for the sweeping labor benefits that followed, it recognized as "unquestionable" the right of the State to intervene as the governing force in labor relations covered by contract and the "right of equality" between employer and employee. This right would assure not only sanitary working conditions, a weekly day of rest, a just wage, and workmen's compensation, but also institutions of social beneficence to care for the sick, aid the crippled, assist the aged, protect the abandoned children, and help the unemployed. Boards of conciliation and arbitration were endorsed for the settlement of labor-management disputes, as was the right of workers to strike if they did so "without violence." The introduction lashed out strongly against peonage, declaring that the law should cancel all debts that workers had incurred with employers or middlemen and prohibit future debts of this kind, "at any time or for any reason, from ever passing to the members of their families."[25] While admitting, on the one hand, that their work was not perfect and would not completely alleviate the country's distressing social ills, the writers believed, on the other hand, that it would provide a promising future for labor and would reduce the growing migration to the United States, due, among other reasons, to the lack of protective labor legislation in Mexico.

The draft was signed by Rouaix and seven others: Góngora; Calderón; President Rojas; Dionisio Zavala; de los Ríos; Silvestre Dorador (Durango); and Jesús de la Torre (Durango). The last two were artisans. Three of the signers—Góngora, Zavala, and de los Ríos—had participated in the debates on Article 5. In addition, fourteen delegates signed as "conforming in general." Among this group are found the names of Macías, Jara, and Gracidas. The latter two, pronounced champions of the proletariat, had also participated in the

---

[24] Rouaix, *Génesis*, pp. 103–107.
[25] *Diario de los debates*, II, 361.

discussion of Article 5. Another of this latter group was Samuel Castañon (Zacatecas), a carpenter. Finally, an additional forty-six delegates signed under the heading "We support the present proposals for reform."[26] Nine of this third group had spoken out on Article 5. Thus, a total of sixty-eight delegates put in writing their support, in varying degrees, of the proposed constitutional labor program. As might be expected, the four delegates who had prepared the Proyecto de Ley sobre Contrato de Trabajo in Veracruz in 1915 were among the signers.

Who were the principal contributors to this first draft of Article 123? Macías, Rouaix, Lugo, and de los Ríos played major roles. Not only did they prepare the initial wording, which served as the point of departure in the discussions, but they also worked each evening, often into the early hours of the following morning, to edit and prepare the remarks made at each meeting for approval the following morning. At the various sessions, Rouaix credits the following as being active participants: Martínez de Escobar; Dorador, de la Torre, Terrones Benítez, and Antonio Gutiérrez of the Durango delegation, all of whom had been Rouaix's collaborators when he was governor; Calderón, Alvarez y Alvarez, Donato Bravo Izquierdo (México), de los Santos, Chapa, and del Castillo, the military delegates; and the workers—Gracidas, Dionisio Zavala, and Góngora.

With the work at the bishop's residence completed, the scene of action now returns to the convention hall. There the draft was read during the afternoon session of January 13 and turned over to the First Committee for study.

Before continuing with the story, however, it is necessary to give brief attention to Article 28, prohibiting monopolies and combinations in restraint of competition in production, industry, commerce, and business. First read on January 12, it was not discussed until the afternoon of the sixteenth. Then, von Versen vigorously attacked the wording for not exempting workers on strike. He feared governmental authorities might act under this article against strikers for restraining "free competition" in production. Von Versen asked the assembly

[26] Ibid., p. 364.

to vote against the article regardless of its other merits. However, to Jara the omission was unimportant. He rightly pointed out that freedom of assembly was guaranteed elsewhere in the constitution (Article 9) and that it was unnecessary to state it again in Article 28 just for labor's benefit. This did not settle the matter, for the delegates, wearied of the debate on the same article's provision for a single banking institution, drifted out of the hall. At 8:20 P.M. the session adjourned for want of a quorum. When discussion resumed on the afternoon of the seventeenth, it was evident that the First Committee had been won over by von Versen's objection, because Article 28 now contained an additional paragraph, which read as follows: "Organizations of laborers formed for the protection of their own interests shall not be considered to be monopolies." There was no objection to this addition, although Palavicini called it a "novelty." By a vote of 120 to 52 the assembly approved Article 28 with the labor paragraph intact.[27]

On January 23, with only one week remaining to finish the constitution, the First Committee presented its draft proposal of Article 5 and the labor code, officially called Article 123 for the first time (see appendices B and C). A superficial examination is sufficient to show the latter's resemblance to and derivation from the proposals drawn up by Pastor Rouaix and his associates. Admitting its indebtedness to the extralegal committee chaired by Rouaix, the First Committee enumerated in the preface to Article 123 the modifications made to the Rouaix draft. The title was changed from Del Trabajo to Del Trabajo y de Previsión Social. To express a greater sense of obligation, the First Committee also changed the Rouaix introductory paragraph, "The Congress of the Union and state legislatures, upon legislating on labor . . . ," to read: "The Congress and the State legislatures shall make labor laws . . ." Although the Rouaix draft called for the eight-hour day in specific occupations, this provision was changed to apply to labor "in general," including artisans, commercial as well as domestic employees, and, by implication, agricultural labor.

The committee accepted the Rouaix proposal outlawing night work

[27] Ibid., pp. 555–556.

for women and children, adding that they should not work in "unhealthy and dangerous" occupations either. The radical concept of profit sharing (paragraphs VI and IX), also added by the First Committee, was considered to pose no threat to capitalism, since the worker, now privileged to share in the company's earnings, would work harder with a personal interest in the success of the enterprise. Furthermore, he would require less supervision, and all disputes concerning wages would become a thing of the past. The First Committee also warned (in paragraph XII) against evasion of the employer's responsibility to provide decent housing for workers even when the business was located in a heavily populated zone where such housing might be difficult to obtain.

Another deviation from the Rouaix draft was the provision outlawing gambling houses and the sale of intoxicating liquors in workers' residential areas. Múgica, a determined foe of alcoholic beverages, gambling, cockfighting, and bullfighting, was undoubtedly responsible for this addition.[28] To prevent abuse by police authorities of the right to strike, the committee specified under what conditions a strike would be considered legal or illegal. To discourage employers from making loans to their workers, the committee added a provision in paragraph XXIV limiting such loans to the amount of one month's wages. Paragraph XXVI, aimed at preventing the abuses suffered by migrant Mexican laborers, was not found in the Rouaix draft. Paragraph XXVIII, concerning the family estate, or *institución del "homestead,"* also new to the Rouaix draft, was added for the benefit of urban workers, although the committee recognized its greater applicability to rural labor. Finally, the committee noted that the preface to the Rouaix draft had proposed the cancellation of all debts workers had accumulated through their work, although the draft itself lacked a specific provision to this effect. To make up for the omission, the committee proposed a transitory article (Article 13), the final wording of which would be as follows: "All debts contracted by workingmen by virtue of their work up to the date of the constitution with masters,

[28] Jaime H. Plenn, *Mexico Marches*, p. 158. The attempt to write prohibition into the constitution is discussed in chapter 6.

their subordinates, or agents are hereby declared wholly and entirely liquidated."[29]

Applause greeted the reading of Articles 5 and 123 on the afternoon of January 23, but not the secretary's announcement deferring discussion to the twenty-fifth. Eager to settle the labor question at once, the delegates demanded that the order of business be changed to permit immediate discussion. By standing vote this was done. Then, to the cry of "Let's vote! Let's vote!" debate began on Article 5.

Federico E. Ibarra (Jalisco), the only one to question the wording, asked why the First Committee had stricken the last line from the Rouaix report. This line, concerning labor contracts, had freed the worker from all but civil responsibility in the event of breach of contract on his part and had prohibited coercion being exercised against him in such a case. Considering it necessary to restore this stipulation, Ibarra reasoned that the Constitution of 1857 had made no provision for a labor contract, but employers had always used coercion against employees when the latter had failed to live up to the terms of a contract. If this had happened under the old constitution, which had not mentioned labor contracts, then what would happen under the new one, which authorized a binding contract for a definite period of time? He thought it necessary to protect the worker against coercion in case of a breach on his part, for without such a provision "we are going to . . . sanction slavery in our country." Ibarra picked up support from Macías, who, reminding all that the Rouaix committee had recognized the need for such a provision, asked the assembly to reinstate it. Although he was sure that limiting workers' liability in case of breach of contract to civil damages alone was guarantee enough, Macías reminded the delegates that "what is understood without being said is understood better if said"; therefore, the addition of a no-coercion statement would remove all doubt on this point. Against such logic, the First Committee could offer no defense. Múgica, indicating that his committee was in agreement, asked to withdraw the

---

[29] H. N. Branch, "The Mexican Constitution of 1917 Compared with the Constitution of 1857," Supplement to the *Annals of the American Academy of Political and Social Science* 71 (May 1917): 113. Transitory articles were those that applied specifically to the first Congress to meet under the new constitution; they dealt with setting up the government, etc.

draft report. Permission was quickly granted. After a brief recess, the committee reported it back with two changes: the last paragraph of the Rouaix report was reinstated, and the phrase "which shall conform to the provisions of paragraphs 1 and 2 of Article 123" was added to the first paragraph. The latter merely imposed limitations on the work day when labor was imposed as a punishment by judicial decree. Acceptance of these amendments ended debate on Article 5, and it was reserved for voting. Although discussion had primarily served as a springboard for ideas that would later find expression in a revolutionary labor program, the delegates to the Querétaro Convention, by agreeing to vote on Article 5 together with Article 123, had given plain recognition to the fact that the former was important for more than just historical reasons.

Discussion of Article 123 began in the early evening hours of January 23, continued after a brief recess at 7:55 P.M., and finally ended shortly before 10:15 P.M., when the exhausted delegates gave their approval to it, together with Article 5 and transitory Article 13, abolishing debt servitude. No opposition developed to the detailed code reported out by the First Committee. The convention accepted most of it without discussion; many delegates were impatient with the reading of it paragraph by paragraph. Múgica answered a few questions of minor importance. Only on paragraph XVIII, concerning strikes, did anything like a debate occur. Because no additions or changes were made from the floor, debate on Article 123 has been dismissed as unimportant, the real discussion having occurred during the deliberations of the Rouaix committee. Nevertheless, the story of Article 123 would be incomplete if it did not include the additional views and sentiments expressed by the labor reformers while the article was before the convention.

In the introductory paragraph, Rafael de los Ríos asked if *trabajo doméstico* referred to servants or to workers engaged in cottage industries. Múgica explained that there was "no difference" between the two, that the provision applied to all who worked for wages. This loose explanation apparently satisfied de los Ríos and the others, for there was no further question. On the reading of paragraph III, concerning labor by those sixteen and under, Saúl Rodiles (Veracruz) asked for special juvenile courts to avoid sending children to jail, where they acquired "vices they did not have before." Rodiles was applauded but told his proposed addition belonged in Article 13, on the extent of court jurisdiction. President Rojas then relegated the proposal to oblivion when he asked Rodiles to put it in proper form for discussion later. To the cries of *adelante, adelante*, paragraphs IV to XIII were read in rapid-fire order, each being reserved for voting without discussion. Thus in a matter of minutes the convention approved such advanced measures as the humane treatment of working mothers; minimum wages; profit sharing; overtime pay; and comfortable and sanitary housing, schools, public markets, and other community services in districts inhabited by workers and their families. Paragraph XIV, on hygienic working conditions and industrial accidents, prompted López Lira to ask if it covered occupational sicknesses that did not incapacitate a person from working. A doctor from a mining state, Guanajuato, he believed that compensation should be made in such cases. Múgica answered that this was a question for state legislatures to decide. No questions were raised on paragraphs XV and XVI and only a minor one on XVII.

    ¡Adelante! The reading of paragraph XVIII, on conditions under which strikes would be considered legal or illegal, produced the only debate on Article 123.[30] Again the *guanajuatenses* were the dissatisfied ones. Nicolás Cano, who knew the meaning of hard work, asked that a striker not be considered as a disturber of the peace simply because he was on strike. Strikes, he said, usually start off peacefully, but when the industrialists, "who are almost always in very close contact with the authorities," cannot break them, they charge the strikers with disturbing the peace or hire persons to create a disturbance that serves as a pretext for police action. This practice, Cano believed, had to be outlawed. Although he thought individuals who destroyed property or disturbed the peace should be punished, he asked protection for those who exercised the right to strike in a peaceful manner.

    Mounting the platform to propose a second addition, Gerzayn Ugarte asked that the right to strike be denied workers employed in

[30] *Diario de los debates*, II, 845–858.

the manufacture of arms and munitions. A strike in this industry, he said, would seriously weaken the country's defense against "external aggression." Calling it "patriotic foresight," he asked that such workers be considered as a part of the army, thus subject to military law and deprived of the right to strike granted other workers under paragraph XVIII. Jara defended the First Committee's draft of this paragraph. Attempting to allay the fears of Cano, he pointed out that strikes would only be considered unlawful when the majority resorted to acts of violence against persons or property. The key word, he emphasized, was *majority*. Destructive acts of five or ten persons in a crowd would not be enough to invoke police action. As for Ugarte's proposal, Jara believed that the munitions workers were already governed by military law; therefore, a special constitutional provision denying them the right to strike was unnecessary.

In a very short but curt speech, Col. Antonio de la Barrera (Puebla) arose to express his dissatisfaction with Cano's request and his approval of Ugarte's proposal. He thought that ample liberty had already been given to the workers. It was now time to give the police the right to apprehend a worker who disturbed the peace. What Cano asked, he said, would lead to unconstrained freedom. As for Ugarte's proposal, if the munitions workers attempted to strike, then let them be drafted into the army. Judging from the many exclamations of *muy bien*, de la Barrera had accurately expressed the mood of the delegates.

At this point Múgica went to the rostrum to calm the fears of the labor sympathizers and to explain why his committee had changed the wording of the Rouaix draft. The committee, he said, had no intention of imposing limitations on the right to strike. Only when "the major part of the strikers might commit abuses against persons and property," added Múgica, could a strike be dissolved. Up to a certain point, he agreed with Cano, who had said that workers rarely behaved so as to invite police action. But he vividly recalled the 1911 strike of streetcar conductors and motormen in Mexico City and the damage they had done, "acts of true violence" that the law in no case could permit. There would be no pretext, he said, under the present wording, for the police to take action against workers on strike unless "a numerous group of strikers should participate in violent acts against property and persons." Unfortunately, according to Múgica, Mexico was still not tolerant of strikes. "The bastard ambitions that capital always has," he said, would try to get the authorities to remove the strikers, who in turn would ask the same authorities for protection. He believed that once the constitution legalized the strike, the police would have to act carefully. As for Ugarte's proposal, the committee had thought that in time of war the workers would be patriotic enough to stay on the job. However, he apologetically explained, the committee had not had time to really look into the matter; and if the assembly wanted to add what Ugarte asked, then there would be no objection.

Immediately after Múgica took his seat, the secretary read an amendment proposed by youthful Fernández Martínez, who had belatedly come to Cano's support. It stated that "no striker shall be considered as a disturber of the peace, and in case strikers commit unlawful acts, they shall be punished individually without responsibility for same extending to other participants in the movement." But this proposal was rejected by a standing vote. The reaction had set in. When Múgica asked permission to withdraw the paragraph and add Ugarte's proposal, it was immediately granted. When presented again, the wording was as follows: "Employees of military manufacturing establishments of the Federal Government shall not be included in the provisions of this paragraph inasmuch as they are a dependency of the national army." Without further ado this was accepted and the paragraph reserved for voting. It was the only addition made to Article 123 from the floor of the convention.

As the reading continued, many paragraphs were reserved for voting without so much as a single question. Paragraph XX provided for boards of conciliation and arbitration with equal representation of labor and management and one member from the government. Gracidas asked whether these boards would be chosen on a permanent or ad hoc basis. In Yucatán, they were permanent, he said, but in Veracruz they were set up as the need arose. Múgica answered that this was a matter for the state legislatures to decide.

Paragraph XXIV outlawed all debts owed employers by employees and prevented the former from ever holding workers' families responsible for these debts. This reform was for the future, but what about the past? Calderón asked why the committee had not canceled all such debts as of the date of the promulgation of the new constitution. Múgica replied that transitory Article 13 declared all such debts null and void *up to* "the date of this Constitution" and that this included "the entire revolutionary period." Together, these two provisions would legally end peonage in Mexico, both past and future. When Rafael de los Ríos innocently asked what it meant in transitory Article 13 to cancel all debts incurred by workers *pleno derecho*, his question drew laughter. Speaking for the committee, Colunga answered that it meant "without need of any proceedings, without necessity of any judicial decision, solely because the Constitution says so." Without further question, the transitory article was reserved for voting.

Despite the increasing restlessness of the delegates, the questions continued. Paragraph XXVIII on the inalienability of the patrimony prompted Doctor Rodríguez to ask if this included the dwelling place of the worker. He said that in some parts of the United States the homestead was not attachable under any circumstances. He thought a similar provision stating that the home, furniture, and other household goods could not be seized for nonpayment of debt would be a "good work" for the constitution. All Múgica could say by way of an answer was that there was no need to add what Rodríguez asked, that paragraph XXVIII included all he desired. No one questioned this interpretation.

Finally, Gracidas, still fighting labor's cause, asked if the First Committee had considered a proposal he had made earlier. Although this proposal is not printed in the *Diario de los debates*, it appears that he had asked for a transitory article affirming the validity of employer-employee contracts made up to the present. Employers in Veracruz and elsewhere, he said, were disavowing these contracts, many of which were favorable to labor. If one transitory article nullified workers' debts, why not add another recognizing the validity of these contracts? Significant gains labor had made during the preconstitutional period should not be lost just because this era was ending and a new one was about to begin. The constitution, Gracidas believed, should especially recognize existing contracts. Backing Gracidas, Epigmenio Martínez arose to speak his mind, saying, "the *señores* jacobins are urging me to . . . (Voices: Bravo! Applause)." He asserted that many workers would be favored by such an article. As for ending debt servitude, he was all in favor "because if it is bad for the capitalists, then it is a good thing for the major part of the workers. (Applause)." From this statement it is difficult to tell whether Martínez was speaking for the transitory article that had just been approved or whether he was really trying to support Gracidas.

Answering Gracidas, Múgica said that the First Committee had taken his proposal into consideration but had rejected it, because, "if it might favor a contract beneficial to the worker, it also might favor a contract that would be harmful to him." Furthermore, said Múgica, "as an act of justice, we believe that from the moment that these bases . . . drawn up for the protection of the working class, as well as to guarantee the rights of capital, take effect, all contracts should be prepared on these bases."[31] Although Gracidas tried again to impress on his fellow delegates the need to protect gains already won by contract, such as "the recognition of unions and even the manner of doing work," he spoke in vain. At this point, no one really cared.

¡A votar! By now the delegates, in no mood for further talk, were impatient, ready to vote approval of an extraordinary labor program. Yet they still seemed in good spirits, as Bojórquez observed just before the vote:

I want to simply state that the good humor of the delegates is not only due to a special condition of the spirit that is always noticeable after the supper hour, but also because in these moments we are approving a true law that fulfills one of the great needs of the Revolution and one of its greatest promises. I want to say to the public that is present at this time that all our manifestations of merriment . . . (laughter) are timely. (Voices: Let's vote!) No; wait a moment. Our demonstrations of joy, on significant

31 Ibid., p. 862.

occasions, ought not to be taken as a joke when such a transcendental matter is discussed, because . . . this same matter was discussed in the previous session, and in heated discussions and at the same time it has been discussed for more than a month in private meetings which were attended by labor representatives. We are, then, completing one of the greatest acts of the Revolution. The good humor of the assembly is justified. (Applause).[32]

When the secretary called for a vote first on Article 5, to be followed by Article 123 and then the transitory article, the assembly demanded that all three be voted on together. So they were. Approval was apparently unanimous, for, as the *Diario de los debates* laconically states, "163 delegates voted for the affirmative."[33] There is no record of any opposition.

It is necessary to recapitulate. The labor program of the Constitution of 1917 was a genuine product of the convention. Carranza's draft contained no such comprehensive proposal; nor did the leftist delegates have a definite plan to place before the convention at the start. Confused as to what should or should not be written into the constitution, uncertain as to where the various proposals should be placed, the delegates were, nevertheless, united in a common goal: to save the worker from further exploitation and offer him and his family hope for a more livable future. Article 5 was the key point in the evolution of the labor program. Only when it was discussed and found wanting were the wheels set in motion for the writing of the proposals later found in Article 123. In the beginning the rightists, or moderates, were opposed to detailed constitutional provisions, preferring a general grant of power to Congress to legislate on labor matters. However, when it was obvious to all that the convention was headed toward a labor code, Carranza's adroit clique of personal followers uncovered their own detailed proposals, mainly from the Proyecto de Ley sobre Contrato de Trabajo published, but not promulgated, in Veracruz in 1915. The leftists forced the reluctant rightists

[32] Ibid., p. 863.
[33] Ibid.

to bring these proposals to the floor, for it is certain that they did not intend to do so otherwise. Persistence on the part of the leftists made Article 123 an enlightened labor code. They accepted the rightist proposals only after Pastor Rouaix and his extralegal committee had made them more acceptable and only after the First Committee under Múgica had hammered them into final form.

It has often been said that Article 123 was written not for the present but for the future, that the provisions were applicable only to a more industrialized society. Discussion in the convention, however, bears testimony to the delegates' determination to eliminate evils already existing in Mexican industry. They knew that men, women, and children worked long hours for low pay under intolerable conditions in mines, mills, and factories, with little or no hope for betterment. Article 123 would protect workers as Mexican industrialization continued, but the problems it was designed to meet were of the present.

Throughout the debates on the labor issue runs a strong racial theme. It is seen in the use of *Indian* as a synonym for *worker*, in the earnest desire to "preserve the race," to make it possible for the worker to develop a strong, healthy body. By giving him the right to a decent wage, a limited work day, safe working conditions, clean housing, and other benefits, the delegates were encouraging the development of a vigorous race from the then diseased, overworked, and impoverished proletariat. For them the constitution would have meaning.

Finally, it may be asked, did the debates on the labor issue reveal a spirit of nationalism? Inasmuch as capital in Mexico was largely foreign, the anticapitalistic bias of the delegates has been variously represented as an attack upon the favored position of the foreigner in Mexico, a call for the emancipation of the Mexican worker from foreign exploitation, and an expression of "Mexico for the Mexicans." Although these may have been conscious motives for the writing of stringent measures into the labor program, a check on unbridled capitalism, there is little if anything in the debates which singled out foreign capital for special attack. Rather, capital in general, both foreign and domestic, was assailed as the enemy of the working man. The predominant theme in these debates was simple humanitarianism. What motivated the delegates more than anything else was the wish to enhance the quality of life for the Mexican worker and his family, to restore his dignity as a human being, and to give him a just share of the national income. The spirit of nationalism, however lacking in the labor debates, would later find full expression in Article 27.

5. Article 27: The Attack on Vested Interests

I say that the agrarian question is the main problem of the
Revolution . . . because now it is on the conscience of all the
revolutionaries that if this problem is not justly solved, the war
will continue.

Juan de Dios Bojórquez
Diario de los debates del Congreso
Constituyente, 1916–1917

When each inhabitant of the Republic has his home and his
piece of land to cultivate, the causes of revolutions in our
fatherland will have been eliminated.

Luis T. Navarro
Alvarez Album

AFTER OBTAINING, in theory at least, the emancipation of labor
through Article 123, the delegates turned to the most pressing of all
national problems, the agrarian. In searching for a solution, they drew
up Article 27, the most distinctive feature of the Constitution of 1917,
the one that has given form and meaning to the Mexican Revolution.
A product of the convention, Article 27 was a frontal attack on
vested interests that had long exploited Mexican lands and waters
at the expense of the rural masses. Strangely enough, it was not presented for debate until near the end of the historic meeting at Querétaro and then was accepted in a matter of hours. At the beginning
there was no plan, no proposal, nothing that could even compare with

the comprehensive article of nearly 2,500 words approved by the convention.

That Carranza contributed little to the finished Article 27 is evident from the record. In his speech of December 1, the First Chief made only passing reference to agrarian reform. Reminding his audience that Article 27 of the Constitution of 1857 authorized the occupation of private property without the consent of the owner when public utility required it, he concluded that this gave sufficient authority to the government to acquire and distribute lands among those who wished to farm them, "thus establishing the small property holding which must be encouraged as the public needs require it." He asked that the declaration of public utility be made by the administrative authority, leaving the value of the expropriated property to be determined by the courts. Condemning the ease with which foreigners had acquired property in Mexico, the First Chief also suggested that Article 33 require them, on obtaining real property, to renounce their citizenship with regard to the property and to submit completely to Mexican law.[1]

Only one reference to agrarian reform appears in the draft proposal of Carranza's Article 27 (appendix D). Its paragraph 5 reads as follows: "The *ejidos* of the villages, whether those maintained subsequent to the Ley de Desamortización, since restored to them, or which have been granted anew in conformity with the law, shall be enjoyed in common by their occupants, while they are divided in accordance with the law to be expedited to that effect."[2] Other provisions authorized property expropriation for reasons of public utility after prior compensation, forbade religious organizations and charitable institutions from owning more property than that destined directly for their use, specified the conditions under which corporations and non-business organizations could own urban and rural properties, and authorized banks to make loans on such properties in accordance with the law. Significantly, Carranza made no reference in his speech nor in the constitutional draft to the famous decree of January 6, 1915,[3]

[1] *Diario de los debates*, I, 392.
[2] Ibid., p. 508.
[3] See chapter 1.

thereby revealing his lukewarm attitude toward the problem and strengthening the fear that this decree had served only as a political gesture to win support for the Constitutionalist cause. In reality, he opposed the writing of detailed reforms into the constitution. A group of determined revolutionaries in the convention, however, did not. Rejecting the First Chief's draft as incomplete and forceless, a betrayal of the national interests, they proceeded to write a new article which "saved the Revolution" and made later reform possible. It was they who forged the decisive feature of the Constitution of 1917.

How was this done? Unfortunately no record was kept of the discussions in the extralegal committee that hammered out the first draft or of the later discussions of the First Committee, which prepared the final draft for the convention. However, some who were present at these historic meetings have told what happened. Prefaces to the drafts of Article 27 emanating from these two committees further reveal what the delegates had in mind. Likewise, the *Diario de los debates* records the discussion on the floor of the convention. From these sources the evolution of Article 27 can be partially reconstructed.

Debate on Carranza's draft article had been postponed because of the complexity of the problem, because no one (least of all Carranza) had the answers, and because its transcendental nature required thorough study. The First and Second Committees, too harassed, too occupied with other matters, could not give it the deserved attention. And, hanging over the convention like the sword of Damocles was the awareness of a fast-approaching deadline: January 31. Under such circumstances the delegates, as in the case of Article 123, again turned to an extralegal committee, which produced a first draft. After studying this draft for four days, the First Committee presented its report on Article 27. Then, during the permanent session of January 29–31, in a matter of hours, the delegates gave it their approval.

Those who played prominent parts in this drama have told the story. One was Lic. Andrés Molina Enríquez. Though not a delegate, this distinguished son of the state of México and intellectual precursor of the revolution was the author of *Los grandes problemas nacionales*, an in-depth study of the agrarian problem resulting from the growth of the hacienda, the failure to protect communal property, and the failure to promote small landholdings.[4] In late 1916 Molina Enríquez served as counsel for the National Agrarian Commission, a creation of the decree of January 6, 1915, under which the Constitutionalists began their agrarian reform program. Ex-officio president of this commission was Pastor Rouaix, secretary of *fomento,* who contributed so to the drafting of Articles 5 and 123. According to Molina Enríquez, one look at Carranza's draft proposal of Article 27 was enough to convince him that "it would require fundamental corrections."[5] The National Agrarian Commission, in a special meeting, readily agreed. With this backing Molina Enríquez explained to Rouaix that as secretary of *fomento* he bore much of the responsibility for the solution of the agrarian problem. He also told Rouaix that it was necessary to find a solution to the whole problem, not just the *ejido* problem as found in Carranza's draft.

At Rouaix's request, Molina Enríquez prepared a draft of Article 27. Read on Sunday, January 14, at a meeting of interested delegates, it produced, as Rouaix says, "complete disillusionment" among those present. Instead of expressing the "revolutionary principles" that all wanted to hear, the Molina Enríquez draft read like a juridical thesis, more theoretical than practical. Missing were the detailed legislative precepts that the reformers believed the constitution should contain.[6]

With valuable time lost in the preparation of the now unusable Molina Enríquez proposals, the delegates would have to work faster. Here the experience of Article 123 served as a guideline. An unauthorized committee, meeting daily from January 14 to 24 in the former residence of the bishop of Querétaro, worked hard to prepare a new draft. Again informality was the theme: no chairman, no set procedure followed in holding the discussions, no voting record kept, no restraint on free expression. Again Rouaix, as the confidant of both Carranza and the radical reformers, served as coordinator at these meetings. Although some forty delegates were usually present,

[4] Moisés González Navarro, "The Ideology of the Mexican Revolution," in *Is the Mexican Revolution Dead?* ed. Stanley R. Ross, pp. 180–181.
[5] Andrés Molina Enríquez, *Esbozo de la historia de los primeros diez años de la revolución agraria de México,* V, 171.
[6] Félix F. Palavicini, *Historia de la Constitución de 1917,* I, 607.

those who most frequently attended and participated in the discussion were four from Durango: Dorador, Antonio Gutiérrez, Terrones Benítez, and de la Torre; three from Veracruz: Jara, Góngora, and Cándido Aguilar; two *poblanos*: Pastrana Jaimes and del Castillo; two from the state of México: Enrique A. Enríquez and Martí; two from San Luis Potosí: de los Santos and Dionisio Zavala; Cano (Guanajuato); Julian Adame (Zacatecas); Chapa (Tamaulipas); Alvarez y Alvarez (Michoacán); Ibarra (Jalisco); Martínez de Escobar (Tabasco); and von Versen (Coahuila).[7] Of this group at least eight were military men, four were lawyers, three were engineers, and two were workers. It is interesting to note that eleven of these men had also participated in the deliberations of the extralegal committee which drew up Article 123. In addition Molina Enríquez and Gen. José Lugo, also of Article 123 fame, were present to give the benefit of their advice.

During the evenings Macías, Lugo, de los Ríos, and Rouaix met to phrase in proper form the ideas expressed during the morning sessions. Their work, together with any new considerations that might have arisen during the evening, was then submitted for approval to the session of the following morning. In this way, Article 27 evolved. On January 24, ten days after the first meeting—ten of the most eventful days in the history of the convention—the draft was ready for submission to the First Committee. Outstanding in the deliberations to this point was Pastor Rouaix. Calling him the bond between Carranza and the assembly, Molina Enríquez says Rouaix "initiated, stimulated, and directed" the efforts which went into the preliminary drafts of both Articles 27 and 123, that "he converted the Constitutional Convention of Querétaro, which was a purely political congress, into one of a social character."[8]

Consisting of fourteen paragraphs, this first draft bore the signatures of eighteen persons, sixteen of whom, including Rouaix and Macías, had taken an active part in the preliminary discussions. The preface, written by Molina Enríquez, expresses clearly the objectives

---

[7] Pastor Rouaix, *Génesis de los artículos 27 y 123 de la constitución política de 1917*, p. 153.
[8] Molina Enríquez, *Esbozo*, V, 172.

the framers hoped to accomplish. They intended to make the State an instrument of social and economic reform. They believed that the welfare of Mexico demanded the complete revision of all property laws passed since independence. During the colonial period the royal authorities had respected the property rights of the Indians. This had changed since 1821 with the passage of laws favoring the upper classes and leaving the Indians without protection. Despoliations, occurring as a result of the well-meaning Laws of the Reform, became so aggravated during the Díaz dictatorship that by 1910 the great property holders had almost eliminated the small and communal holdings. How were these wrongs to be righted? First, it was necessary to return to the basic feature of colonial property law: the king's right to "absolute ownership," a right now considered as having passed to the nation. Under this concept, the nation would gain full rights over lands and waters under its jurisdiction and would only recognize or grant to private persons direct ownership under the "same conditions in which it was exercised by private persons during the colonial period" and under the same conditions later recognized by the republic. The nation would "retain under its domain as much as may be necessary for social development, such as mines, petroleum, etc., not bestowing upon private persons more than the exploitation of these properties which the respective laws authorize."[9]

The phrase "same conditions in which it was exercised . . . during the colonial period" refers to the granting of property rights to private persons by the king, in whom original ownership was considered to have been vested. If the king wished, he could dispossess the grantee of the property and return it to the royal patrimony. Recognition of the retention of ownership by the nation of property "necessary for social development" was derived from colonial legislation, according to a subsequent analysis of Article 27: "The subordination of the rights of ownership by private persons . . . to the social rights which the Nation now represents, also comes from the colonial period, for the Nation has taken the place of the King; the application of these social rights now represented by the Nation to impose on the rights of private ownership such limitations as the public interest may demand,

[9] *Diario de los debates*, II, 1224–1225.

likewise comes from the colonial period."[10] As the preface to Article 27 stated, this retention of ownership would "permit the Government, once and for all, to solve with ease the most difficult part of all the property matters involving the agrarian problem, which is the division of the large estates without loss to the owners." Reserving for itself the "supreme ownership over all property," the government would now have the weapon whereby it could "regulate the status of all property with payment of the respective compensation."[11]

Deploring the inadequacy of existing property laws to provide protection for the underprivileged components of Mexican society, the preface further stated that

civil law, as we have already said, only recognizes a perfect title in private property; in the civil codes of the Republic, there is hardly any provision for the communities under constitutional law than full private property; in none of them is there a single provision that can regulate either the existence, or the functioning, or the development of all those communities which throb in the depths of our social structure; the laws ignore the fact that there are *condueñazgos, rancherías, pueblos, congregaciones, tribus*, et cetera; and it is truly shameful that, when there is some matter concerning the above mentioned communities, one has to search for the applicable laws in the compilations of the colonial period which no more than five lawyers in all the Republic know well.[12]

The first draft of Article 27 clearly reveals that the framers saw the agrarian problem as stemming from the abuse of property rights. In accepting this premise, they rejected the thesis of reactionary elements who held that the problem did not involve the land as much as the need for irrigation, agricultural credit, and scientific agricultural education. Such a view completely overlooked the fact that a few persons owned so much land and so many of the rural inhabitants had so little, or none at all.

The *Diario de los debates* records that the Rouaix committee turned over its draft to the First Committee on the afternoon of January 25,

10 "El artículo 27 de la constitución federal," *Boletín de la Secretaría de Gobernación* (September 1922), quoted in Eyler N. Simpson, *The Ejido, Mexico's Way Out*, p. 64.
11 *Diario de los debates*, II, 1225.
12 Ibid.

having finished it by the afternoon of the preceding day. For the next four days, the distraught committee studied it as best it could. According to Rouaix, Enrique Colunga was in charge of preparing the report. By the afternoon session of the twenty-ninth, Article 27 was ready.

Before proceeding with the story, it is necessary to analyze the preface to the committee report. In it the framers revealed that they had utilized various studies in preparing the famous article, but singled out for special mention the draft prepared by Pastor Rouaix, who had "effectively assisted the Committee, taking part in its deliberations."[13] In general it followed the theme developed by Molina Enríquez in his expository remarks to the Rouaix draft, although the solution to the agrarian problem received greater emphasis than the redefinition of property rights. The First Committee got to the point in the first paragraph by asking three fundamental questions: if property must be considered a natural right, what is the extent of that right? Who has the right to acquire real property? What are the bases for the solution of the agrarian problem? In regard to this last question, the harassed members admitted that they had not had time to find "a complete solution to so transcendental a problem."

The preface strongly denied the concept of an "absolute" right to private property, reaffirmed the principle of eminent domain, and stated that what constituted private property was only what the nation had granted to private persons, "a cession which has not included the right to the products of the subsoil." This was frank admission that the law of November 22, 1884, vesting in the owner of the surface the rights to subsoil minerals, and the law of June 4, 1892, granting the surface owner free exploitation of mineral resources without need of concession, were invalid.[14] The framers fully accepted the Rouaix committee thesis that at independence the rights to all private real property reverted to the nation as the successor of the Spanish crown.

[13] Ibid., p. 1070. For the complete text of the committee report, see pp. 1070–1072.

[14] M. G. Villers, *El artículo 27 de la constitución mexicana de 1917*, pp. 121–122, 127–128.

The nation now had the right to recover this property if it so desired, this being no more than the same right exercised formerly by the king. But what were the limits to which the committee was willing to go in remolding private property rights? Clearly they did not wish to abolish private property, for they said that "the eagerness to abolish individual real property cannot be considered in its essence as anything but utopian." Nevertheless, there existed strong sentiment to socialize all property.[15] In the end, the framers reached a compromise: they socialized subsoil rights while creating multiple forms of private ownership of surface rights.

The framers were determined to destroy the great estates, for monopolization of land in the hands of the few had not only obstructed the "progressive development" of the country but had also brought misery to the rural masses, even resulting at times in food production insufficient to meet the demands of local consumption. To solve the agrarian problem, the revolutionaries called for measures aimed at "reducing the power of the *latifundistas* and raising the economic, intellectual, and moral level of the workers." Specifically, they proposed raising to constitutional status the law of January 6, 1915, and breaking up "the *latifundios* through expropriation, but with respect for the rights of the owners." They did not fear burdening the country with a heavy debt, since the expropriated land "will be paid for by the same ones who acquire it, [thus] reducing the role of the State to that of a simple guarantor." The framers also sought to encourage individual ownership of the divided lands, but they concluded that this privilege should not be conceded to everyone, for "it would be childish to seek the solution of the agrarian problem in the transformation of all Mexicans into landowners; the only thing that can and must be done is to facilitate the conditions under which all who have the will and aptitude to do so may become owners." Concluding with an enumeration of the bases for dividing the large estates, the preface expressed confidence that this would result in material improvement in the standard of living of the rural workers and an increase in agricultural production to the point where it would be greater than consumption.

15 Frank Tannenbaum, *Peace by Revolution: Mexico after 1910*, pp. 166–167.

So much for the preface. How was Article 27 written into the Constitution of 1917? When it was first read during the early evening hours of January 29, President Rojas asked that discussion be deferred, since it was a matter of "extraordinary importance," until sufficient copies were at hand. This was a reasonable request, for only a handful of delegates were fully aware of the significance of what they were about to debate. Those who had participated in writing the Rouaix draft had undoubtedly discussed their work with others, but few knew what changes the First Committee had made. The work was largely unknown, not understood. The delegates, however, were unwilling to wait. Andrés Magallón (Sinaloa) expressed their sentiments. Declaring to the assembly that he had just heard Palavicini say outside the hall that the solution to the agrarian question should be left to the next Congress, not decided in the convention, Magallón asked that debate begin immediately. Furious at Magallón's reporting from the rostrum what he had said on the street, Palavicini explained that he had only stated his opinion that the First Chief's draft of Articles 27 and 33 contained the general principles for the solution of such an important question and that it would be very difficult to discuss thoroughly all the details involved in a short time. This cinched the matter. The delegates were in no mood to accept Palavicini's view, which could result in blocking all discussion of the most important article of the constitution. Terrones Benítez and Jara promptly moved that the convention resolve itself into permanent session until all pending matters had been dealt with, "beginning with the agrarian question." This motion carried immediately. At the same time freedom of debate, without limit on the number of speakers or the time allotted each, was agreed on. Years later Palavicini wrote that the majority, forewarned to oppose any attempt to postpone debate, showed their disapproval of his suggestion by a "great demonstration." As a result, the article was discussed and voted on the same night "without separating the good from the bad."[16] Hence, with only three or four copies of the draft available, deliberation began on an instrument of far-reaching social and economic reform. To add to the

16 Félix F. Palavicini, *Política constitucional: Artículos y discursos*, p. 50.

drama, the lights went out, and the hall had to be lit with candles and oil lamps.

It will be remembered that the First Committee viewed the problem in three separate parts: the nature of property, who could acquire it, and the bases for the solution of the agrarian problem.[17] On paragraphs (1) through (6) there was nearly full agreement, an almost complete lack of discussion. In a long, rambling speech, which he prefaced by stating, "I want to be even more radical than the Committee," Ing. Luis Navarro asked that paragraph (1) be changed to declare that the nation was the only owner of lands and that these should be made available to those who worked them. Although he contradicted himself on whether this should be done by sale or by grant, Navarro stressed the need for the division of the great estates and for assurances that, once divided, they should never be re-created. If the government provided plots of ground to those who worked them, they in turn should pass the plots on to their children, thus making it impossible for the family to ever alienate its holdings. Revolutions in Mexico, he said, would then end, for once an Indian had his own land, he would never leave it to follow some revolutionary leader. Although the assembly turned down his request, Navarro, in the course of his speech, succeeded in becoming the only spokesman in the convention for Zapata and the "revolution of the South." As a *renovador* of the Twenty-sixth Congress, persecuted by Huerta and forced to flee the capital, he had sought refuge with *zapatistas* in Morelos, where for some months he witnessed the strength of an indigenous struggle based on a "principle of justice," i.e., that the land should belong to those who worked it. In spite of this association with *zapatistas*, Navarro had qualified for admission to the convention by virtue of subsequent service in the Constitutionalist Army, in which he had shown distinction as an engineer. Now, speaking in praise of Zapata, he gave a brief résumé of his movement, mentioning its respect for the small property holding, the genuine support it received from the people who furnished supplies, its cooperative retailing of merchandise, and the strong military discipline of the *zapatista* units, who were severely punished

[17] See appendix E.

if they harmed civilians. Navarro could not help but contrast this with the actions of *carrancistas*, who used force to extend control over an area, who razed dwellings, looted, and killed.[18] Judging from his account, the *zapatistas* had learned principles of guerrilla warfare, while the *carrancistas* had not. Although eyebrows were raised and Navarro received no applause for his pro-Zapata statements, his sincerity was beyond question. The ideals of the "revolution of the South" had penetrated the Querétaro Convention.

Silence greeted the reading of paragraphs (2), (3), (4), and (5). Except for a minor question on paragraph (2), there was no discussion. All were accepted as read and reserved for voting. The delegates gave unanimous approval to provisions affirming national ownership of natural resources, the right of the State to impose such limitations on private property as the public interest might demand, and the expropriation of private property for reasons of public utility with payment of compensation. No one questioned the meaning of the phrase "by means of compensation" in paragraph (2). Whereas the Constitution of 1857 had specified "prior compensation," the delegates to the Querétaro Convention simply stated "by means of compensation." Worthy of note is the confirmation of all grants of land made up to the present under the decree of January 6, 1915. Some delegates, including Múgica, had sought the confirmation of all grants made since the start of the revolution, but they did not press the point.[19] As to the meaning of *dominio directo* in paragraph (4), Pastor Rouaix later gave a concise explanation of what the delegates had in mind: "In treating of the products of the subsoil, the Constitutional Convention wished that the rights of the Nation should be even more precisely expressed, and for this reason employed the words 'Dominio Directo' . . . That is to say, the complete proprietorship that it has over these products is inalienable and imprescriptible, and only by means of concessions and subject to determined conditions may it cede the use of these to private individuals."[20]

[18] *Diario de los debates*, II, 1083–1084. For biographic data on Navarro, see *La Herencia del Constituyente*, no. 2 (October 5, 1963).
[19] Juan de Dios Bojórquez [pseud. Djed Bórquez], *Crónica del constituyente*, p. 625.
[20] Letter from Pastor Rouaix, March 13, 1918, in Ministry of Industry, Commerce,

In regard to paragraph (6), Ibarra questioned the granting of concessions by the federal government for the exploitation of mineral resources. He believed royalties should be paid the government on the minerals produced. In lieu of the insignificant amount received from the mining tax, royalties, he affirmed, would provide a rich source of revenue. Furthermore, Ibarra reasoned, since the nation owned all subsoil wealth, that alone justified the payment of royalties to the government rather than to those who leased lands to the exploiting companies. The whole tenor of his complaint indicated unfamiliarity with Article 27, thus strengthening the belief that many delegates had not yet read it and were unfamiliar with its provisions. Answering Ibarra, Rouaix said that the framers had rejected royalty payments to the government in favor of taxes on the value of the company property or on the profits made. Speaking for the committee, Colunga said Ibarra's request was of secondary importance, one not to be decided in haste, more appropriately the concern of the Congress in drafting the next mining law. Although rebuffed, the persistent Ibarra did not give up so easily. Shortly before debate ended, when the weary delegates were preparing to vote, he presented the following amendment: "The Nation, on granting a concession for the exploitation of any of the substances which are referred to in the cited paragraph, must impose on the concessionaire the obligation of paying the Nation a certain percentage of the value of the production, the amount to be determined by law."[21] Pleading that "millions of pesos" were at stake, Ibarra tried to arouse support for his addition, but no one paid any attention. Paragraph (6) was approved as presented.

Although the delegates had rapidly endorsed the foregoing paragraphs, the rest of Article 27 was not approved so simply. To reaffirm state ownership of mineral and other resources was easy. To accept the First Committee's recommendations on who had the legal capacity to acquire ownership of land and waters would be more difficult. The seven clauses of paragraph (7) concerning this ownership provoked the most comment and debate.

---

and Labor, *Documentos relacionados con la legislación petrolera mexicana*, p. 390, quoted in Frank Tannenbaum, *The Mexican Agrarian Revolution*, p. 191.

[21] *Diario de los debates*, II, 1124.

As initially presented, clause I read as follows: "Only Mexicans by birth or naturalization and Mexican companies have the right to acquire direct ownership in lands, waters, and their appurtenances in the Mexican Republic. The State shall concede the same right to foreigners when they agree before the Secretary of Foreign Relations to renounce their status as such as well as the protection of their governments in all matters which pertain to the said properties, remaining fully subject in this respect to the laws and authorities of the Nation."[22]

This differed from the corresponding clause of the Rouaix draft in that it was drawn up on a more reduced scale. Yet, when debate had ended and it was reserved for voting, the clause contained all the provisions of its Rouaix counterpart, but with one significant modification. How this came about reveals the nationalistic bias of the delegates. Although determined to impose safeguards against plunder of Mexican resources by foreigners, they feared intervention if restrictions on the foreigner were too strong. Where could the dividing line be drawn? No sooner was the clause read than Terrones Benítez asked: "Why were the words 'by means of their agents or diplomatic representatives' added?" This question by Terrones Benítez, who had participated in the preparation of the Rouaix draft, indicates that what was read to the delegates on the night of January 29 contained the above line (inserted after the words "Secretary of Foreign Relations"), which did not appear in the written text. Had the First Committee taken advantage of the few copies circulating on the floor to insert additional matter? Apparently they had, because later Múgica admitted that the committee had been "enchanted by the idea" expressed. Affirming that they "had not had sufficient time to consider seriously all that had been proposed to them," Múgica explained that some delegates had advised the committee that a partial renunciation of the rights of citizenship would be valid only if taken before the diplomatic representatives of those concerned. Others, he said, had warned that such partial renunciation of citizenship had been condemned by the International Court of Justice at The Hague. The committee only wanted to do what was best, said Múgica, but now

22 Ibid., p. 1091.

that the addition had been made, it could not be withdrawn without the permission of the assembly.

Two speeches were enough to convince the First Committee of its error. Terrones Benítez arose to say that no foreign official would permit any such renunciation by a national of his country, that diplomacy did not recognize the partial renunciation of rights. Citing a case in Mexico in which such a renunciation had not been heeded, he asked how the First Committee expected the requirement to have any real effect. Believing that the framers did not have strong convictions in the matter, that they had only added the phrase at the suggestion of "various lawyers," he asked the committee to withdraw the objectionable part, leaving the renunciation to be made before Mexican officials only. Cándido Aguilar agreed with Terrones Benítez, saying that no country had recognized the Carranza Doctrine, which embraced this innovation in international law.[23] Furthermore, he did not believe that foreign diplomats should interfere in Mexican internal affairs. Speaking briefly, but to the point, Aguilar received the applause of the assembly when he asked the committee to withdraw the objectionable phrase. This was quickly done.

Further debate on clause I revealed the delegates' nationalistic spirit, their determination to keep Mexican lands and waters out of the hands of foreigners. Three delegates from the state of México were particularly concerned. Enrique Enríquez believed clause I could be easily violated by foreigners wishing to acquire real property. An effortless way, for example, would be through marriage. Consequently, he and Juan Manuel Giffard proposed to prevent foreigners from marrying Mexican women who were owners of real property without first renouncing their nationality before the Ministry of Foreign Relations. The assembly applauded but took no action on this proposal.

[23] Aguilar was probably referring to Carranza's decree of August 15, 1916, which required foreigners to renounce the diplomatic protection of their governments as a condition for the acquisition of real property in Mexico. This was considered to be an extreme application of the "Calvo Clause," which generally holds that foreigners are not entitled to rights and privileges other than those normally granted to the nationals of a country. Hence, they may not seek the redress of grievances except before authorities of the host country. See Frederick Sherwood Dunn, *The Diplomatic Protection of Americans in Mexico*, pp. 391–394.

Finally, José Reynoso mounted the rostrum to carry the matter to its logical xenophobic conclusion: only those who obtained Mexican citizenship, he said, should be allowed to hold real property or obtain subsoil rights.

After a one-hour recess, the committee presented a new draft of clause I, and debate began at 10:30 P.M. This text read as follows:

Only Mexicans by birth or naturalization and Mexican companies have the right to acquire ownership in land, waters, and their appurtenances, or to obtain concessions to exploit mines, waters, or mineral fuels in the Mexican Republic. The State may grant the same right to foreigners whenever they agree before the Ministry of Foreign Relations to be considered as nationals with respect to the said properties, and to not invoke, for the same reason, the protection of their governments with respect to the same, under penalty in case of breach, of forfeiture to the nation of property so acquired. Within a zone of 100 kilometers of the borders, and of 50 kilometers from the coasts, no foreigner shall under any conditions acquire direct ownership of lands and waters.[24]

The controversial phrase had been removed, and the wording was less harsh. Now, foreigners were not to renounce their capacity as such but were to agree before the Ministry of Foreign Relations to consider themselves as Mexican nationals in respect to such property. Rather than having to renounce the protection of their governments, they were simply not to invoke it. If they did, they would run the risk of forfeiting their property to the nation. The committee also took advantage of the opportunity to add the provisions of the Rouaix draft forbidding foreigners to own property within certain distances of the borders or the coastline.

In the opinion of Macías, an experienced lawyer, the restriction on foreigners would be completely ineffective, because they would always ask for protection from their governments. If, he declared, permission to acquire real property was granted to foreigners on the condition that they first renounce their nationality, "foreign governments will come . . . to protect them, and as we are, whether we want to be or not, a weak people with respect to foreign nations, they will drag

[24] *Diario de los debates*, II, 1098.

us to the Hague Tribunal, and there they will condemn us."[25] He
suggested following United States practice. American law, said
Macías, held that foreigners could not acquire real property without
becoming naturalized or declaring their intention of doing so. If they
did not carry out their intention, they forfeited all rights to any real
property that might have been acquired. Speaking for the First Committee, Múgica admitted that the point was a very difficult one to
cover adequately and said that his committee was only too willing to
accept the most appropriate wording that was acceptable to the assembly. When President Rojas asked if the convention wished to take
Macías's proposal into consideration, the answer was affirmative.
Again the committee withdrew its draft. Upon its resubmission
shortly thereafter, however, there was no change. Why? On behalf of
the committee, Colunga explained that they had not accepted Macías's
suggestion because to have done so would have "absolutely closed
the door to the country to foreign capital," a significant admission.
Macías, however, far from being displeased, thought the objective had
been accomplished; whereas the original draft stipulated renunciation
of nationality, the new wording simply required that the foreigner
agree before the ministry to consider himself a national should he
wish to acquire property. Stating that this was acceptable to him,
Macías pointed out that the obligation could be considered as a pre-
requisite to a contract, and no foreign government could compel its
nationals not to enter into a contract. Furthermore, he said, The Hague
would now recognize that no obligatory renunciation was provided
for, and, since private agreements were not brought before the tribunal, the desired effect would be achieved. This ended the discussion. No one dissented, and the disputed clause was immediately
reserved for voting. Fearful of foreign intervention, but recognizing
the necessity of foreign capital, the convention had decided that the
foreigner would be welcome to invest in Mexico, but on Mexican
terms, not his.

Clause IV was approved in a short time, but not without a change

25 Ibid., p. 1099.

in wording.[26] The Rouaix committee had forbidden "civil or commercial companies owned by bearer instrument" (*sociedades civiles o comerciales de títulos al portador*) from acquiring, possessing, or administering rural property. The committee had deleted the word "civil" and accepted the remainder. However, Rafael P. Cañete (Puebla), an elderly lawyer, objected to the words "bearer instrument," fearing that either this form of ownership or that by specific persons (*títulos nominativos*) would open the door again to the clergy to convert their wealth into rural property. This possibility was enough for the jacobin Múgica to request permission to withdraw the whole clause for further study. When it was presented again shortly thereafter, the phrase "commercial stock companies" (*sociedades comerciales por acciones*) had been substituted for "civil or commercial companies owned by bearer instrument." To Pastrana Jaimes, also a lawyer, this wording was unacceptable, because he believed it did not represent the delegates' views. In his opinion, they only wanted to prevent stock companies (*sociedades anónimas*) from acquiring real property. The revised wording, he affirmed, was too severe, even unreasonable, because it prohibited all companies, even cooperatives, from owning real property.

Answering the two *poblanos*, Colunga said that the committee had interpreted opinion in the assembly as wanting to prohibit all kinds of commercial stock companies from acquiring real estate. Colunga explained that the committee "had, in the beginning, limited the prohibition to stock companies, to companies with silent partnerships whose ownership is in the form of a bearer instrument [*sociedades en comandita con títulos al portador*]; but since ownership of these companies can also be in the name of specific persons, the prohibition must be interpreted as including all [*para unos y para otros*]."[27] On these nuances of Mexican corporate terminology, there was no further question as to whether the First Committee had selected the most suitable wording or not. The clause was promptly reserved for voting,

[26] Clauses II and III, primarily concerning the religious issue, were discussed in chapter 3.
[27] *Diario de los debates*, p. 1108.

although Pastrana Jaimes could hardly have been satisfied. Worthy of note is the fact that he and Colunga were referring to ownership of real property (*bienes raíces*) whereas the prohibition in clause IV only concerned rural agricultural properties (*fincas rústicas*). The intention of the First Committee to prevent concealment of ownership and management of rural agricultural properties by foreigners, clergy, or other unauthorized groups through commercial stock companies is clear. As finally approved, however, the wording of clause IV was considerably more lenient than the corresponding clause of the Rouaix draft, which covered civil organizations as well as commercial stock companies.

Discussion of clause V, regarding mortgages on urban and rural property, brought forth different views of the role of banking and credit institutions under the property provisions of Article 27. Initial criticism of the First Committee draft came from Rafael Nieto, subsecretary of the Ministry of the Treasury and one of the few in the convention knowledgeable in banking and finance. He pointed out that the committee had lumped under the general term "banks" such institutions as mortgage banks and banks of issue, whose functions in the national economy differed greatly. He believed the committee had banks of issue in mind, because it would be redundant to state that mortgage banks could impose mortgages. There were cases, he said, in which banks other than mortgage banks could temporarily hold properties. Under a law of 1895, even the bank of emission could hold real property when its assets were not liquid in other form. To clarify the wording, he proposed the following amendment: "Mortgage banks duly organized under the laws governing institutions of credit may make mortgage loans on real properties, and hold and administer the said properties as the laws shall determine. In regard to banks which are not mortgage banks, they may only possess buildings necessary for their immediate purposes . . ."[28] According to Rouaix, this motion motivated him, Nieto, and Truchuelo to reword the proposal as follows: "Banks . . . may not possess more real proper-

28 Ibid., p. 1107. Brief biographical data on Nieto may be found in Eugenio Martínez Núñez, "Don Rafael Nieto," *Boletín Bibliográfico de la Secretaría de Hacienda y Crédito Público*, no. 357 (December 15, 1966): 4–5.

ty than that necessary for their immediate purposes, and temporarily, for the brief period fixed by law, those properties which may be assigned judicially to them in payment of their loans."[29] Although no record of this motion appears in the *Diario de los debates*, the First Committee apparently accepted it, for the next reading, which came a few moments later, retained the original wording with the following addition: "and temporarily for the brief period that the law determines, those real properties awarded to them by the courts for the nonpayment of their loans."[30]

During this period of the discussion of Article 27, considerable confusion reigned. While the beset members of the First Committee were discussing among themselves proposed changes to one clause, another would be up for debate on the floor. Hence, before clause V could be reserved for voting, debate began on clause VI. When discussion of clause V resumed, Luis Espinosa voiced dissatisfaction with the addition reported out by the First Committee. Instead of referring to banks in general, he proposed that the wording be changed to "duly authorized banks which are not mortgage banks." In answering Espinosa, Colunga acknowledged that the "banks" understood in this clause were of three categories: mortgage banks, banks of issue or discount banks, and *refaccionarios*. For the sake of brevity the First Committee had included all three under one term. Concerning the proposed addition authorizing banks to temporarily hold foreclosed property, Colunga thought this could be done without any danger since it was to be for a short time. This explanation, however, did not satisfy Macías, who promptly mounted the rostrum to criticize the clause, thereupon engaging in a personal debate with Truchuelo.

According to Macías, to permit banks of issue to make mortgage loans was "highly dangerous" and contrary to the whole nature of their operations, since they needed liquid funds, which should not be tied up in mortgages. Banks of issue holding mortgage loans on rural property, said Macías, had exerted detrimental influence on Mexican agriculture. These banks should be primarily concerned with business operations, not those involving rural property, since farmers usually

[29] Rouaix, *Génesis*, p. 202.
[30] *Diario de los debates*, II, 1108.

did not have funds available to liquidate their debts in a short period of time. To continue this practice, warned Macías, would place all farmers under the control of a bank of issue, which would soon "take over all agriculture." In his opinion, if agricultural finance were to progress in Mexico, the government emerging from the revolution must establish a bank solely for that purpose. Furthermore, he argued, neither banks of issue nor mortgage banks should be permitted to hold mortgaged properties. This practice was what had ruined Mexico, he alleged. As a consequence, the major part of the nation's property was now controlled by banks and would remain so, since the banks were powerful and could influence the law in their favor. In conclusion, Macías urged that Mexico follow the course taken by other countries and forbid banks to hold rural properties attached for nonpayment of loans. When the mortgages fell due, the owners should not let the banks keep the properties. Furthermore, banks would want to sell the properties at high prices, "thereby making a considerable profit, and this we must not permit."[31]

In rebuttal, Truchuelo reaffirmed his support for the right of banks of issue to invest their funds in real property, because there would be only one bank of this type and it would be "controlled by the government." As for the addition permitting banks to hold for a short time property judicially assigned to them in payment of their loans, Truchuelo declared that this would prevent banks' taking advantage of debtors. But Macías was to have the last word. More knowledgeable than Truchuelo on Mexican banking practice, and more persuasive in his argument, he referred to himself as "the lawyer of the poor, who comes to plead . . . against the lawyer of the banks, because Señor Truchuelo must have been the lawyer of some bank." Vigorously opposing the addition, Macías said that banks should not be permitted to hold temporarily any rural properties, or they would soon have them all. The only way to protect the debtor, or owner of the property, he affirmed, was to deny the bank possession of the property and require its immediate sale at public auction. This cinched the matter. When the president asked the assembly if Macías's proposal should be taken into consideration, the answer was affirmative. When clause V

31 Ibid., p. 1121.

was resubmitted, the wording was identical to that of the original draft, and the controversial addition had been removed. In this form the clause was quickly reserved for voting before any further questions could be raised. All in all, the discussion had been long and boring. Twice the chair had had to ask the delegates not to leave the floor. The will of the majority, however, had been expressed: banks, regardless of what kind, were not to own any more property than that essential for the immediate conduct of their business. In denying them the right to acquire additional property, the delegates, according to Molina Enríquez, relied on the principle that since the existence of corporations was founded on a legal fiction, they could not acquire a real right in property.[32]

Clause VI, concerning the right of communal groups to hold and utilize lands and waters, was first presented in the following terms: "Properties held in common by co-owners, hamlets situated on private property, villages, communities, tribes and other settlements which in fact or by law conserve their communal character, shall have legal capacity to enjoy in common the lands, woods, and waters which belong to them or have been restored to them in accordance with the Law of January 6, 1915. The law will determine the manner of making the division of only the lands."[33] Comparison with the corresponding clause of the Rouaix draft reveals the latter to be more comprehensive in that it specifically provided for the future restitution of lands, forbade community members to dispose of their properties to others, and stipulated that laws to be passed in the future for the division of communal lands should contain provisions to prevent the holders from losing their plots, since such losses could possibly result in the re-creation of "undesirable *latifundios*." During the brief discussion of this clause, three questions came up. First, Macías expressed his preference for the Rouaix draft, which provided for the future return of lands, woods, and waters, inasmuch as many settlements and villages (*pueblos*) had not yet received anything. The committee report took care of the past, but what about the future? Al-

---

[32] "El artículo 27 de la constitución federal," *Boletín de la Secretaría de Gobernación*, p. 19, cited in Tannenbaum, *The Mexican Agrarian Revolution*, p. 196.

[33] *Diario de los debates*, II, 1109.

though the *Diario de los debates* does not indicate that the First Committee ever considered this proposal, and it is missing from the final reading, the official copy of the constitution as signed on January 31, 1917, provides that communal groups should have legal capacity to enjoy in common lands, woods, and waters "which belong to them, or which may have been or shall be restored to them . . ."[34]

Next, Luis Espinosa questioned the provision for the division only of lands, pointing out that the clause provided for communal enjoyment of lands, woods, and waters but at the end provided exclusively for the division of lands. Was this not a contradiction? Answering for the committee, Múgica explained that lands could be divided, but that woods and waters would always be enjoyed in common, "not being divided under any circumstances."

Finally, Cañete said that if communities were given the right to possess lands, the constitution should also grant the right to defend them legally and by other means. Did communities have legal personality to defend their interests? This is what Cañete wanted to know. Since many communities had been stripped of their lands in the past for this reason, he thought it imperative that clause VI clearly state this right. In answering Cañete, Múgica evaded the question by declaring that the clause concerned only the capacity to acquire lands, nothing else. Medina added that, in his opinion, paragraph III of Article 115, which stated that municipalities were to be regarded as enjoying corporate existence for all purposes, covered the matter. Cañete, quite rightly, replied that a municipality was one thing and a community was another. To this assertion Medina answered that difficulties in the past, at least in cases that had reached the Supreme Court, had not arisen from the communities' lack of legal personality but from the way they had been represented. Without going into detail, he stated that the law provided for the naming of a legal representative in case the community should seek to recover or defend its lands. In his judgment, communities were accorded the full protection of the municipality, but in case they were not, there would be no problem in according them the necessary "political personality." On the other hand, it would be curious, he said, if the constitutional

[34] Ibid., p. 1188.

grant of legal capacity to acquire real property did not include the right to defend it at law "or in any other way." Finally, Colunga said that, if the property of the communities remained undivided, each co-owner had the right to defend the plots of all the others. Without further question, the clause was then reserved for voting. The legal and political personality of communal groups and their right to self-defense had been affirmed.

An important feature of this clause, one not brought out in the debate, is the provision for the eventual division of communally held lands, the first step toward ownership and another indication that the convention did not intend to abolish private property. In recognizing the old communal form of landholding, the delegates were admitting the need to give legal status to the only kind of property rights understood by the large primitive part of the population. At the same time, they were making it possible for the individual members of the communities in the course of their social development to eventually acquire outright ownership of the land which they tilled.[35]

With clause VI reserved for voting, the framers of Article 27 had achieved their second objective: to prescribe who would be permitted to acquire, hold, and administer real property. The right to private property had not been destroyed, only modified in accordance with the needs of the component sectors of Mexican society. The form of ownership would vary for such distinct groups as Mexican nationals and Mexican companies, foreigners and foreign companies, and primitive communal groups; it would be determined by state and federal laws in accordance with the constitutional provisions of paragraph (7). The delegates had sketched the general outline. Details would be filled in as time went on.

The remainder of Article 27, paragraphs (8) through (12), contained a series of measures for the solution of the agrarian problem: expropriation of private property for reasons of public utility with payment of compensation; restoration to communal groups of lands, woods, and waters that had been illegally taken from them; division of the *latifundios*; recovery of public lands and waters that had been

[35] Simpson, *The Ejido*, p. 73.

alienated since 1876. These provisions correspond to paragraphs VIII, XII, and XIV of the Rouaix draft, the major difference being that the Rouaix proposals contained neither detailed provisions for dividing *latifundios* nor a declaration that all contracts and concessions made since 1876, resulting in the monopoly of national lands, waters, and natural resources, would be subject to revision. Thus the draft of the First Committee was much broader in scope.

In the discussion of agrarian reform, few questions were raised. Why, when the most eventful moment of the convention had arrived? Three reasons may be given. First, a considerable number of delegates were solidly in favor of the proposals. This group included those who had worked with Rouaix in preparing the first draft and were familiar with the contents. Second, many delegates were unaware of the significance of the committee report, since so few copies were in circulation. Finally, there were others too exhausted to show interest. At one point the chair had to ask them to wake up, or they would not know how to vote when the time came. This brought the retort, "Who are the ones asleep?" followed by the impatient: "Let's vote, let's vote!"

Two who spoke on this great Mexican problem were revolutionaries of the left: Bojórquez and Jara. Bojórquez showed a keen appreciation of the agrarian problem and the need for a solution if there was to be peace. In early 1916 he had helped establish in Sonora the first local agrarian commission, which sought to return *ejidos* to the people and form agricultural colonies. Governmental bureaucracy, however, had frustrated the commission's work. After praising the committee for incorporating the decree of January 6, 1915, into Article 27, Bojórquez went on to say that the decree's objective would be attained not solely by the restoration of the *ejidos* but also by the development of the small property holding. The most effective way to do this, he believed, was to authorize state legislatures to scrutinize the titles to land held by the large landowners and to draw up the best laws for the formation of agricultural colonies. He advocated local governments rather than the federal government as the most qualified agent to accomplish these reforms. Furthermore, he pointed to the need to give *campesinos* the concept of association in order to promote their common good, to educate them to accumulate savings and to form cooperatives. Land was essential for the masses, but they had to develop the idea of property ownership, that the land belongs to the person who works it. Capital necessary for the development of the land should be made available by the government. Heretofore, Bojórquez said, there had really been no agriculture in Mexico, only great landowners who had exploited labor, dedicating themselves to "the wealth of *pulque*," which needed no cultivation or science to develop. He believed the real future of Mexico lay in its agricultural resources, the development of which meant "true wealth, true welfare, and effective progress." Jefferson himself could not have made a stronger plea for agriculture and the small property holding. Unfortunately, the youthful Bojórquez went on and on, and the restless delegates began stamping their feet. In the end the confusion was so great that President Rojas was forced to state that in discussing such an important matter the convention should not turn into a "cattle branding."

Jara, too, defended the committee report and the need for an agrarian law. Reminding the delegates that influential landowners, like the Terrazas and Creels of Chihuahua, had defeated proposals for meaningful agrarian reform in the Twenty-sixth Congress, he asked:

Who will assure us that in the next Congress all these evil influences will not be put into play? Who will assure us that in the next Congress there will be revolutionaries sufficiently strong to oppose that tendency . . . the objection has been made that within the framework, let us say of the Constitution, this [agrarian reform] does not fit . . . I want someone to tell us, someone of the most illustrious, of the *científicos* (laughter), of the statesmen, who has laid down the model for constitutions to follow? . . . the writing of constitutions has been nothing else but the result of experience . . . if we complete this book with a law of this sort, concerning the agrarian question, we will protect the national interests; the plot of land will be assured for the small farmer; this law will clearly say: no longer will you be the slave of yesterday but the owner of tomorrow . . . it was the cry of land which aroused many Mexicans, many who before were slaves; the cry of land furnished the greatest number for the Revolution; we owe to that cry the honor we now have of attending this Constitutional Convention. Therefore, *señores diputados*, vote for the report as the Committee has drawn it up, with the assurance that you will be voting for the true freedom of the Mexican *patria*. (Applause).[36]

Although filled with rhetoric and demagoguery, Jara's speech was just what the delegates wanted to hear.

Applause also followed the reading of paragraph (9), nullifying all actions or proceedings that had deprived communal groups existing since passage of the law of June 25, 1856, of their lands, woods, or waters. The decree of January 6, 1915, providing for the return of these lands, was raised to the status of constitutional law. The only exceptions to the nullity provision concerned lands to which title might have been acquired in divisions made by virtue of the law of June 25, 1856, or to those held in undisputed ownership for more than ten years, provided they were not larger than fifty hectares (123.5 acres). Any excess was to be returned for communal use and compensation paid the owner.

Only on this paragraph did anything like a debate occur. When Navarro questioned the ten-year exemption period and the fifty-hectare size, claiming that this was "too large" and that many illegally acquired haciendas would still remain, Colunga replied that the objective was to preserve the small property holding, the ideal size being considered fifty hectares. In Guanajuato, said Colunga, this was not even a *rancho*; hence it was well under the size of the typical small farm in that state. As for the ten-year period, Colunga declared that some *campesinos* had acquired title to property within the *ejidos* but had no written record of the transfer. In such cases, the word of the owner would be accepted, provided that he had held the property for ten years. In regard to compensation for expropriated property, Cepeda Medrano asked who would be responsible for the payment. It would be an injustice, he said, to expect the wretched Indians to have to pay for lands that had been snatched from them years before. Why should they pay large sums for false titles to lands that were rightfully theirs to start with? Furthermore, valuable farm lands were at stake, and the rightful owners were poor. Although Múgica answered that it was "not the members of the *congregaciones* but the

[36] *Diario de los debates*, II, 1094–1097.

Government" that would pay the compensation, Cepeda Medrano replied that the government was bankrupt, that the present owners would never take the nearly worthless *infalsificables* for payment. In his opinion the matter of compensation needed clarification.

Cepeda Medrano was right. The agrarian decree of January 6, 1915, now a provision of Article 27, provided that lands "indispensable" for communal groups should be provided at government expense, whereas paragraph (9) simply stated that the present owner would be indemnified for the amount over fifty hectares that would be expropriated. It will be remembered that the preface to the committee report had declared that those obtaining expropriated lands would pay for them, the State merely guaranteeing payment. Apparently the framers believed that ultimately the State would have to assume this obligation. In answering Cepeda Medrano, Múgica pointed out that the question really concerned lands taken by force and that these would be returned to their rightful owners without any question, "by the sole fact that the Constitution decrees it."[37] Furthermore, he said, in furnishing lands to villages having none at present and unable to identify specific tracts seized from them in the past, the law of January 6, 1915, provided that those presently in possession of the lands to be furnished to these villages would have no right to indemnification. Actually, the law did not say this, but Múgica was correct in adding that the same law permitted an individual dispossessed of lands returned to a village to go to court for redress. If the court upheld his claim, the owner could demand compensation, which would be paid by the government. As to the kind of money to be used in making payment, Múgica asserted that this did not concern the convention. Expropriation decrees issued up to 1937 indicate the intention of the government, in the case of properties expropriated for *ejido* grants, to pay the cost of expropriation, but to be reimbursed by those receiving the land.[38] Despite the wishes of the framers, those who could least afford it were the ones who ultimately paid.

The sharpest attack on paragraph (9) came from Medina, who criticized it as a travesty on reason and justice because it went to the

[37] Ibid., p. 1113.
[38] Simpson, *The Ejido*, pp. 218–219.

extreme of declaring null and void all proceedings, court decisions, surveys, transactions, and auctions since 1856 that had deprived communal groups of their lands. In his opinion many of these were legal transactions, completed with the free consent of the parties. To approve this paragraph, said Medina, would be tantamount to saying that no legitimate government had existed in Mexico since 1856. Although he accepted the premise that the convention had the right to examine past actions contrary to the principles of the revolution, he urged that this be done with caution and that the problem be studied calmly from the points of view of "justice, morality, and public stability." Practical guidelines for solving the problems of the past were necessary, but not a "principle so destructive as this . . . a retroactive law which alters the whole system of individual property rights."[39]

Furthermore, Medina objected to the statement declaring illegal all future decisions, resolutions, surveys, and concessions that would deprive villages of their lands, woods, and waters. This edict, more properly a matter of legislative concern, with the courts available to redress wrongs, was just too drastic to accept. Would there be any possibility of judicial action if the constitution declared that all future concessions were, ipso facto, null and void? Medina also thought that the terms "hamlets, communities, and villages" needed to be defined more clearly. The constitution should not go to the extreme of granting them more rights than they previously had. Individuals and communal groups should be equal before the law. If an individual legally transferred property, that contract was irrevocable. But if a communal group legally disposed of its lands and later wanted them back, the contract could be revoked. Calling this "absurd," he asked the convention to study the matter carefully before incorporating such a precept into the constitution. Obviously the alert Medina, fully aware of the revolution in property rights engineered by the authors of Article 27, believed too firmly in the inviolability of the right of private property to accept a measure jeopardizing this right in favor of an unfortunate component of society.

Replying to his fellow lawyer and *guanajuatense*, Colunga argued

[39] *Diario de los debates*, II, 1115.

that in the main the people had lost their communal lands by the illegal actions of those who had acquired them. Paragraph (9) did no more than recognize this truth by declaring null and void all the acts which had resulted in depriving the people of their lands. As for the future, a similar provision was necessary considering the ultimate objective of dividing the *ejidos* among those who worked them. Tenants would not be allowed to transfer their plots to anyone. Hence, to protect these landowners, Colunga declared, "it is just to prohibit any action that might tend to thwart this plan and again deprive the people of their lands."[40] Múgica added that, although many transfers of rural property from one owner to another had been legally made, the result had been disastrous for the rural communities. The problem was not how something had been done but what had been the consequence. Speaking with emotion, he asked,

Are we going to let that happen just because the law permits it? Are we going to consent to that? If we agree to that injustice, then cursed be the Revolution, may it be cursed a thousand times! (Applause) . . . revolutionaries who at one time were consistent with their principles used to write in the newspapers: "If the law is in the way of justice, then down with the law." This explains what we came here to do tonight on regaining possession of all those lands taken under the protection of a law drawn up to favor the wealthy and under whose protection great injustices were committed. Let us undo those injustices now and return to each his own, voting this paragraph as we have presented it.[41]

Without further discussion, paragraph (9) was reserved for voting. Social justice had triumphed over strict legality. Humanitarian motives, more than any other consideration, had guided the framers of the agrarian reform program.

The remaining paragraphs were reserved for voting without change. No one questioned paragraph (10), providing for judicial and administrative procedures in matters affecting the national interest under this article. Only a minor question was asked on paragraph (11), providing for the division of the large estates. One of its clauses gave preference to soldiers of the Constitutionalist Army, or their widows

[40] Ibid., p. 1117.
[41] Ibid., p. 1118.

and children, and to "those who had served the cause of the Revolution or public education," in obtaining benefits under Article 27. Although readily approved, in the final draft of the constitution this clause appears as a transitory article. Paragraph (12), on the revision of all contracts and concessions made by previous governments since 1876 that had resulted in a monopoly of the lands, waters, and natural resources of the nation by a single individual or company, was steam-rollered through without discussion.

The voting of Article 27 took place about three o'clock on the morning of January 30. Various writers have stated that approval was unanimous. The *Diario de los debates* states that all 150 delegates present voted in favor. Molina Enríquez, who had played a prominent role in the preliminary discussion, states that this was not so, that the first fifteen votes were against. Juan Manuel Giffard, he asserts, cast the first affirmative vote, Enrique Enríquez, the second. Their votes were "received with applause."[42]

The importance of Article 27 contrasts markedly with the attention accorded this extraordinary document by the assembly. Only a few typewritten copies were available for consultation. Twice during the discussion the First Committee admitted that there had been insufficient time to examine fully the issues involved. Some of the provisions later causing national and international controversy were approved without question. In a matter of hours, in a hall dimly lit by lamps and candles, the convention accepted the article with only minor changes.

Did the delegates fully realize the significance of their handiwork? Many probably did not. A small but influential minority, however, did. Nationalists and reformers of both the right and the left, they quickly realized the inadequacy of Carranza's draft, realized that his proposals failed to solve the agrarian problem and that drastic steps had to be taken to save the revolution. Under Rouaix's leadership, with Molina Enríquez as adviser, and backed by Múgica, this group forged an acceptable draft. That a handful of delegates were able to impress their views on the others may be partially explained by the

[42] Molina Enríquez, *Esbozo*, V, 179.

fact that the latter had, exclusive of Carranza's proposals, no plan of their own.[43]

Article 27, the ideas which it contains and the frame about which they were woven, came from the convention itself. More than any other article of the new constitution, this article represented the break with the Porfirian past, embodied the cry for economic independence, proclaimed the destruction of vested interests, and gave hope of a better future to the rural masses. In short, it was the convention's most singular achievement.

[43] Frank Tannenbaum, *Mexico: The Struggle for Peace and Bread*, p. 104.

6. The Prevailing Winds of Reform

Local progress is the basis of national progress because the *municipio* is to the organism known as the Nation what the cell is to the person; and it is evident that a body whose cells are poor and feeble will never acquire vigor.

Francisco Martín del Campo (Jalisco)
Fernández Martínez Album

. . . in this unfortunate country, in which industry is so anemic, bullfights are a national sport and we even flaunt the largest and most modern bull ring in the world; even the most wretched town may not have schools but there will surely be a bull ring, cockfights and some cheating gamester [*desplumadero del prójimo*].

Federico E. Ibarra (Jalisco)
Diario de los debates del Congreso Constituyente, 1916–1917

THE WAVE OF political, social, and humanitarian reform which swept the world during the first two decades of the twentieth century left its mark on Mexico. Although locked in its own fratricidal revolution and largely isolated from the family of nations during World War I, Mexico could not escape the reform that was in the air. Feeling its influence, the Constitutional Convention sought to right wrongs of the Díaz regime and to chart the national course for the future. In doing so the delegates expressed concern for more than secular education, labor welfare, and agrarian reform. In the political field, efforts to broaden the concept of the *municipio libre* indicated faith in the principles of local self-government and grass-roots democracy. In coming to grips with the problems of alcoholism and gambling, abolition of the death penalty, and woman suffrage, the delegates further revealed regard for the underdog and less fortunate components of Mexican society and a strong determination to lay the bases for true political, economic, and social justice.

MUNICIPAL REFORM

A major political reform of the revolution was the establishment of the self-governing municipality by Carranza in his decree of December 25, 1914. Declaring that "the independent municipality is the base of the political liberty of the people," the First Chief ordered the states to adopt it as the unit of their territorial subdivision and political organization. The *municipio libre* was to be administered by an *ayuntamiento* elected by direct popular vote and without authorities interposed between it and the state government.[1] Why was this decree necessary? Although the Constitution of 1857 was silent in regard to the *municipio*,[2] it continued to be one of the administrative divisions of state government, but with decreasing autonomy. During the Díaz regime, in many states the oppressive *jefe político* usurped powers of local officials and effectively stifled municipal liberties. Revulsion toward the *jefe político* coupled with the people's longing to regain control of local government convinced Carranza that reform not only was overdue but would have popular approval as well. By his decree of December 25 he emerged as champion of the cause of municipal autonomy.[3]

[1] The text of this decree may be found in *Cincuentenario de las adiciones y reformas al Plan de Guadalupe, del 12 de diciembre de 1914*, pp. 37–39.

[2] A rural-urban political subdivision of the state, the *municipio* resembles the American county or township more than it does a city per se. A typical *municipio* consists of a *cabecera municipal* (seat of government of the *municipio*) and a surrounding area, which may include towns, villages, and other communities. Because of the difficulty in translating this word accurately into English, it is left in Spanish, although frequently the adjective "municipal" or the noun "municipality" is used in reference to the *municipio*.

[3] For a concise account of the evolution of the *municipio* to 1917, see Leonard

In his address of December 1, the Constitutionalist leader reminded the delegates that the independent municipality was "one of the great triumphs of the revolution, as it is the basis of free government, a triumph which not only will give political liberty to municipal life, but which will also give it economic independence, since it will have funds and its own resources to meet all its needs, thereby freeing itself from the insatiable greed that the governors have regularly shown toward it."[4] His draft proposal (Article 115, paragraph I), almost identical to the decree of two years earlier, read as follows: "The States shall adopt for their internal government the popular, representative, republican form, having as the basis of its territorial division and of its political organization, the free municipality, each one administered by a council elected directly by popular vote and without intermediate authorities between this body and the state government."[5]

In the convention the Second Committee of Reforms studied the Carranza proposal. Noting that "*municipios* are coming to life after a long period of oblivion" and that the constitution must guarantee their finances, "the *sine qua non* of life and their independence, the measure of their effectiveness," the committee proposed the following municipal reforms (Article 115):

The States shall adopt for their internal government the popular, representative, republican form which shall have the free [self-governing] municipality as the basis of its territorial division and its political and administrative organization in accordance with the three following principles:

I. Each municipality shall be administered by a council chosen by direct, popular vote and there shall be no intermediate authority between the latter and the state government.

II. The municipalities shall freely administer their finances, shall collect all the taxes, and shall contribute to the public spending by the State in the proportion and according to the terms which the local legislature shall

Cárdenas, Jr., "The Municipality in Northern Mexico," *Southwestern Studies* 1, no. 1 (Spring 1963): 3–15.

[4] *Diario de los debates del Congreso Constituyente, 1916–1917*, I, 394.

[5] Ibid., p. 528.

determine. The executives shall name inspectors to receive the States' share and to watch over the bookkeeping in each municipality. Financial conflicts arising between the municipality and the branches of a state government shall be settled by the Supreme Court of Justice of the Nation in accordance with the provisions of the law.

III. The municipalities shall be invested with juridical personality for all legal purposes.[6]

The *Diario de los debates* devotes nearly fifty pages to discussion of the committee report, for agreement on the degree of political and financial independence to grant the *municipio* did not come easily. In spite of the seeming clarity of the wording, paragraph II raised numerous questions. Was the *municipio* to collect its own taxes as well as those of the state? Were there to be two collecting agencies or only one? Why should the *municipio*, which was generally poorer than the state, contribute to financing state services? Could it freely administer its finances under supervision of inspectors appointed by the governor? Could the local legislature be counted on to determine impartially sources of state and municipal taxable wealth? In the course of the attempt to answer these questions, as well as others which arose during the discussion, the issue became one of states' rights vs. municipal rights. Unfortunately, delegates spoke more from emotion than from knowledge of a practicable state-municipal financial relationship, more about what they did not want than what they did want.

First read during the afternoon session of January 20, Article 115 was not debated until immediately after the second reading on the afternoon of January 24. The preamble and paragraphs I and III were approved without question, but paragraph II came in for harsh criticism from José Rodríguez González (Coahuila), Martínez de Escobar, Reynoso, Cepeda Medrano, and Calderón.

To Rodríguez González, the *norteño* educator, the principle of the *municipio libre* was noble, but the effect on education could be harmful, a possibility which the framers—two lawyers, one doctor, and one general—had undoubtedly not considered.[7] Contending that poli-

---

[6] Ibid., II, 695.

[7] Dr. Agustín Garza González (Nuevo León), fifth member of the committee, was on sick leave and did not sign the report. For biographic data on Rodríguez

tics and education did not mix, Rodríguez González feared municipal freedom would subject teachers to undue political pressures. Ever since the First Chief had decreed the *municipio libre, ayuntamientos* throughout the country had been appointing teachers, and the effects, said Rodríguez, had been harmful. Furthermore, if teachers were to be paid from municipal funds, *municipios* should be obligated to assign a certain percentage of their revenue to education. Although he pleaded for adequate teachers' pay, Rodríguez González's main concern was that the states not lose administrative and supervisory control over public education.

Martínez de Escobar, who began his speech with the announcement that he was in "good spirits," an indication that he had enjoyed his *mescalitos* and dinner, attacked the entire paragraph. In his opinion, states should collect their taxes and *municipios* should collect theirs. If inspectors were named to check municipal accounts, they would surely intervene in local matters and destroy the very autonomy that the framers sought for the *ayuntamientos*. Equating municipal liberty with the *municipio*'s freedom to manage its own finances, he deplored the fact that the *municipio* was not represented before the legislature in regard to tax matters, and he opposed municipal contribution to state needs in accordance with the dictum of the legislature. If the *municipio* had to turn over half, or two-thirds, or even all of its funds, then, he asked, "where is municipal financial freedom?" Finally, he criticized as illogical and a clear violation of state sovereignty the provision authorizing the Supreme Court to settle financial disputes arising between a *municipio* and a state.

José Reynoso, a native of Guanajuato but a delegate from the state of México, nearly forty-nine, a mining engineer by profession, had served as undersecretary of finance and public credit in the Madero government. A *renovador*, he had suffered imprisonment following dissolution of the Twenty-sixth Congress. To Reynoso, municipal freedom had several disadvantages. Either the states, through their inspectors, would meddle constantly in municipal matters, or the *municipio*, drinking heavily of the wine of freedom, would become a

González, see *La obra de una vida: Homenaje de admiración y gratitud al maestro José Rodríguez González.*

thorn in the side of the state. Urging that each level of government collect its own taxes, he foresaw all kinds of problems if the *municipio* had to turn over to the state part of what it collected. Furthermore, if it turned to the national Supreme Court whenever financial problems arose with the state, then neither governor, legislature, nor judiciary would ever be able to exercise any authority over it. The *municipio* would always look to the Supreme Court as the champion of its rights.

The most damning attack on municipal financial autonomy came from Cepeda Medrano, who had been an employee of the Coahuila state treasury since 1913, serving as inspector, fiscal agent, tax collector, inspector of public offices, and finally as state treasurer. His experience had revealed the incompetence of municipal employees in carrying out financial responsibilities. In "all the *municipios*" in Coahuila he had found apathy, rank confusion and disorder, no knowledge of accounting, and dishonesty on the part of employees. Perhaps this was due to the upset caused by the revolution, but Cepeda Medrano could only ask how anyone could confide in *ayuntamientos* or entrust them with management of public funds without state intervention. He emphatically declared that the *municipio*, on gaining a measure of autonomy, must not become the *papa grande* (big daddy), a power within the state, and that the settlement of state-municipal financial conflicts by the Supreme Court was contrary "to all common sense." In conclusion, he warned: "If we approve the proposal of the Second Committee, we will simply have signed the death sentence of the majority of the states of the Mexican Republic."[8]

Another strong critic of paragraph II was Calderón. In recognition of his ability as an officer of the Constitutionalist forces in the battle against *villistas* in Guadalajara in early 1915, he had later been appointed chief tax officer (*director general de rentas*) of Jalisco. An advocate of state authority, he believed it would be disastrous to approve paragraph II in its present form. He contended that the only competent body to make state laws was the legislature, which should specify the sources of taxable wealth available to both state and local governments. Furthermore, asserted Calderón, each level should have its own separate offices for collection purposes. Characterizing as "im-

[8] *Diario de los debates*, II, 892.

practical" the solution of state-municipal financial problems by the Supreme Court, he said state problems should be settled within the state, or the federal republic would cease to exist, because *ayuntamientos*, like spoiled children who cry when they do not get their way, would always be appealing to the Supreme Court in Mexico City. Nor did he believe *ayuntamientos* could competently manage their fiscal affairs. Citing Jalisco as an example, Calderón said that of the 108 *municipios*, only 12 had "enlightened *ayuntamientos*." All the rest were under the tutelage of the legislature, which had to approve their budgets and set up their schedule of excise taxes. The *municipios*, he believed, could not be counted on to do the job without close supervision.

In face of such an offensive against paragraph II, the surprised defenders reacted with grim determination to uphold it. "Political liberty cannot be conceived of when financial freedom is not assured," warned Jara. He complained that the state had always dominated municipal affairs, leaving to the *municipio* only such responsibilities as care of the town and maintenance of the police force. Heretofore, he said, if a *municipio* had wanted to authorize an increase in its budget for education, the state had been able to veto the increase. Surely inhabitants of the *municipio* best knew what services they needed. In a plea for home rule, Jara put the matter in simple terms that all would understand:

We want the state government to stop being like papa who, afraid that his child would buy so much candy that it would make him sick, takes from him money that his godfather or grandfather has given him and then returns it a cent at a time so that the candy will not do him any harm. The *municipios* must not be [put] in this situation. If we grant political liberty on one hand, if we boast that a social revolution has helped them and that with this help such an important freedom has been obtained and what for so many years had been snatched from it has been returned to the *municipio*, we must be consistent in our thinking; let us not grant freedom on one hand and then restrain it on the other . . .[9]

If municipal governments in Coahuila and Jalisco could not func-

9 Ibid., p. 879.

tion effectively without state supervision, this was not the case in Michoacán. According to Alvarez y Alvarez, it had been the first state to put into practice the system proposed by the Second Committee. There *municipios* were collecting all taxes and turning over to the state amounts set by the legislature. The result was successful. The previous system of state approval of municipal budgets had been a calamitous failure because all state authorities did was look at the total amount requested. He then cited a case typical of this system: "How much does the *municipio* of Zamora ask? Thirteen thousand pesos. No, it is a lot, let us give it half, say six thousand pesos."[10] According to Alvarez y Alvarez, this was not enough to pay police, lighting, and salaries of schoolteachers. The only answer was to give *municipios* the right to decide for themselves budgets of proposed expenditures and income as well as to indicate how much they might contribute to the state. Commenting further on conditions in Michoacán, Alvarez y Alvarez said he had noticed such political apathy in the remote areas that voters refused to take part in local elections. Why? It was because a vote meant nothing if those elected had no funds at their disposal to pay police or schoolteachers, and "instead of having a schoolhouse for them all they had was a corral."[11] In all or most of the states, said Alvarez y Alvarez, *municipios* just did not have funds to provide essential services. If they had the freedom to manage their own finances, he argued, voters would respond; they would overcome their apathy, take pride in the community, and pay taxes, knowing that money collected would go toward betterment of the *municipio* instead of for the construction of the state theater or the paving of streets in the state capital. In his opinion, true municipal independence meant giving to the *ayuntamiento* the right to collect enough to meet all its expenses, not to take in what it had been told it could and no more. As for two collecting offices, this would result in an "impossible mess" because the taxpayers would not know to which office they should make their payments. As for the Supreme Court settling differences arising between state and *municipio*, Alvarez y Alvarez supported this proposal because he did not see how

10 Ibid., p. 884.
11 Ibid., pp. 884–885.

an organ of state government could ever be impartial in a dispute involving the state.

Subsequent speakers defending the committee report stressed the need for municipal financial autonomy as well as the need to reorganize the whole tax system in order to see that the *municipio* received a fair share of revenue. In Cayetano Andrade's opinion, the *municipio* simply had to manage its own finances in order to count on sufficient funds for the support of education. Complaining that salaries were so miserable that no one wanted to become a teacher, he quipped that, if a man failed in business or a student could not make his grades, or a professional could get no clients, as a last resort, he could always say, "I am going to become a schoolteacher; at least to be one you do not have to know anything. (Applause. Laughter)"[12] Let the states decide what to teach and how it should be taught, but *municipios*, he believed, should select the teachers and pay them from local revenue.

According to Hilario Medina, a member of the Second Committee, all the speakers agreed that the only true basis of municipal liberty lay in the free management of funds available to the *municipio*. Where they differed, he believed, was on the sources of wealth available for taxation. These needed to be identified. If the constitution granted the *municipio* the right to manage its own finances, it would be necessary to reform the tax structure so as to know what it could or could not tax. As for the *municipio*'s getting its just share of the tax base, Medina naively declared that this would present no problem, because the members of the legislature that decided the matter were all residents of *municipios* and they would surely look after municipal interests! Dismissing as improbable the objection that state-appointed inspectors would meddle in local affairs, Medina went on to justify the solution of state-municipal financial conflicts by the Supreme Court. As the *municipios* emerged into freedom, they would face many problems. Enemies from the old regime would probably slip into public office and work to their detriment. Therefore, some system of vigilance would have to be established to prevent this. Further-

12 Ibid., p. 889.

more, if the *municipio* were engaged in a dispute with a branch of state government, it could never be assured of justice, because a certain degree of "solidarity" always existed among the three branches. Recourse to the national Supreme Court, affirmed Medina, was the only answer.

In the opinion of Fernando Lizardi, the genial *guanajuatense*, who followed Medina to the rostrum, paragraph II had its good and bad features. Although registered to speak in favor, he announced that he did not know whether to speak for or against. By the time he had finished, he had done both. Agreeing that *ayuntamientos* would never enjoy real liberty if they could not freely administer their finances, Lizardi saw the major problem as failure to define the nature of the municipal financial system. Moreover, this definition should not appear in the constitution, because conditions varied from one state to another. He thought the solution was to leave to state officials, who best knew state resources and how to manage them, complete liberty to determine a system of municipal finance best suited to the people of that state. He would eliminate from paragraph II the *municipio*'s responsibility for collecting "all" taxes. Disagreeing with Cepeda Medrano about whether *municipios* were capable of administering their finances, Lizardi made a plea for home rule for those that were. The decision, however, rested with the state. Let the state legislature expedite laws governing municipal finances, he reiterated, but grant the *municipios* freedom in administering these laws. *Municipios* should be free, he logically reasoned, but within the limits set by each legislature.

Last to defend the committee report on the evening of January 24 was the wearied Medina, who could offer nothing new in support of paragraph II. The committee proposal for the *municipio* to collect all taxes and turn over a part of the amount to the state was best in theory and practice, he said, as he made a passionate appeal for municipal liberty, assuring the delegates that it would not lead to an absolutism endangering state sovereignty. The revolution sought to break the bonds linking the past to the present, to provide municipal freedom through "absolute financial independence." By now Medina had run out of argument. In conclusion, he could only appeal to the "patriotism" and "deep revolutionary sentiment" of the delegates to approve paragraph II.

Sincere as the appeal was, it did not convince the assembly. Sensing the rejection of paragraph II, Palavicini suggested adoption of Article 115 of Carranza's draft. No one supported him on this point; and the president ruled that, if paragraph II was disapproved, it should be returned to the committee. In the voting which followed, Article 115 was approved, but paragraph II was rejected by a vote of 110 to 35. Only a handful of delegates had sided with Jara, Medina, and Paulino Machorro y Narváez, committee chairman, in favor of the measure.

Now the assembly was back where it had started with the first reading on January 20. When the paragraph was reported out on January 29, it was obvious that even the Second Committee could not agree on the wording. Signed only by Machorro y Narváez and Arturo Méndez, it provided for municipal liberty based on financial independence and the *municipio*'s right to have its own taxable resources, which, the authors believed, would be both "difficult and dangerous" to enumerate in the constitution. Municipal government was to be funded from three sources: payments by residents for current public services; an amount provided by the state, which would not be less than 10 percent of the total revenue collected by the state for its own purposes in that *municipio*; and an additional amount to be provided by the state to finance services the *municipio* had not customarily provided. Conflicts arising between a *municipio* and the executive branch of a state government would be settled by the state legislature; conflicts arising between a *municipio* and the legislature would be resolved by the state supreme court.[13] The framers now believed the state must bear responsibility for support of the *municipio*. This position was a far cry from that of the original version, in which the *municipios* were to contribute to state treasuries.

Disagreeing with their colleagues, Jara and Medina submitted a minority report, which they believed more closely reflected the wishes of the assembly. It read as follows: "The *municipios* shall freely administer their finances which shall be composed of municipal taxes

13 Ibid., pp. 1065–1066.

necessary to meet their diverse needs and from the sum that the state assigns to each *municipio*. All disputes that arise between the branches of a state government and the *municipio* shall be settled by the Supreme Court of each state in accordance with the terms of the respective law."[14]

Unfortunately, discussion did not resume until several other articles, including Article 27, had been reserved for voting. By then, early on the morning of January 30, the weary delegates were little inclined to continue. Debate promptly broke down into a three-cornered struggle among those who opposed the minority report, those who favored it, and those who urged its rejection in favor of Carranza's draft. The Machorro y Narváez–Méndez report received little consideration. When Cepeda Medrano asked that the matter be postponed for further study, Palavicini retorted that, after discussing the most important problem before the convention (Article 27), it was inconceivable that the delegates would spend more time on this paragraph. Although the chair announced that delay would make it difficult for the calligrapher to finish the constitution on time, since he still had the long Article 27 to do, five delegates promptly presented a motion asking that debate be suspended and resumed at 10 A.M. The proposal failed to carry; and, as the secretary implored the delegates not to leave, final debate commenced on the status of the *municipio* in the new order.

Little could be added to what had already been said. To pleas by Palavicini and Chapa that the assembly reject the pending proposals in favor of the First Chief's draft, the delegates turned a deaf ear, despite the fact that some, including Calderón, were willing to accept Carranza's wording as a last resort. In the end, Calderón, Jara, and Medina summed up the respective positions in the argument. Calderón, a defender of state sovereignty, conceded that the *ayuntamientos* should administer their own resources, but only under conditions imposed by the legislature. He pointed out that the concept of the *municipio libre* implied political, not financial, freedom, that the *jefe político* had been swept away, leaving the *presidente municipal* without hierarchical superior. Just because the *municipio* was free, said

14 Ibid., p. 1067.

Calderón, this did not mean that it would have to take over all public services, thereby requiring additional financial support. For example, the *municipio* should be concerned with seeing that parents sent their children to school and that new classrooms were built, but responsibility for the technical supervision of education would have to remain with the state. As for the right of the *ayuntamientos* to levy taxes without legislative approval, this, concluded Calderón, "will bring about chaos throughout the State. (Voices: *¡A votar! ¡A votar!*)"[15]

Answering Calderón, Jara, a fellow leftist but now on the opposing side of the debate, hammered on a now-familiar theme: municipal freedom without financial liberty meant nothing. Criticizing Calderón for his conservative views on municipal finance, Jara said that, if *municipios* were going to remain subject to the will of the state, there would be no improvement; they would continue to suffer. Appealing for support of the minority report, he stressed that the wording was simple, that no percentages of tax support were involved as in the majority report, that all it asked was for the *municipio* to administer its own fiscal affairs and have sufficient funds to meet its needs.

Finally, Medina reminded his audience that the committee had removed the two most objectionable items from the original report: municipal responsibility for collection of all taxes and settlement of municipal-state disputes by the Supreme Court. Now, he said, it was necessary to declare that the *municipio* would be supported from taxes on its resources in addition to a state subsidy in case local revenue was insufficient. Refuting Calderón's statement that the *municipio* could decree its own taxes, he pointed to the minority report, in which this right was not stated at all. In conclusion, he emphasized that the question was one "of life or death" and that the decision of the assembly could "mutilate municipal liberty forever."[16]

Mounting the platform to break the impasse was Gerzayn Ugarte, Carranza's private secretary, *renovador*, and no friend of the leftists. As late as January 4, Bojórquez and twenty-six other delegates had presented a petition charging Ugarte with conflict of interests and asking that he either resign his position as secretary to the First Chief

15 Ibid., p. 1134.
16 Ibid.

ustiano Carranza, leader of the Constitutionalist movement that gave Mexico the Con-
tion of 1917. (Photo by José Mendoza)

The Iturbide Theater (today, Theater of the Republic), Querétaro, scene of all sess of the convention, December 1, 1916–January 31, 1917. (Photo by José Mendoza)

First Chief of the Constitutionalist Army in Charge of the Executive Power of the Na Venustiano Carranza delivering his speech at the inaugural session of the convention, De ber 1, 1916. At Carranza's right is Convention President Luis Manuel Rojas (Jalis (Photo by José Mendoza)

Prominent delegates to the Querétaro Convention. (Photos by José Mendoza)

is Manuel Rojas (Jalisco), convention pres-
nt and co-author of Carranza's draft of
orms to the Constitution of 1857.

Pastor Rouaix (Puebla), chairman of the
extralegal committees that prepared first drafts
of Articles 27 and 123.

ncisco J. Múgica (Michoacán), spokesman
the leftists.

José Natividad Macías (Guanajuato), coauthor with Rojas of the Carranza draft proposals.

Three friends, prominent leftists of the Constitutional Convention of 1916–1917: *left to right*, Hilario Medina (Guanajuato), Heriberto Jara (Veracruz), Francisco J. Múgica (Michoacán).

Félix F. Palavicini (Federal District) speaking during the debate on Article 3, December, 1916. (Photo by José Mendoza)

Four of the spokesmen for the proletariat in the Constitutional Convention. (Photos by José Mendoza)

Esteban B. Calderón (Jalisco).

Luis Fernández Martínez (Guanajuato).

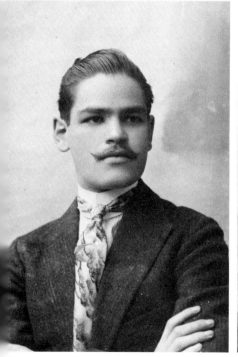

Froylán C. Manjarrez (Puebla).

Carlos L. Gracidas (Veracruz).

Delegates who participated in the preparation of the Rouaix draft of Article 123 and ot
labor sympathizers at the Querétaro Convention: *seated, left to right*, Carlos L. Graci
(Veracruz), Jesús de la Torre (Durango), Federico E. Ibarra (Jalisco), Luis G. Mon
(Sonora), Pastor Rouaix (Puebla), Francisco J. Múgica (Michoacán), Nicolás C
(Guanajuato), Cándido Aguilar (Veracruz); *standing, left to right*, Dionisio Zavala (
Luis Potosí), Victorio E. Góngora (Veracruz), Andrés Molina Enríquez (lawyer for
National Agrarian Commission), Jorge E. von Versen (Coahuila), Silvestre Dora
(Durango), José Inocente Lugo (director of the Office of Labor, Ministry of Fomen
Antonio Gutiérrez (Durango), Heriberto Jara (Veracruz), Porfirio del Castillo (Pueb
Héctor Victoria (Yucatán). (Photo by José Mendoza)

Participants in discussions of the preliminary (Rouaix) draft of Article 27: *seated,*
to right, Alberto M. González (Hidalgo), Rafael de los Ríos (Federal District),
Inocente Lugo (director of the Office of Labor, Ministry of Fomento), Pastor Ro
(Puebla), Porfirio del Castillo (Puebla), David Pastrana Jaimes (Puebla), Dionisio
vala (San Luis Potosí); *standing, left to right*, José Alvarez y Alvarez (Michoacán),
vestre Dorador (Durango), Antonio Gutiérrez (Durango), Jesús de la Torre (Duran
Rafael Martínez de Escobar (Tabasco), Alberto Terrones Benítez (Durango). (Phot
José Mendoza)

The original of the Constitution of 1917, showing
the authentic title. (Photo by José Mendoza)

Three "jacobins" of the Querétaro Convention. (Photos by José Mendoza)

ιis G. Monzón (Sonora).

José Alvarez y Alvarez (Michoacán).

Juan de Dios Bojórquez
(Sonora).

Delegates taking the oath to protect and defend the new constitution, Iturbide Theater, Querétaro, January 31, 1917. (Photo by José Mendoza)

or ask for leave of absence from the convention. More than resentment at Ugarte, it was a slap at Carranza himself. Nothing, however, had come of this petition. Now Ugarte was to demonstrate once again his ability as a compromiser. Agreeing with Calderón that an unconditional grant of autonomy to the municipal councils would be the equivalent of allowing them the right to legislate for themselves on administrative, financial, and other matters, he reminded the assembly that *municipios* had always had the right to propose budgets to the state legislatures and to inform them of the extent of municipal taxable resources. Under the concept of the self-governing municipality, Ugarte believed that this right would certainly not be taken away. A harmonious working relationship had to be preserved between *municipio* and branches of the state government. The *municipios* would have to observe the laws made by the legislature, just as the executive branch would have to enforce them. On behalf of various delegates, Ugarte then presented a new draft of paragraph II, which read as follows: "The *municipios* shall freely administer their finances which shall be composed of the taxes determined by the state legislatures and which, in all events, shall be sufficient to meet their needs."[17]

It was a shrewd move, made at the right moment, and took the proponents of unlimited municipal fiscal authority by surprise. In presenting an entirely different wording, Ugarte had boldly usurped the Second Committee's power. The assembly, in no mood for further debate, agreed to consider this new proposal; thereupon, Jara, to the applause of the delegates, requested permission to withdraw the minority report. The new version was promptly reserved for voting, despite Jara's final lament that Ugarte had proposed nothing new, because state legislatures had always reviewed municipal budgets. Then, as one of several articles, including Article 27, voted on in the final minutes of a session that ended at 3:30 A.M. on January 30, Ugarte's proposed paragraph II of Article 115 was approved by a vote of 88 to 62. Jara, Medina, and Méndez, all disillusioned and worn out from the fight they had lost, voted against.[18]

[17] Ibid., p. 1135.
[18] Ibid., p. 1136.

In writing Article 115 into the constitution, the delegates did little more than confirm that the *municipio*, as a territorial, political, and administrative division of the state, would be free of the hated, authoritative *jefe político*. A group of delegates, however, anxious to instill new life into Mexican local government, seized on the opportunity to demand financial independence as well. To them the words *municipio libre* signified a panacea for all the ills of municipal existence. Motivated by their own idealism, they were also influenced by Don Venustiano himself, who, in his inaugural speech of December 1, had spoken optimistically of benefits accruing to the *municipio* if it were permitted to have its own financial resources and manage them as well. The First Chief's draft of Article 115, as has been seen, however, was considerably more sobering. It remained for proponents of municipal liberty to try to elevate the principle they sought into the constitution. In drafting their measure they tried to walk a narrow line between states' rights and municipal freedom. In a sense they were seeking municipal home rule. This quest resembled a contemporary movement in the United States aimed at freeing cities from legislative domination and endowing them with sufficient powers to meet the demand for greater local services. On the other hand, the enthusiasm of the reformers for more freedom in local government was more than matched by those who feared establishment of autonomous enclaves within each state. The result was a compromise. Municipal autonomists were forced to settle for a measure granting free administration of local finances, but within limits set by the legislature. Jara and members of the Second Committee, who longed to establish a free-functioning unit of local government, a showcase of democracy governed by its own legislative, executive, and judicial authorities, were defeated. The revolutionary principle of the free municipality was written into the constitution, but it was more a goal for the future than an achievement in strengthening the Mexican municipality.[19] Curiously, few of the delegates qualified to speak on the matter actually did so. Most were content to listen to others. For example, Luis Ilizaliturri (Nuevo León), who had long served as legal adviser to

[19] Sergio Francisco de la Garza, *El municipio, historia, naturaleza y gobierno*, p. 202.

the *ayuntamiento* of Mexico City and who was presumably well informed in the field of municipal finance, remained silent throughout.

PROHIBITION

During the convention a group of delegates persistently attempted to write the prohibition of bullfights, cockfights, gambling, and the manufacture and sale of intoxicating liquors into the constitution. As in the case of the free municipality, opposition to these measures forced them to settle for less. Their touching yet unsuccessful efforts, however, evoke admiration for the reformers who sought to heal running sores of Mexican society.

That alcoholism was a problem cannot be denied. As early as 1904 the Second Catholic Congress of Mexico had pointed to the need for a campaign against drunkenness. Little was undertaken, however, until the revolution, when various provisional state governments decreed prohibition. During the debate on Article 5, Luis Monzón declared that all the saloons and gambling houses in Sonora were closed, "with the approval of thousands of families who before lay in dire need and today bless the revolution . . ."[20] Salvador Alvarado, military governor of Yucatán (1915–1917), boasted that he had left that state "without alcohol, without gambling, without bullfights, without raffles, without lotteries, without red-light districts, and without vagabonds."[21] Although Carranza took no step to combat alcoholism, by a decree of October 7, 1916, he outlawed bullfighting in the Federal District and territories and prohibited it in the states pending the re-establishment of constitutional order.[22]

In the convention a temperance movement surfaced the morning of December 11, 1916, with the reading of Article 4. Whereas the First Chief's draft had simply stated that everyone had the right to choose his own profession or occupation, as long as it was legal, the reform-minded First Committee had added a line declaring the liquor busi-

[20] *Diario de los debates*, I, 1030.
[21] Salvador Alvarado, *Mi actuación revolucionaria en Yucatán*, p. 76, cited in Wilfrid Hardy Callcott, *Liberalism in Mexico, 1857–1929*, p. 259.
[22] *Memoria de la Secretaría de Gobernación correspondiente al período revolucionario comprendido entre el 19 de febrero de 1913 y el 30 de noviembre de 1916*, pp. 386–387.

ness and the operation of gambling houses to be unlawful and, therefore, prohibited. Undoubtedly Múgica, a known prohibitionist, inspired this provision. The preface to Article 4 acknowledged that enforcement would be difficult, but not impossible, since "in some areas the revolution has succeeded in almost completely putting an end to the business of intoxicating beverages."[23]

Discussion of Article 4 did not occur until the afternoon of December 18. In the interim the First Committee, with second thoughts, had withdrawn the prohibition on drinking and gambling, stating that this subject lay more appropriately in the realm of congressional action. Nevertheless, it announced its intention of studying measures to combat the "vices of drunkenness and gambling" so as to place them in the most suitable place in the constitution. Although this sounded reasonable enough, it failed to satisfy Federico Ibarra. He asked for an addition to Article 4 prohibiting the preparation of *pulque*; the importation and distillation of alcohol for the making of beverages; the consumption of intoxicating liquor at the place of sale; bullfights, cockfights, and games of chance; and "houses of pimping in community" (*casas de lenocinio en comunidad*), by which it is presumed he meant prostitution.[24] In a long speech, accentuated by references to newspaper articles and special studies on vice, Ibarra blamed the moral degeneration of the Mexican people on the Díaz dictatorship. Exploitation of gambling and prostitution by men surrounding the old leader had left the people in "the greatest misery, the saddest debauchery, indifferent to everything, without hope, profoundly wounded in soul, with a frightful number engaged in criminality or relegated to insane asylums, or hospitals, or buried in cemeteries."[25] Mexico was quickly drinking itself to death, and it was the duty of the revolution, especially of the Constitutional Convention, to extirpate such evil, to redeem the people. Certainly, Ibarra believed, this was the intention of the First Chief in his famous decree of December

[23] *Diario de los debates*, I, 545.
[24] Ibid., p. 788. "We shall never have a great and strong citizenship if we do not raise our people from the state of barbarity in which they are held by vices, savage amusements, and fanaticism; everything we do against these calamities which afflict us will be little" (Federico Ibarra in Ruiz Album).
[25] *Diario de los debates*, I, 789–790.

12, 1914, which served as the basis for many of the reforms of the preconstitutional period.[26] The convention, the last act of the preconstitutional period, was obligated, he thought, to look to the future, to lay the basis for moral regeneration.

Replying to the argument wielded by opponents of Article 3 that the section on individual rights should only contain limitations on governmental action, Ibarra said that it was perfectly proper in this section to outlaw abuses committed by some individuals against others, crimes "against the preservation of the human species and which among ourselves have reached alarming proportions." Since prohibition was being debated in the American Congress and in France, Ibarra thought Mexico would do well to follow suit. Refuting charges that vested interests would suffer and revenue would decrease, he pointed out that *pulque* was not the only product of the maguey; its honey, sugar, and fiber were also marketable. But if the capitalists were harmed, that was not important, "because it is a principle of law that the interests of a few must be sacrificed for those of society." As for the loss of revenue, Ibarra said that big business could well afford to pay higher taxes and that assessments on rural properties were ridiculously low. States that had decreed prohibition had not suffered financially. Furthermore, with the prohibition of liquor, gambling, and prostitution, all levels of government would henceforth incur less expense in maintaining large police forces, jails, insane asylums, and hospitals. In conclusion, Ibarra drew applause as he pleaded for support of the measures that would "redeem our people, removing them from the utter degradation into which they have fallen."[27]

Only idealistic Doctor Andrade supported Ibarra, arguing that the precept had to be placed in the constitution in order to receive the respect it deserved. If it were only a legislative prohibition, companies producing alcohol would bribe officials, and the law would be unenforceable. Like Ibarra, Andrade believed that prohibition would not

[26] In this decree Carranza stated that he would expedite and put into effect laws and measures aimed at satisfying the "economic, social, and political needs of the country." For the full text, see *Cincuentenario de las adiciones y reformas al Plan de Guadalupe*, pp. 31–36.

[27] *Diario de los debates*, I, 788–792.

be out of place among the individual rights. Article 3 had set the precedent. Why could not the assembly write it into Article 4?

Other speakers, not necessarily against prohibition, tried to bring out the problems involved with such a drastic measure. One Herrera spoke for the committee report—that is, against Ibarra's proposal—because he believed it ridiculous to write into the constitution a maxim that really fell under the police power of the states. They should regulate drunkenness, "the cause of so many evils," and keep it from getting worse. As for gambling, he reminded the delegates that not a single gambling house existed in most of the republic. If an old *tahur* was arrested, he paid the penalty and left the area, not to return. Herrera's criticism of the Ibarra proposal also drew applause.[28]

Speaking in defense of the report, Colunga commended the humanitarianism of those who attacked the problem of alcoholism in Mexico but argued against a constitutional provision on the subject. The proposal to prohibit *pulque* and grain alcohol would only eliminate competition for producers of tequila in Jalisco, *mezcal* in Zacatecas, and brandy in Parras (a wine-producing area of Coahuila). Nor would a general prohibition be appropriate, because alcohol was used in industry as well as for medicinal purposes. Furthermore, Colunga asked, "with what right can you keep a person from drinking who is accustomed to a moderate use of wine?" Affirming that the problem of alcoholism was complicated and had to be studied with care before taking any action, he categorically stated that the First Committee could not accept Ibarra's proposal.[29]

A final blast against Ibarra's proposed addition came from Cepeda Medrano. Speaking for the moderate drinkers, he claimed that it was "illegal and uneconomical." It was illegal because alcoholic beverages had to be classified before their sale could be prohibited, since various kinds were consumed, many of which could be easily manufactured. Every maguey in the Federal District was a potential bar, since it could produce a great quantity of *pulque*. Furthermore, it would be

---

[28] The *Diario de los debates* does not indicate whether this was Alfonso Herrera (Federal District) or Manuel Herrera (Oaxaca).

[29] *Diario de los debates*, I, 799.

hypocritical to prohibit in the constitution the sale of alcoholic beverages when tomorrow not only delegates but the greater part of the people were apt to be intoxicated! He did not think the delegates had come to Querétaro to violate the constitution they were about to sign when they should be the first to comply with its provisions. As for the economics of prohibition, he reminded his audience that the manufacture of alcohol brought in great amounts of revenue not only to the national treasury but also to those of states and *municipios*. Under present conditions, Mexico could not do without this income. Furthermore, a great number of people depended on the liquor business for a livelihood.

It was clear to all that Ibarra's proposal had no chance of acceptance. By a vote of 145 to 7 on the evening of December 18, Article 4 was approved as reported out. Ibarra and Andrade were among the minority voting against. The prohibitionists had met defeat, but they would be heard from again.

The full force of the dry movement in the convention was brought to light on January 23 with the reading of a proposed amendment to Article 117 on powers denied the states. Signed by seventy-one persons, rightists as well as leftists (including Múgica, Monzón, Macías, Bojórquez, and Ibarra), the text read as follows:

In the States, Federal District, and Territories the following will always be prohibited:

1. The manufacture and sale of *pulque*, as well as the manufacture of alcohol from maguey and sugar cane for the preparation of intoxicating beverages and from cereals for whatever purpose. 2. Games of chance, bullfighting, cockfights and all kinds of games or diversions in which there is the inevitable shedding of blood. 3. The sale of drugs, use of which is harmful to the health or results in the degeneration of the species, except as dispensed by prescription of a physician.

Violations of the above listed provisions shall be punished by law and prosecuted by the authorities. The latter will be considered as coauthors of said violations in case they are committed with their permission, authorization, or tolerance; and they will be considered as accomplices when they are less than diligent in pursuit of said violators.[30]

[30] Ibid., II, 827.

As might be expected, Múgica's name appeared at the head of the list. Three others, perhaps less abstinent than their colleagues, signed as favoring prohibitions 2 and 3 only. They were Ramón Ross (Sonora), Miguel Rosales (Puebla), and José L. Gómez (Morelos).

The preface to the amendment asserted the need for governments to work against those customs and habits that led to the degradation and weakening of society. More cultured peoples, especially those of the "Saxon" race, recognized the need to take care of the body and did so. They were also concerned with eradicating alcoholism and sports reminiscent of their savage past. Mexico had to do the same. The aboriginal race had been strong and vigorous, and, although it had had its defects, servility, drunkenness, and gambling had been unknown. Alcoholism had resulted from the Spanish conquest, encouraged as a means of holding the natives in bondage. The revolution, which had "the noble task of awakening all Mexicans held back from civilization," would carry out a program of reforms aimed at uplifting the degraded. Nothing would be accomplished toward physical and cultural betterment, however, if vices were allowed to flourish beside the school. The delegates had already shown themselves concerned with measures to protect the working class, "saving it from the avaricious and pitiless exploitation of the capitalists." Now it was time to do something about vice. Attempts had been made to extirpate gambling and bullfighting, but they still persisted, "and surely they will continue to exist in the future if a constitutional precept does not prohibit them." This, the framers idealistically believed, was the sure solution to the problem. As a last exhortation, they urged the convention to follow the example of the many states of the American union that had recently enacted prohibition measures.[31]

Why was the amendment offered at this time? Although prohibitionist sentiment was certain to find expression sooner or later, it is probable that the sponsors were strongly influenced by the speech of Dr. José María Rodríguez during the evening session of January 18. Dedicated to the cause of improving public health, this conscientious medic, a native of Saltillo, forty-six years old, had studied in the National School of Medicine and in the Military Hospital, both of

31 Ibid., pp. 825–827.

Mexico City, receiving his doctor's degree and commission as a major in the army in 1895. As one of the founders of the Liberal party of Coahuila, he early allied himself with Madero. Elected mayor of Torreón in 1912, he resigned after the *decena trágica*, later serving as personal physician to Carranza and as Constitutionalist consul in San Antonio, Texas, where he bought arms and supplies for the revolutionary army. In 1914 he organized the Army Medical Corps and served as its first head.

Doctor Rodríguez was best known, however, for his service as president of the Superior Council of Public Health in Mexico City. From this experience, he urged the convention on January 18 to create a Department of General Public Health responsible to the president and with power to enforce health measures that would also be binding on the state governments. A responsibility of the department would be to conduct a campaign "against alcoholism and the sale of substances which poison the individual and cause the degeneration of the race." During his long speech, he cited statistics to show the frightful toll alcohol had exacted from his people. Crime was less in Paris, Vienna, and Berlin together than in Mexico City, "perhaps the deadliest [*la más mortífera*] city of the world." Eighty percent of the crimes involving bloodshed were committed by persons in a state of drunkenness. In 1901 alone, he said, there had been 113,607 arrests for drunkenness in the eight police districts of the capital.[32] Nine-tenths of the lower classes were habitual drunkards. The high mortality rate of Mexico City, Rodríguez asserted, was largely due to alcohol and its effects on the human body. Consequences of the seven trainloads of *pulque* consumed daily in the capital were untold occupational accidents; jails, asylums, and hospitals filled to capacity; and weakened bodies susceptible to sickness and contagious diseases. Rodríguez also deplored the production of alcohol from cereals, which deprived the people of needed food and caused Mexico to have to import grain. In conclusion, he stated that he had revealed these facts for the "patriotic and disinterested consideration" of the delegates in

[32] The census of 1900 listed Mexico City as having 367,777 inhabitants. On the problem of drunkenness, see Moisés González Navarro, *El Porfiriato: La vida social*, vol. 4 of *Historia moderna de México*, ed. Daniel Cosío Villegas, pp. 72–82.

the hope that they would support his proposal for the "benefit of the *patria*, the race, and humanity."[33] It was a strong appeal, one which the convention could hardly overlook.

Late on the evening of January 18 the delegates rejected naming under Article 90 the ministries of the executive branch, thereby accepting the First Chief's draft, which left the matter to Congress to decide. The way was now open for Doctor Rodríguez to propose, under paragraph 16 of Article 73, on the powers of Congress, an amendment making the Superior Council of Public Health a direct dependency of the president, hence free of interference from any ministry. The amendment specified that measures put into effect in "the campaign against alcoholism and the sale of substances which corrupt the individual and cause the race to degenerate" would later be reviewed by Congress. It bore the signatures of Rodríguez, Dr. Miguel Alonzo Romero, Rubén Martí, and thirty-nine others.

Speaking for the proposal, Doctor Alonzo Romero said that a strong campaign against this "scourge of humanity" was direly needed. He believed the problem was so serious that 90 percent of the people "owed their lack of development, their weak and miserable condition to the disastrous ravages of alcohol on their systems."[34] The only opposition came from Pastrana Jaimes and Eliseo L. Céspedes (Veracruz), two young lawyers, who feared that the grant of power to the Superior Council was excessive, that it would violate the sovereignty of the states. In addition, Céspedes believed that the salvation of the race lay in the school, not in a campaign against alcoholism. Sentiment, however, was overwhelmingly in favor of the proposal, which was approved on the afternoon of January 19 by a vote of 143 to 3. The convention had written into the constitution the first measure aimed at controlling a social malignancy of great proportions.

By the second reading of the prohibition amendment to Article 117, on January 25, the convention had approved another measure against alcoholic beverages. Article 123, paragraph 13, prohibited the sale of intoxicating beverages and the establishment of gambling houses in workers' centers. As previously noted, this article was ac-

[33] *Diario de los debates*, II, 616–624.
[34] Ibid., pp. 651–652.

cepted without discussion by the affirmative vote of 163 delegates on the evening of January 23.

Thus the seventy-one sponsors of the amendment to Article 117 had good reason to believe that the convention was psychologically prepared to accept prohibition. Curiously, the first to speak against was none other than Doctor Rodríguez, who previously had so aroused the delegates with his exposure of the evils of drink in Mexico. Although professing opposition to alcoholic beverages, Rodríguez pointed out to the sponsors the full consequences of their action. First, Mexico, almost bankrupt, could not afford prohibition because of the resulting loss in revenue. Second, more than 400,000 persons in the *mesa central* depended on the *pulque* trade alone for a livelihood. What was to become of them? They would surely suffer terribly, since, for want of plows, oxen, mules, etc., destroyed during the fighting, they could not turn immediately to agriculture. Third, the way to deal with the problem of alcoholism was not to declare it illegal overnight but to eliminate it gradually throughout the republic. Here the Superior Council could play a key role by controlling excessive consumption of liquor, by prohibiting drinking on the streets and at places where liquors were sold, by improving the sanitary quality of alcoholic beverages, and by cleaning up the *pulquerías*. These measures, Rodríguez believed, would soon raise the price of the drink to a level that low-paid workers could not afford. He also urged that the alcoholic be treated as an *envenenado* and not as a lawbreaker. In his opinion, with decreasing demand for *pulque*, the landowner would be forced to turn to the other uses of the maguey—making sugar and fiber. But the changeover had to be carried out slowly, for the country could not survive the economic dislocation of doing it immediately.

Next Rodríguez proceeded to tell the delegates why he was opposed to a constitutional prohibition on bullfighting. This turned out to be another blow to the puritanical reformers. As he saw it, the measure's sponsors had probably never fought bulls as amateurs or perhaps had got dizzy at the sight of blood. But, he said, "bullfighting . . . is a *fiesta de la raza*; it is a *fiesta* attended by the best and most illustrious of society; it is a true 'sport,' the top sport of all, where exhibitions of valor are seen, where skill has its greatest and most beautiful manifestations, . . . the only sport in which intelligence, bravery, and skill are seen to dominate brute force, a useful example in general which might be put into practice in everyday life."[35] When delegates questioned the killing of a brave bull, which, they said, might serve to work the soil, they did not think of the brutal way thousands were killed daily in the slaughterhouses. "These thoughts never come to them when they put in their mouths the delicious beef-steaks that they eat with pleasure." Nor had they protested against even more abominable acts. "Why not put in the constitution that castration of animals is also prohibited?" asked Rodríguez. This he considered a "thousand times worse, a thousand times more painful, a thousand times more wicked" than death itself. Rodríguez also took to task those delegates who bewailed the killing of horses during bull-fights. Most were just nags, he said, destined to die in the countryside of sickness or old age and become carrion for birds of prey, crows, and coyotes, a scavenging process that he vividly described, to the disgust of many present. In conclusion, he commended the efforts of those who wanted to abolish sports in which animals are killed, but said:

This in no way should be put in the Constitution. This will come by example, with the gradual change of this kind of sport for another; if you wish, change it for the turkey trot or the American dance; change then, if you wish, our *fiesta de raza* for the innocent entertainment of the civilized country to the north. Copy from its dances and its movies, where the audience is taught to abuse the authorities, to assassinate, to kill in order to rob; change it for all this, teach the people to dance and to play football, but do not use the pretext that the bullfight is immoral, calling it a barbarous festivity.[36]

It was a speech inappropriate for the high level of debate that should characterize a constitutional convention, but Rodríguez had made his point, and there was little inclination to refute him. Only Andrade replied that if a lot of people lost their jobs from the outlawing of bull-fights, this would not matter. It was necessary for the progress of

---

[35] Ibid., pp. 941–942.
[36] Ibid., p. 943.

Mexico. Later, to an accusation from Ibarra that he owned a bull ring in Saltillo, Rodríguez made no reply.

Another who spoke against the prohibition amendment to Article 117 was Rubén Martí. He was sure that of all the delegates present there were not more than two or three who had never got drunk. "I am sure that yesterday more than ten signers of the amendment were . . . (Laughter. Murmurs.)" Although he praised the sponsors for their good intentions, Martí warned that laws could not change people's customs, nor was it right for a minority to impose itself on the great majority of individuals who really liked to drink *pulque*. When the state of México enacted prohibition, there were few if any drunks around the first few days. Then illicit traffic developed, and a short time later, "instead of there being a *pulquería* on each corner, there was a *tinacalito* [vat] in each house; although no one could find where *pulque* was sold, there were drunks everywhere." Martí asked where the government would get the "thousands of inspectors necessary to keep the people from drinking." When he said he had never found men who did not drink, he was interrupted by the youthful Bojórquez, who said: "Go to Sonora." Well, Martí hoped Bojórquez was right, but he doubted it. Admitting that consumption of alcohol in Mexico was terrifying, Martí stood firm in his belief that prohibition was not the answer, for people just drank more under prohibition. A campaign against alcoholism was necessary, but not outright prohibition. His own antialcoholism campaign among the soldiers stationed along the Mexico City–Toluca line had ended in failure. As a consequence he had opened a *pulquería* in his own regiment, where he could keep the drinking under control. Furthermore, if prohibition was voted, the loss of revenue to the new government would be disastrous. Mocking the measure's supporters, he said they could do more for the cause by solemnly pledging not to enter another bar, not to drink any more *pulque*, and to refrain from ever getting drunk again. This, he thought, would set a good example for others to follow. If the manufacture of *pulque* were prohibited, said Martí, this would deprive the poor of the only liquor they could afford, and "by what right are we going to establish the exclusive privilege that

in order to get drunk one must be rich?" This would only confirm
what the *peladitos* were saying already: "What for the rich is happiness, for the poor is drunkenness." Martí also agreed with Rodríguez that the juice and fiber of the maguey plant should be more
fully utilized, not almost exclusively tapped for *pulque*. As a last
resort, he tried to get his colleagues to take the pledge not to drink
any more during the rest of their stay in Querétaro (one week).
Reminding all that he was not asking for lifelong abstinence, but
"only until you reach México," Martí decided to set the example himself, saying, "From today on I will not take another drink. (Applause)."[37] Said with more humor than conviction, it was an appeal
that the delegates liked, whether they were willing to go along with
him or not.

Predictably, the indomitable Múgica arose to plead the cause of prohibition. Speaking with emotion, he questioned why anyone should
even sign the new constitution if it was going to be worthless as an
instrument for opposing vested interests and eradicating evils deeply
rooted in the Mexican social milieu. In his opinion, prohibition was
so important that, if for some reason the delegates had to leave
Querétaro with their work unfinished, this would be the provision
he would most wish to see in the constitution, where it would have
the sanctity it deserved, something that could never be obtained by
legislation alone. Vested interests and the distillers were sure to violate the regulations of the Superior Council. Even though its officials
were honest, bribery would soon tempt them. When Múgica asked
Rodríguez how much the *pulque* producers had offered him not to
oppose its sale in Mexico City, he replied: "Four hundred thousand
pesos silver to me alone."[38] Fortunately, Rodríguez could not be
corrupted.

Next, Múgica belittled the importance of liquor excise taxes as a
source of revenue, although he was promptly challenged on this by
Ernesto Perusquía (Querétaro), who informed the delegates that the
sale of *pulque* alone brought in four million pesos in taxes each

37 Ibid., p. 947.
38 Ibid., p. 948.

month. Conceding that it was this much or more, Múgica countered: "How many millions of pesos does the nation spend keeping drunks in jail and the sick, whose illnesses are due to the excessive use of alcohol, in hospitals?"[39] Concerned about the states that had prohibition, he believed the failure of the constitution to provide the same would leave them in a ridiculous situation. Admitting that this grave social problem could not be solved by a single stroke of the pen, he asked the delegates not to wait for "evolution or education, which reduce the evil little by little," but to "grip the lance once and for all, prepare it for action, and attack those factories which are not windmills, but really some great enemies of the Mexican race (Applause)."[40]

Once over this quixotic outburst, he told how prohibition had benefited two states. In Sinaloa, field hands who once cultivated maguey were now producing cereals, so much that there were not enough workers for the harvest. In Sonora, workers who once spent all their earnings on drink had even started a savings bank. Underestimating the opposition to prohibition, Múgica said that only a handful of delegates were really against it. The real enemies, he believed, were distillers, who had always defrauded the government of its revenue while unloading impure alcohol on the public. If prohibition brought about their ruin, it was a deserved punishment that the revolution should not fear, because the effect would be for the benefit of the Mexican people. But, in conclusion, Múgica weakened, asking: "Do you believe, gentlemen, that someone of the delegates who signed that addition does not intend to enter a bar again to take a drink? Nevertheless, gentlemen, the idea is altruistic and redeeming. Vote for it! (Applause)."[41] It was a frank admission that, noble as the cause was, prohibition would never be effective in Mexico. Even Monzón, another of the signers, agreed. Only yesterday, he said, the Sonora delegation had offered a *convivialidad* to the jacobin group in the convention, and he, "after fourteen months of cruel abstinence," had quenched his thirst. In effect Monzón was saying that, if a man felt

[39] Ibid., p. 949.
[40] Ibid., p. 950.
[41] Ibid., p. 952.

like drinking with friends, he would. Prohibition would be no deterrent.

The debate continued with Doctor Alonzo Romero, who thought it a mistake to enumerate the prohibition of only certain alcoholic beverages. Either all should be quashed, he said, or none. Every alcoholic drink had a harmful effect, whether on the stomach, the nervous system, or the liver. The delegates, however, were little interested in the pathology of alcoholism; and, when Alonzo Romero had finished, the secretary asked if the matter had been sufficiently discussed. Before there could be a show of hands, Gerzayn Ugarte asked to be recognized. He was the last speaker of the opposition.

As had been his custom during previous sessions, Ugarte had refrained from speaking until the end of the debate, when he could offer a compromise solution. After praising the visionary sponsors of the measure, Ugarte asked the delegates to come down from the beautiful realm of theory to reality and think of the consequences of their action for the Mexico of the present. All the states producing *pulque* and alcohol, especially those in the *mesa central,* would be deeply harmed by a measure that the convention had written into fundamental law. It would be impossible to transform the liquor industry in those states in a few days or weeks or months to one producing sugar or molasses or utilizing maguey fiber. Meanwhile, the law would be in force. These states would see themselves as ruined and would hold the federal government responsible. As for the loss of revenue, he rebuked Múgica for saying that the country could get by without it. The budget, only half of what it was in normal times, was based on a monthly income of 12½ million pesos, of which 9 million went to the War Department. A loss of 4 million pesos to a prosperous country would mean nothing; but to a country bankrupt like Mexico this was an enormous amount, especially when the real loss was probably closer to 8 million. The next government would need all the financial help it could obtain. In Ugarte's own words: "This is the practical necessity: to take care of the financial needs of the government so that it can survive and the revolution can consolidate, to keep us from sweeping the government and the revolution, in a moment of sentimentality, to disaster."[42] Furthermore, Ugarte decried prohibition as a violation of the principle of federalism. Regulation of the manufacture and sale of intoxicating beverages and prohibition of bullfights were matters that fell under the police powers of the states, not the federal government. Carranza had imposed the federal ban on bullfighting only for the duration of the preconstitutional period, said Ugarte, because he respected state sovereignty and knew that it was the states' obligation to "regulate vice, or, if it is possible, to exterminate it, decreeing restraining measures and increasing taxes, so that not only the manufacture of alcohol becomes impossible but all that is immoral and harmful to society as well."[43]

In conclusion, Ugarte stressed the need to leave the states fully at liberty to legislate on prohibition so that they would not be deprived of revenues "on which they depend for their survival." Signatories of the prohibition amendment to Article 117 would lose nothing, argued Ugarte, if they took his views into consideration. Let "their beautiful dreams" become reality at the proper time. They could then rest assured that they had not contributed to the financial weakening of the national and state governments that would surely occur if the measure were approved immediately.

By now there was little more that could be said on either side. The issue had been fully discussed, from the financial consequences of prohibition to the pathological effects of alcohol, from criminal statistics on drunkenness to arguments about the degeneration of the race, and from the gory effects of bullfighting to the danger of suppressing a national sport. Calderón had the final word when he said that, although Jalisco recognized that it would lose a strong source of revenue, "the state government was determined to uproot the last maguey." He was applauded, but it would take more than that to change the minds of some. By a vote of 98 to 55 the amendment was rejected. Not only had the puritans lost the vote, but only thirty-eight of the original signers had voted in the affirmative. The rest, for reasons best known to them, had voted against or not at all.

[42] Ibid., p. 955.
[43] Ibid., p. 956.

In spite of this setback, the temperance movement in the convention lived on. No sooner had the above vote been taken than Bojórquez announced that, since there was a "real inclination" to prohibit the sale of *pulque* and the manufacture of alcohol, perhaps there should be a measure empowering the state legislatures and the Congress to act. Calderón interrupted him to say that many delegates wanted to "restrict, combat, or exterminate" the vice of drunkenness. What he regretted was that the matter had not been sufficiently studied beforehand. Although his fellow *tapatío*, Ibarra, had authored a worthwhile measure, it was poorly drafted. He then announced that the next day concerned delegates would submit a new draft, for "it would be shameful for this Constitutional Convention if it were believed that sentiment is not unanimous here against the vice of drunkenness."[44] The *Diario de los debates* records that Alonzo Romero, Calderón, Ancona Albertos, Bórquez, and Bojórquez submitted such a proposal on January 26. Immediately referred to the Second Committee, the measure was reported out on January 30, as the convention was drawing to a close. It simply stated that "the Congress of the Union and the state legislatures shall immediately dictate laws aimed at combatting alcoholism."[45] Although Calderón complained that it should have read "laws aimed at the suppression of alcoholism," the proposal was reserved for voting and approved during the morning session of the thirty-first by a vote of 185 to 2.

One further attempt to legislate morality occurred in regard to Article 33. As originally reported out on January 18, it defined foreigners and their rights, stated that they could be expelled from the country by the president if their presence was considered "undesirable," and listed certain transactions in which they were forbidden to engage. A minority report, however, signed by Múgica and Román, enumerated special circumstances in which a foreigner might suffer presidential expulsion; among these were engaging in bullfighting or gambling and being a vagrant or habitual drunkard. Although various provisions of Article 33 were discussed on January 24, no one brought up the proposal concerning foreign bullfighters, gamblers, and tip-

44 Ibid., p. 961.
45 Ibid., p. 1141.

plers. During the permanent session (January 29–31), the secretary ruled that the majority report on Article 33 would be voted on first, and, if it were rejected, the minority report would then be debated. This proved to be unnecessary. By a vote of 93 to 57, the majority report on Article 33 was approved early on the morning of the thirtieth.

It is not surprising that the convention rejected the attempt to impose, by constitutional provision, prohibition and the suppression of bullfights and cockfights in Mexico. What is surprising is that the problem received such attention. Reform-minded delegates persistently attempted to institute prohibition as a step toward uplifting and moralizing the people. Other delegates, more realistic, convinced the convention that outright prohibition was impossible for economic, political, and social reasons. In the end the crusaders had to accept a compromise solution which empowered Congress and the state legislatures to adopt measures aimed at combatting alcoholism. For Mexico, there would be no "noble experiment" like the prohibition movement in the United States.

THE DEATH PENALTY

Another reform that received consideration at Querétaro was abolition of the death penalty. How should evildoers pay their debt to society? Debate on this question evoked humanitarian sentiment and concern for the unfortunate elements of society, who deserved uplifting rather than the gallows. In discussing capital punishment, however, attention focused not on full abolition but on which crimes deserved the death penalty and which did not.

As reported out by the First Committee on January 8, the third paragraph of Article 22, on punishment, outlawed the death penalty for political crimes but authorized its imposition on "the traitor to the country during a foreign war; the parricide; the homicide who kills through treachery, by premeditation, or for profit; the arsonist; the kidnapper; the highwayman; the pirate; the rapist; and on those guilty of grave military offenses."[46] To the list of transgressors subject to capital punishment under the Constitution of 1857 (Art. 23),

46 Ibid., p. 230.

Carranza's draft had added the rapist and the kidnapper. The First Committee accepted this wording without change.

Devoting more than half of the preface to Article 22 to justification of the death penalty, the framers sought to refute the arguments of Gaspar Bolaños (Jalisco). In committee hearings, he had urged abolition of capital punishment in all cases save treason. A thirty-three-year-old native of Michoacán, Bolaños had served as secretary of development in the revolutionary government of Jalisco, and, at the time of his election to the convention, was holding a position of responsibility in the Ministry of Gobernación in the Carranza government. Here, perhaps, he developed his strong repugnance for the death penalty. According to the committee, Bolaños had given all the reasons commonly cited by the abolitionists: the death penalty was a violation of natural law, was contrary to the theory that punishment should be imposed only as a corrective measure, was useless as a warning, deprived the innocent family of the victim of its source of income, prevented amends if it were later found that the person executed had really been innocent, and treated the criminal and the mentally ill the same. Since delinquency was the result of ignorance, which society had not succeeded in eliminating, society had no right to impose punishment by death. Finally, Bolaños had reminded the First Committee of the promise of the Constitutional Convention of 1856–1857 to abolish the death sentence upon the establishment of the penitentiary system. Now that this system had become a reality, with the approval of Article 18, "the fulfillment of that solemn promise should be delayed no longer."[47]

Admitting that time was too short to fully answer Bolaños, the committee prepared its own justification for retention of the death penalty. Society, so the reasoning went, had the right to determine the degree of punishment in order to prevent repetition of the crime.

[47] Article 23 of the Constitution of 1857 provided for abolition of the death sentence upon the establishment of the penitentiary system. In the 1917 convention, debates centered on the political question of whether this system should be under state or federal control. As finally approved, Article 18 of the Constitution of 1917 delegated responsibility to both levels of government to set up a system consisting of *colonias* (penal farms), penitentiaries, and *presidios* (places of punishment by hard labor) based on work as a means of regeneration.

Capital punishment was justifiable if it resulted in greater security for the people. The fact that some countries had abolished execution only to reinstate it later proved that humanity had not reached the level of perfection that rendered the death penalty unnecessary. Mexico had not reached this "superior social state"; hence the extreme penalty had to be kept. As for the new capital offense of *violación*,[48] this crime deserved the death sentence because it could leave the victim in such a miserable and pitiful situation as to have made death more preferable. The harm done, said the committee, could be worse than that of a homicide.

An event that occurred in Querétaro about this time focused attention on punishment by death. On New Year's Eve an army officer, Capt. José Trinidad Ramírez Llaca, brother of delegate Carlos Ramírez Llaca (Guanajuato), had discharged his pistol in a restaurant, probably to celebrate the coming of 1917. In the struggle to disarm him, other shots had been fired, and two persons had been wounded, but not seriously. Once apprehended, Ramírez was court-martialed and, although he was ably defended by delegate Juan Sánchez (Oaxaca), was sentenced to death. Considering this to be excessive punishment, a group of delegates brought the matter to the attention of the convention on January 10, asking that a commission be named to plead with the First Chief for clemency. In the discussion that followed, it turned out that the indictment had been improperly prepared. With the humanitarian spirit of many delegates aroused, Ramón Frausto asserted that if this sentence were permitted, it would be a blot on the new constitution. Others, however, objected to the convention's having to consider matters outside its competence, Múgica declaring that military authorities should rule on the case. Finally, as the assembly returned to its business of writing a constitution, it was informally decided that a delegation, mainly of

[48] In legal and medical parlance, *violación* is defined as having carnal knowledge of a woman by force or when the woman is unconscious, mentally deranged, intimidated, or a minor less than twelve years old. While this is analogous to rape, "rape" is translated into Spanish as *violación* or *estupro* (carnal knowledge of a young, unmarried woman by abuse of confidence or deception). To avoid error, the word *violación*, which was used during the debate, is left untranslated.

guanajuatenses, would try to save the unfortunate captain's life by appeal to the First Chief. This brief discussion served to arouse compassion for those condemned to death; as Frausto said, "I do not want a man to be killed as if he were a dog."[49]

When debate commenced after the second reading on January 12, various objections were raised to the death penalty for certain crimes. In a direct interrogation of the committee, Cravioto asked why *violación* had been made punishable by death. This, he said, was a novelty. The crime was not the same if committed on a girl of fifteen, a *joven núbil* of eighteen, or a "*jamona* of forty, widowed and happy." Also, *violación* could be committed by brutal force, or with the aid of narcotics or intoxicating liquors, or by gradual suggestion through promises. Yet the punishment would be the same: death. Had the committee forgotten, asked Cravioto, that it was the custom for youth to receive their "initiation into passion through violent intercourse with servants and cooks? (Laughter and applause). Has the Committee thought about the detestable blackmail that will occur if that article is approved?"[50]

Answering the facetious Cravioto, Román said that the committee had considered the objections raised by Cravioto but that no one had cared to submit a minority report. Therefore, the article was reported out as found in the Carranza draft, accepting the death penalty "as a necessity, as a sad and painful necessity, above all for our country."[51] Even Bolaños, he said, had not exempted death for treason in time of war. Criminals who killed with premeditation, by treachery, or for profit were dangerous to society and had to be put away. Likewise, death for highwaymen was necessary to bring order out of the chaos resulting from the revolution. The committee was convinced, continued Román, that this was the only solution, especially in states like Morelos. History had shown that after three or four known criminals were put to death, there was greater security on the roads. As for parricide, despite its low incidence around the world, death was

[49] *Diario de los debates*, II, 279.
[50] Ibid., p. 331.
[51] Ibid., p. 332.

imposed, not as a deterrent, but because it was "truly a shocking crime that affects the sentiment and the conscience of multitudes."[52] The committee urged death for the crime of *violación* only in case the victims were minors, although this limitation was not in the text, a point that prompted Luis Ilizaliturri to say he was sure that no state would ever write the death penalty into its penal code for the crime of *violación*.

Delegates registering to condemn the death penalty were de los Ríos, del Castillo, and Jara. De los Ríos, an active participant in the writing of Articles 27 and 123, a native of the Federal District, and twenty-six years old, had studied law, taken part in the political campaign against Díaz, and opposed Huerta. He had contributed to opposition newspapers and since 1914 had held positions in the Ministry of Fomento, first as interim director of mines and petroleum and later as private secretary of the secretary of *fomento* (Rouaix). A firm believer in human rights, he attacked the death penalty as useless and unjust, as a punishment that belonged to the past. Mexico, now under the penitentiary system, should strike it from the penal code. Segregation of the "gangrenous member" from society by death was unjustifiable, for once imprisoned he was no longer a danger to society. The death penalty amounted to an act of vengeance of the strong against the weak, a war declared by the nation against one of its citizens. Who had given the right to an individual or to society to take life? Even the exemplary benefits of capital punishment, he said, were illusory. They rarely if ever deterred an individual from committing the same crime; the scaffold did not discourage the person who killed for hate, revenge, or jealousy. Furthermore, "the individual whom they kill cannot perform any useful service to his family (Laughter). The individual who is permitted to live can, even in prison, sustain his kindred with the fruit of his labor." De los Ríos also cited the example of the United States, saying that a large number of states had abolished the death penalty. In conclusion, he appealed to the sentiment of all present by repeating the words of a member of the revolutionary French Convention during its debate on the abolition of

---

[52] Ibid.

slavery: "Let us not discuss this, gentlemen, because we disgrace ourselves. (Applause)."[53]

In del Castillo's opinion, death for treason during war was almost
too mild a punishment, but he rebelled against it for other crimes.
Parricide was so horrible that only a mentally ill person could commit
it; one found guilty of this crime should be confined to a mental
institution, not put to death. Piracy and kidnapping were such rare
crimes that the constitution should not specify the death penalty, since
they were more the exception than the rule. The same he believed to
be true of highway robbery, which would die out as soon as law and
order were restored. Speaking with pathos, del Castillo lashed out at
society for its indifference toward the unfortunates who were driven
to crime because of ignorance, vice, and their miserable surroundings.
Society, instead of succoring those who went astray, was deaf to pleas
for help. Quick to punish, it never tried to save the offender from a
life of crime or uplift him once he had become trapped in it. He also
opposed death as punishment for insubordination in the army, believing that abuse of authority on the part of superiors was frequently
a cause. Finally, in a dramatic plea for the underdog, he condemned
capital punishment, saying,

It will be for the weak . . . never will it be for the prominent, never will
it be for high society; for the poor man, death will be unavoidable, because the poor suffer all the severity of the law, because there is no defense
for him; he has no resources for support, and when he begs justice, justice
turns its back . . . do we not know many cases in which the *hacendado*
takes out his pistol to take the life of a peon and after two or three months
in jail, during which all aspects of his defense are prepared, during which
lawyers perform miracles, society runs to his assistance; the wealthy man,
who has gold at his disposal, goes free to show his impudence about
town, insulting the same society and mocking the same justice?[54]

Last to air his views against the death penalty was Jara. Although

[53] *Diario de los debates*, II, 335. By the end of 1916 eight American states had
completely abolished capital punishment in the course of their history, and six more
retained it only for a few specific crimes. Three states had restored the death penalty
and one had reabolished it by that time, leaving six states with the abolition still
in effect. See *The Death Penalty in America*, ed. Hugo Adam Bedau, p. 12.

[54] *Diario de los debates*, II, 343.

in favor of its retention for treason, even in time of peace, Jara opposed execution for the arsonist, the kidnapper, the highwayman, and the rapist, because he feared many who were innocent would suffer at the hands of immoral officials, as had happened during the Díaz regime, when, if someone wanted to eliminate someone else, he would get the support of the *jefe político* and accuse the person of robbery. The unfortunate was then apprehended by *rurales* and the *ley fuga* administered. Nor did Jara believe that capital punishment was a palliative for evils that afflicted society. The guilty person was rarely penitent. Death was a feeble punishment, in Jara's opinion, because it did not serve as a corrective measure, but deprived the culprit of his life. Capital punishment was, perhaps, permissible during times of stress, as at present, but "we are drawing up a Constitution that, in reality, has to be put into practice during normal times."[55] Furthermore, he deplored the fact that the committee had increased the number of offenses punishable by death over those specified in the Constitution of 1857. This made it appear that crime had increased through the years in Mexico. As for *violación*, Jara, strong nationalist that he was, opposed stating in the constitution that death was the penalty, because it would appear to the world that this punishment was necessary due to "the temperament of the Mexican males," that what Antonio de la Barrera had said was true when he opposed the employment of a female stenographer at the convention, given "the nature of the *señores diputados*."[56] Jara thought that *violación* should be covered by statutory law. He favored retention of the death penalty for serious military crimes; otherwise, he believed, discipline would suffer. As for parricide, only someone really insane could commit this crime, and such a person should be committed to an asylum. Jara concluded that limiting capital punishment to treason and serious military crimes would keep "those who enjoy killing, those who enjoy shedding blood [executioners] from doing so under the protection of the Constitution."[57]

Defenders of capital punishment made a strong case for its reten-

[55] Ibid., p. 346.
[56] Ibid., p. 347.
[57] Ibid., p. 348.

tion in the constitution. Marcelino Cedano (Tepic), an army officer, believed that abolition was great in principle but too visionary to be put into practice in Mexico. As distasteful as the Díaz regime had been, he said, banditry, the unavoidable heritage of revolutions, had been eliminated. Now, with the constitution almost ready to be promulgated, it would be impossible to reduce brigandage without the death penalty, for "what then would be the dam which might hold back this overflow of violent emotions . . . in which everyone, by virtue of seeing himself ensured against the death penalty, would want to commit all kinds of wrongs?"[58] Furthermore, persons prone to commit crimes punishable by death could not be cured by medicine or imprisonment. Nor did delinquents ever respect the rights of others. The death penalty had to persist for those who took life with premeditation. In conclusion, Cedano argued that abolition of the death penalty would be tantamount to accepting a foreign institution, one completely unadaptable to the Mexican milieu.

According to José Rivera (Puebla), capital punishment, as detestable to him as to others, was still necessary. Those who thought only of saving the condemned man never considered his innocent victim and how he had suffered, whether it was a case of assassination, of a lover who had killed his girl friend, or of one killed in the derailment of a train by *zapatistas*. Many chief executives, he pointed out, granted clemency, and some of the crimes punishable by death, like piracy and parricide, had practically disappeared. As for the allegation that only the lower classes paid the supreme sacrifice, while the wealthy and influential went free, he reminded the delegates of what the First Chief had recently said: "Have faith in Constitutionalist justice and remember García Granados who, in spite of his riches, fell beneath the unbending justice of Constitutionalism."[59]

Fernando Lizardi, last to speak in favor of the death penalty, thought it unnecessary to defend capital punishment, since, like the reproduction of the species, it was a social necessity. Abolition would eventually come, but *zapatistas* were still blowing up trains, and they

[58] Ibid., p. 337.
[59] Ibid., p. 345. The reference is probably to Ing. Alberto García Granados, secretary of *gobernación* in the Huerta cabinet.

had to be dealt with harshly. Stating that countries that had abolished the death penalty had had to reinstate it, he refuted the allegation that it was not a deterrent. Those who said it was not asserted that, for everyone who paid the penalty for murder, there were two others who committed the same crime. But, argued Lizardi, did those opponents of capital punishment know how many had heeded the lesson and refrained from committing a crime punishable by death? Referring to the death penalty for *violación*, Lizardi agreed that all young men had had their first sexual experience with the cook or the maid. Affirming that he did not presume to be a saint in this respect, he asserted, to the amusement of the delegates, that he did not imitate Cravioto either. "On the other hand," he concluded, "how many times instead of it being the youth who violates the cook is it the cook who violates the youth! (Laughter)."[60] In Lizardi's opinion, not everyone who had contact with a woman violated her. As for one in love who seduces through promises or "one who through the literary beauty of his manner is capable of winning the heart of a lady, whether she is a stenographer or not, one who is capable of winning the love of a woman, I admire him, I respect him, and I envy him." The crime of *violación*, he asserted, was very rare. The woman who said she had been violated almost never had been. It was almost always a case of blackmail that she tried to exploit. One who deserved death, however, was the rapist who used force. In the Mexico of 1916 and 1917, Lizardi continued, bands of outlaws entered towns solely for the purpose of taking off girls to satisfy their lust. Directing himself to Machorro y Narváez, who was entering the hall at that moment, he asked if this was not true. Machorro y Narváez replied affirmatively, citing the town of Tapalpa as an example.[61] In conclusion, Lizardi stated that the penal code distinguished clearly between seduction, rape, and *violación*, and, when the convention authorized the death penalty for *violación*, this did not mean that it was obligatory except in certain cases to be determined by law. It was necessary, he said, for Mexicans to be considered by foreigners not as barbarians but as civil-

[60] *Diario de los debates*, II, 349.

[61] Tapalpa, Jalisco, municipal seat of a *municipio* of the same name, is 141 kilometers (88.1 miles) south-southwest of Guadalajara.

ized people, "as men who wish above all to guarantee what is most
sacred to man: the inviolability of his home. (Applause)"[62]

By now it was obvious to all that the majority was in favor of re-
taining the death penalty, despite determined opposition to it for the
crime of *violación*. How to separate this crime before taking a vote
on the entire Article 22 was the next question. Calderón, seconded
by Palavicini, asked that the penalty for *violación* be voted on separately, and this separation was agreed to. In the end, Calderón, smart-
ing over Machorro y Narváez's statement about conditions in Tapalpa,
assured President Rojas, also of the Jalisco delegation, that, "if a
bandit of that kind falls into our hands, he will not even get to town,
whether there is an article in the Constitution or not. Aside from this,
I think it is dangerous . . . to state in the Constitution that the punishment for this crime [*violación*] is death, because, unfortunately, the
moral level of our people is not as high as we would like it to be."[63]
Although Federico Ibarra attempted to have the crimes of treason,
murder with premeditation, and *violación* with violence voted on
separately, his plea was in vain. Considered sufficiently discussed,
Article 22, minus the crime of *violación*, was put to a vote and approved, 110 to 71. Then the death penalty for *violación* was voted on
separately and rejected, 119 to 58. Thus the issue of capital punishment was resolved by the Querétaro Convention. Three speakers had
courageously defended the humanitarian proposal of Gaspar Bolaños,
only to be received with general apathy by their colleagues. When
debate centered on whether to authorize the death penalty for *violación*, the humanitarian appeal became less important. In reality, absolute abolition of capital punishment was doomed before it was even
considered. Mexico, as the defenders of the death penalty asserted,
was not yet ready for such a radical reform.

WOMAN SUFFRAGE

Finally, attention must be given to woman suffrage and how the
convention dealt with this issue, the reform era's step toward woman's
liberation. By 1912 eight states of the American union had granted

---

[62] *Diario de los debates*, II, 351.
[63] Ibid.

full suffrage, and soon the movement would culminate in congressional acceptance of a proposed amendment to the U.S. constitution. The crusade, however, was far ahead of that in Mexico. Traditionally, Mexican women had been confined to the home more than American women. Toward the end of the Díaz regime, however, more and more were found in the professions and in the business world. Nevertheless, their participation in the political life of the country was nil. Not only did they not have the vote, but they were also ineligible for holding office. A Latin American Feminine League had branches in Mexico, but one of its principles was to "abstain carefully from direct or indirect connection with politics."[64] One of the results of the upheaval of 1910 was an increased interest in political rights for women.[65] Mexico's first feminist congress was held in Mérida, Yucatán, in November, 1916. Under these circumstances, it was only natural that the issue of woman suffrage should come before the Querétaro Convention.

The *Diario de los debates* records the submission of three proposals on this subject. On December 12 one Hermila Galindo presented a request that women be granted the right to vote for representatives to the lower house of Congress. Applause interrupted the reading of several of the paragraphs, after which the proposal was dutifully turned over to the First Committee.[66] Three days later the committee received a proposal from delegate Salvador González Torres on the need to grant Mexican women more rights, one of which was suffrage. A native of Michoacán, González Torres had worked in the antireelection movement against Díaz in 1909, had been involved in the abortive uprising of November 20, 1910, had later fought for Madero, and after the advent of the Constitutionalist movement had served with distinction in the army and had been promoted to general. A man of pronounced liberal, if not radical, sentiments, he had participated in the debate on Article 3 in support of Monzón's minority

---

[64] *Liga Femenil Latino Americana*, pp. 11 ff., cited in Wilfrid Hardy Callcott, *Liberalism in Mexico, 1857–1929*, p. 219.

[65] Ward M. Morton, *Woman Suffrage in Mexico*, p. 2.

[66] L. Melgarejo Randolf and J. Fernández Rojas, *El Congreso Constituyente de 1916 y 1917*, pp. 435–436.

report on "rational" education. Curiously, the third proposal, presented on December 16 by one Inés Malváez, was against woman suffrage.

As reported out on January 23, the First Committee's draft of Article 35, which enumerated the rights and privileges of citizenship, included the right of citizens to vote, to be voted for, and to associate together to discuss the political affairs of the country.[67] Although by inference these rights might be extended to women, the committee, in its report on Article 35, went out of its way to deny this, as the following excerpts indicate:

The doctrine [of restricted suffrage] can be invoked to settle negatively the question of female suffrage. The fact that some exceptional women have the necessary qualifications for satisfactorily exercising political rights does not lead to the conclusion that these can be conceded to women as a class. The difficulty of making the selection authorizes the negative.

The difference between the sexes determines the difference in their respective activities; in the state in which our society finds itself, the activity of the woman has not gone beyond the confines of the home . . . the disruption of family unity has not occurred among us, as happens with the advance of civilization; women, then, do not feel the need to participate in public affairs, as is shown by the lack of all organized movement toward that end.

On the other hand, political rights are not based on the nature of the human being but on the regulatory functions of the State, on the functions that it must exercise in order to maintain the coexistence of natural rights of all; under the conditions in which Mexican society finds itself, the granting of the vote to women is considered unnecessary.[68]

When debate commenced on Article 35 during the afternoon session of January 26, Palavicini, the only one to speak up for woman suffrage, asked why the committee had not taken into consideration the various proposals on the subject. It was a reasonable question, and Palavicini, advocate of woman suffrage, deserved a more relevant answer than the one he got. Speaking for the committee, Luis Monzón

[67] *Diario de los debates*, II, 830.
[68] Ibid.

said that various delegates had approached the committee, asking that the question not even be considered. Consequently, for this reason, and because of the "traditional question," the matter was not given any attention. The inference is that the radicals, fearing the traditional influence exerted by the Church over women, wanted nothing that would enfranchise the fairer sex.[69] When Palavicini chided Monzón for not answering, the latter sarcastically replied, "So it happens that now you come to defend the feminine vote. . . . (Laughter)."[70] However, the persistent Palavicini refused to be silenced. Pointing out that the article declared that all citizens had the right to vote, he wanted to know how this affected women. Again Monzón avoided a direct answer, simply stating that the committee did not take the question of woman suffrage into consideration. The discussion ended on this arbitrary reply. Palavicini, commenting later that Múgica, the First Committee's chairman, was not present for the session, thought it strange that the leader of the jacobins never remembered having signed the report on Article 35, although it bore his name.[71] Palavicini implies that, had Múgica been present, he might have given him some support or at least given a more complete answer than did Monzón, especially since Múgica had granted scholarships to women while serving as military governor of Tabasco and was known to favor granting them the right to vote.[72] Ironically, in summing up the arguments for Article 35, Monzón appealed to the "truly democratic impulses" of the delegates and to those who felt "within their breasts the beating of a markedly revolutionary soul" to support the article. No further urging was needed. Article 35 was approved as reported out by a vote of 136 to 5, despite the fact that the assembly, according to Bojórquez, was generally in favor of granting women the right to vote.[73] In rejecting all consideration of woman suffrage, the delegates showed how little importance they attached to the matter. For

[69] Morton, *Woman Suffrage in Mexico*, p. 8.
[70] *Diario de los debates*, II, 983.
[71] Félix F. Palavicini, *Historia de la Constitución de 1917*, II, 98.
[72] Magdalena Mondragón, *Cuando la Revolución se cortó las alas*, pp. 86, 264.
[73] *Diario de los debates*, II, 997; Juan de Dios Bojórquez [pseud. Djed Bórquez], *Crónica del constituyente*, p. 531.

all the manifestations of adherence to democratic ideals and revolutionary principles made during the convention, it is evident that there were limitations on their enjoyment. However much the delegates hoped that the fruits of the revolution would be for all Mexicans, regardless of sex, the right to vote would continue to be a privilege reserved for males alone.

7. Concluding Sessions: The Politics of Discord

Respect for the Constitution is the best signature that we who have worked on it can affix.

Gaspar Bolaños
Ruiz Album

Don Benito Gómez Farías* was present at the funeral of the Constitution of 1857. I hope that the one of 1916–1917 will be present at the funeral of the last one of us.

Marcelino Dávalos
Alvarez Album

Hurrying to complete their work within the period specified by the First Chief, the delegates had entered into permanent session on the evening of January 29 to discuss Article 27. At 3:30 A.M. on the thirtieth they voted approval of this article along with the much debated paragraph II of Article 115 and seven others of lesser importance. At this time the exhausted assembly recessed until 3:30 P.M. When they were again called to order, there was no quorum; and Jorge von Versen and Emiliano Nafarrate were authorized to round up the absentees, searching "the whole city of Querétaro" if necessary. Twenty minutes later they had a quorum; and, in a session

* Benito Gómez Farías, delegate from Jalisco to the Constitutional Convention of 1856–1857, died in 1914. He was the son of the famous liberal, Valentín Gómez Farías, also a member of the Jalisco delegation and president of the same convention.

that ended at 7:05 P.M., most of the remaining business was disposed of. Although scheduled to reconvene at 11 A.M. on the thirty-first, the last phase of the permanent session began forty-five minutes late because the delegates were busy having their pictures taken.

The most dramatic event of the final moments came during a speech by Gerzayn Ugarte, who pulled from his pocket the fountain pen used to sign the Plan of Guadalupe nearly four years before, the same one Don Venustiano had used throughout the Constitutionalist movement. The First Chief, he said, was providing the pen so that it could be used to sign the constitution. Then, addressing Múgica, he extolled his enthusiasm and the strength with which he had sustained his convictions. As Múgica signed the new charter, said Ugarte, he would receive the "applause and affection" of his fellow delegates on behalf of those who had signed the historic plan. Implicit in his words was the respect Don Venustiano had for the young radical who had led the fight to modify his proposals.[1] The only delegate to have signed the Plan of Guadalupe, Múgica had sought at that time to make it more than a purely political document. In the convention he had led the successful fight to transform a political draft into a document of socioeconomic power, one embodying the goals of the revolution. Ugarte's tribute was justly deserved.

Not easily overcome by sentiment, Múgica admittedly found it difficult to control his emotions on this occasion. After thanking Ugarte, he recalled the events of March, 1913, which had launched the Constitutionalist movement. After the defeat in Saltillo at the hands of the *federales*, the small band of partisans had retreated northward to the hacienda of Guadalupe to lick their wounds and reorganize. There, in a heated meeting, they had written the plan, which "epitomized in those moments the national will represented by a few patriots." Then they had gone on to successfully avenge the national honor desecrated by a "habitual drunkard" (Huerta). In conclusion, Múgica received thunderous applause as he exhorted the delegates "to

---

[1] During the first sessions, Carranza is reported to have ordered Múgica to return to Tabasco. When Múgica, accompanied by Gen. Jacinto Treviño, visited the First Chief to tell him that the reason for the order was his fear that Múgica would defeat his draft proposals, Carranza rescinded the order. See Magdalena Mondragón, *Cuando la Revolución se cortó las alas*, pp. 81–82.

fall on the battlefield defending this Constitution in the same way those fell on the battlefield defending the clauses of the Plan of Guadalupe."[2]

The signing ceremony, the last notable act of the Querétaro Convention, commenced at 2:05 P.M., January 31. President Rojas signed first, followed by the two vice-presidents, Cándido Aguilar and Salvador González Torres. Next the delegates, in the alphabetical order of their states, proceeded to the tribunal to affix their signatures. Unfortunately, Don Venustiano's pen ran out of ink, or broke, as Gaspar Bolaños was signing, and the remainder of the delegates signed with Bolaños's pen. Last to sign were the secretaries and alternate delegates. At the end came the rush for souvenirs. Saying he deserved it because he had talked so much, Palavicini took the glass that had always been on the podium. No one disputed his right to it. Jesús López Lira took the water bottle used to fill the glass; and Adolfo Villaseñor Norman, who had always sat on the front row, got the plate on which bottle and glass had rested. Appropriately enough, Rojas got the bell he had used to call for order.[3]

Before the convention concluded its only period of sessions and passed into history, the delegates and Carranza had to swear to defend the constitution. A little after 4 P.M., with all delegates and visitors standing, President Rojas took the oath, saying: "I swear to defend the Political Constitution of the United Mexican States issued today which reforms that of February 5, 1857, and see that it is defended. If I do not do so, the nation will demand it of me." When applause had subsided, Rojas administered the same oath to the delegates.

Shortly thereafter, the spectacled First Chief arrived at the theater. Acclaimed by public and delegates alike, he was escorted to the front, where he took his seat by the president. In what was to be his last speech before the convention, Rojas hailed the "extraordinary importance" of Carranza's draft proposals in the preparation of the new constitution. Handing over the completed constitution to the First

---

[2] *Diario de los debates del Congreso Constituyente, 1916–1917*, II, 1165–1166.

[3] Juan José Manzano and Emma Villaseñor, interview, Mexico City, March 27, 1965.

Chief, Rojas said that all his ideas had been accepted, including the agrarian and labor decrees issued in Veracruz in 1915. Considering that Articles 27 and 123, missing from the Carranza draft, were products of the convention, it was a very diplomatic, yet deceptive, statement. None present must have known this more than Carranza himself. In an almost apologetic tone, Rojas told Carranza that, if "on some points it [the constitution] has gone a little beyond what your wisdom had indicated as a norm," this was due to the revolutionary enthusiasm of the youthful followers of the Plan of Guadalupe and their eagerness to break old social patterns. In spite of flaws in their work, he said, all the delegates had labored on behalf of the less fortunate, in keeping with their convictions on great social problems, and guided by "the idea of making the Mexican Republic great and happy."[4]

In reply, the First Chief acknowledged that he had had some doubt on December 1 as to whether he had rightly interpreted the needs of the country in his draft of reforms to the Constitution of 1857. Now, however, since the convention had accepted his proposals, he was satisfied to know he had been right. If his proposals had lacked something here or provided too much there, this was unimportant because the convention had ironed out the defects. The constitution would assure the future stability of Mexico. With the dissension that had threatened to split the convention obviously on his mind, Carranza said the time had come to put aside grudges and hatreds, to put into practice the supreme law that will "lead us to live the tranquil life of free peoples, through respect for liberty and the rights of each other." As visitors and delegates applauded wildly, he took the oath to protect and defend the constitution.

On behalf of the assembly, Hilario Medina then delivered a farewell address, one that was too long, more rhetorical than substantive, and more notorious for what he did not say than for what he said. As he saw it, the constitution contained four principal features: Article 3, Article 5, Article 24, on the "religious problem," and "Article 129 [sic] which has given organization to that social class which is called the clergy." Fanaticism would henceforth be controlled through

4 *Diario de los debates*, II, 1173.

education. As for clericalism, it too had been exposed and must never be allowed to regain its strength. Curiously, he made no mention of Articles 27 and 123, the most distinctive features of the new supreme law. Almost as an afterthought, he reminded all present of the importance of the individual's rights. Praising Carranza, whom he compared to Washington and Juárez, he concluded by exhorting all present "to spread . . . the seed of the revolution made law and to see that each and every one of our fellow citizens feel it, live it, understand it, and respect it."[5] By now there was nothing left to say or do except to officially close the session, which President Rojas did. He was followed by shouts of "Long live the Revolution! Long live Carranza! Long live the Constitutional Convention!" Thus ended the most important single event of the Mexican Revolution, the most notable gathering in Mexican constitutional history.

Before scattering to all parts of Mexico, never to reunite, the delegates offered a banquet to Don Venustiano, the spiritual father of the constitution, whose unseen presence they had felt throughout the convention. It was held at the Centro Fronterizo on the evening of January 31 and attended by many distinguished revolutionaries, including Gens. Alvaro Obregón, Benjamín Hill, Pablo González, and Manuel Diéguez. The delegates ate and drank heartily, collected signatures on group pictures, and exchanged final *abrazos*. At the end, in a spontaneous display of regard for Múgica, a group hoisted the young intellectual to their shoulders and carried him to his residence.[6]

What had been accomplished in such a brief period, with so much time lost in dispute and personal allusions, was in many ways remarkable. The "more revolutionary than thou" syndrome that appeared during the discussion of credentials had split the assembly into two hostile groups, a division that lasted through the final session. In a way this was unavoidable. A schism had developed early in the Constitutionalist movement between the military and the civilian bureaucracy grouped around the First Chief. It became more pro-

[5] Ibid., p. 1178.
[6] For glowing testimonials to Múgica from his fellow delegates, see Francisco José Múgica Velázquez, *Hechos, no palabras*, II, 229–246.

nounced during the withdrawal to Veracruz and subsequently found its way into the convention. To the soldiers, many of the civilians were Johnnies-come-lately who had boarded the Constitutionalist bandwagon when Huerta's defeat appeared imminent. Especially despicable, from their point of view, were the *renovadores*, who had remained in Congress following the assassination of Madero and Pino Suárez. Carranza's telegram of November 20, 1916, on behalf of the *renovadores* seeking admission to the convention stirred controversy.[7] How could their approval be justified under the Plan of Guadalupe? The fact that Rojas, Macías, Palavicini, and Cravioto had played important roles in drafting Carranza's proposed constitutional reforms exacerbated the situation, especially when Rojas attempted to pack the all-important First Committee with Macías and others sympathetic to the Carranza draft. The fact that the First Chief had allotted to the convention only two months in which to draft the constitution further heightened the tension, for it implied ratification rather than debate.

Although General Aguilar, as early as November 28, charged from the floor that General Obregón was exerting influence on the approval of credentials, battle lines between the opposing factions were not clearly drawn until discussion of the controversial Article 3. On December 13, Rojas stepped down from the presidency to speak against the committee report. Charging that a group of delegates headed by Manuel Aguirre Berlanga had failed in their duty as revolutionaries and in their loyalty to the First Chief by opposing his draft proposals, he went on to accuse Obregón of having sent a message to the Jalisco delegation and those of the other western states urging them to maintain an "intransigent attitude" in opposing the Carranza draft. He was possibly mistaken, he said, in regard to Aguirre Berlanga, because Carranza had made him secretary of *gobernación*, but he was positive about Obregón. To all assembled in the Iturbide Theater the warning was clear: those opposing the First Chief were considered obstructionists, and the prestigious Obregón was branded their leader. Although admitting that opposition was indispensable to the democratic process, Rojas complained that the questioned loyalty of Aguirre Berlanga, who at that moment was on the floor with some members of the leftist

[7] *Diario de los debates*, I, 49.

faction, Obregón's telegram, and the bitterness of the discussion of Article 3 had had a disquieting effect throughout Mexico. At this crucial moment in its history, the country needed unity and harmony, and this could best be obtained by supporting the First Chief, not opposing him.

More than a demonstration of jacobin strength, the vote on Article 3 on December 16 was a resounding defeat for Don Venustiano, a clear indication that his close followers could not control the convention, that the delegates would vote according to the dictates of their individual consciences. On December 18, Rojas again stepped down from the presidency to discuss convention alignments. He referred to two major groups: *liberales carrancistas* and *jacobinos obregonistas*. The former, consisting of fifty to sixty delegates, were determined to support faithfully the First Chief's draft, either because they had helped write it, because they were personal friends of Carranza, or for other reasons. The latter, consisting of approximately the same number, constituted the opposition—a designation which brought immediate protest from the leftists, for it insinuated that unwillingness to accept the Carranza draft without change or discussion implied disloyalty to Don Venustiano. In reality, this was an unfair imputation, for all the delegates, regardless of their views, had shown and would continue to show respect and loyalty to the First Chief. Rojas also indicated the presence of a third group, the independents, whose members might vote with either faction.

Obviously he could not get away with such accusations. Trembling with anger, Calderón arose to deny emphatically that Obregón was leader of the jacobins. "We do not have any chief, least of all in this Convention," he said. As for Aguirre Berlanga, a former governor of Jalisco, he was a friend of the *tapatío* delegation. Was it cause for alarm for him to be seen with its members? And was it strange that delegates from Tepic, Colima, and Sinaloa should fraternize, when many were army officers who belonged to the Division of the Northwest of which Obregón was the commanding general? Calderón undoubtedly spoke for many of his fellow delegates when he said: "We simply want to discuss this Constitution with independent judgment; . . . we [do] not consider this draft [Carranza's] infallible." Deploring the classification "oppositionists" for those who believed as he did, he concluded by saying, "If we are not going to discuss the draft with an open mind, we will not be loyal to the First Chief (prolonged applause)."[8]

The next exchange of fire involved Obregón and Carranza directly. On December 20 the famous general sent a message to the convention asking the *renovadores* to stop making reckless charges in attempting to discredit the "radical revolutionaries" who had tried to keep them out. Opposition to the group, said Obregón, did not come from individuals alone but from the "national conscience." In a decree of August 7, 1913, issued from Durango, the First Chief had stated that those who failed to attend the next session of Congress would be exempt from punishment. The *renovadores*, however, had returned to Congress and remained there, ostensibly on instructions from the First Chief himself. Obregón thought it strange that these instructions could have been issued prior to August, 1913. Impugning the group as untrustworthy, Obregón said with sarcasm that, if they had been instructed to betray Huerta, perhaps they were now betraying the First Chief on instructions from José Mora y del Río (the archbishop of Mexico) or Emiliano Zapata! In conclusion, he urged each "honorable revolutionary" to remember "that men are mutilated and die for principles, but principles do not die nor are they mutilated for men."[9]

Although the reading of this message evoked pleas for harmony from both factions, Obregón had made serious charges that only Don Venustiano could refute. This he did in a letter dated December 23 addressed to Heriberto Barrón,[10] editor of the newspaper *El Pueblo*, in which he attempted to explain the apparent contradiction between his decree of August 7, 1913, and his telegram of November 20, 1916, requesting the seating of the *renovadores*. Apparently a copy of the

[8] Ibid., p. 787.
[9] Ibid., pp. 861–862.
[10] Venustiano Carranza to Heriberto Barrón, Querétaro, December 23, 1916, in *Diario de los debates*, I, 920–921. Elected as a delegate from Guanajuato, Barrón was accused on November 29, 1916, of having forcibly dissolved the meeting of a group of liberals in San Luis Potosí in 1901 and of having been a collaborator of Huerta. Although he presented evidence that he had early disavowed Huerta, so strong was the feeling against him that he was denied a seat by a unanimous vote.

letter was sent to President Rojas, for he ordered it read to the assembly at the beginning of the afternoon session on Christmas Day, the secretary prefacing his reading with the remark that he hoped this was "the last word that is spoken on this matter."

According to Carranza, in April, 1913, in the border town of Piedras Negras he met Lic. Eliseo Arredondo, a *renovador* and confidant of the First Chief, who informed him that a number of delegates to the Twenty-sixth Congress sympathized with Carranza and would do his bidding. Recognizing that they would be of little use in the campaign against Huerta, unless serving in the army, Carranza told Arredondo to advise them to remain in Congress and obstruct Huerta in every way, especially to deny him loans and to try to force him to dissolve Congress. Out of touch with Mexico City for the next four months, as he began the campaign from Sonora, Carranza said he did not know until he reached Durango in late July that Huerta had not dissolved the body. Therefore, he issued the decree of August 7, 1913. He hoped that Huerta, chagrined by the opposition in Congress, would carry out a coup d'état, thereby further weakening his regime's appearance of legality and possibly resulting in its disavowal by army elements and some state governors. Although this did not happen, Huerta did dissolve Congress on October 10, an act that caused his government to lose what little credibility it had. Subsequently, Arredondo revealed the names of Carranza's supporters in the Congress, several of whom later served in different branches of the Constitutionalist administration. In conclusion, Carranza said he was leaving to the people of Mexico the decision as to whether he had done the right thing or not.

Not to be outdone by the reading of Don Venustiano's letter, Bojórquez and three fellow leftists immediately protested the activity of some of the *renovadores* as a "blot" on the assembly's record, in which the people might see complicity on the part of other delegates. Therefore, he and his friends wished to affirm that the admission to the convention of certain *renovadores*, "who had remained in Mexico City during the Huerta dictatorship," was due to the appeal made on their behalf by General Aguilar during the discussion of credentials.[11]

[11] See chapter 2.

Ridiculing Aguilar's action as a *golpe teatral*, Bojórquez said it had caused the delegates, in a moment of weakness, to vote for admission. Since neither he nor his colleagues wished to be considered "accomplices" of such a detestable group, the young Sonoran asked that their protest become a matter of record so that historians could judge each member of the controversial group on his individual merits.[12]

Although the bickering continued for the remainder of the sessions, the wrath of the leftists reached its peak on January 31 with the issue of a "Manifesto to the Nation" that denounced four *renovadores* in harsh terms. Signed by 94 delegates, a sizable number, considering that the average daily attendance was 140 to 150, it reproached President Rojas for having shown partiality to the *renovadores*, for having concealed congratulatory telegrams to the leftists, for not having observed the bylaws of the convention, for having changed the order of speakers on different articles, and for having tried to create a schism between Carranza and Obregón. Next, the signers railed at Macías for having been a *gonzalista*, a *porfirista*, a *corralista*, a *huertista* "for fear of the Revolution," and finally a *carrancista*. He was also described as being a tiring speaker with a "false reputation for knowledge," inconsiderate of the "independent delegates who were desirous of sound advice, hungry for education." As for Palavicini, "with his audacity *sui generis*, his glittering eloquence, with his unheard of cynicism, he sought to crush, to ridicule and restrain . . . the patriotic, radical labor that the revolutionary element began immediately in favor of the new Magna Carta, but his crazy accumulation of Italian atavism only earned for him the virile protest of the honorable delegates." The remainder of the venom was saved for Gerzayn Ugarte, "the most dangerous one because of his insincerity," since he professed friendship for the leftists from the podium but, as private secretary to the First Chief, reported to him "false impressions" of the delegates' opposition, disrespect, and unfaithfulness. More in hypocrisy than sincerity, the signers praised Don Venustiano for seeing through the *renovadores* to the aims of the jacobins, which were boldly summarized as follows: "to condense in the Fundamental Charter all needs of the nation . . . satisfy the dreams and ideals of the dead soldiers and

[12] *Diario de los debates*, I, 923–924.

the living . . . to put an end completely to capitalism, economic slavery, clericalism, and ignorance." In conclusion, the signatories branded the group of *renovadores* as "not worthy of consideration for any elective post, nor in any administrative position, because they only seek their personal interest and gain."[13]

The "Manifesto to the Nation" exemplifies the intensity of feeling against these *renovadores* and close friends of Don Venustiano, each of whom had made no little contribution to the writing of the constitution. On the last day, when the document had been signed and a spirit of camaraderie might have prevailed, the jacobins unleashed a vituperative attack on Rojas, Macías, Palavicini, and Ugarte.

The issue of the *renovadores* had widened the basic split in the convention. Rojas had rightly denied in his December 18 speech the presence of a conservative group in the convention, a denial reiterated by Lizardi, who said, "We are all liberals, some black [*negros*], others brown [*pardos*]." The liberals, however, were divided. A right wing, whom Rojas dubbed *liberales carrancistas*, held the traditional nineteenth-century view of liberalism. Moderately anticlerical, strongly dedicated to individual rights, determined to preserve the spirit of the Constitution of 1857, and believing that governments should exercise a limited role in national development, they also took the American view that a constitution should be written in general terms for subsequent implementation by statute. On the other hand, the leftists, or *jacobinos obregonistas*, more radical in their views, more rabidly anticlerical than the rightists, saw government as a vehicle for effecting fundamental changes in the Mexican social and economic structure. They were inclined to stress societal rights over those of the individual, to place faith in detailed rather than general constitutional provisions. Lines of division between right and left were indistinct, although more pronounced in the debate on Article 3 than in any

[13] For the full text of the manifesto and names of the signers, see Juan de Dios Bojórquez [pseud. Djed Bórquez], *Crónica del constituyente*, pp. 555–562. Over a month earlier Rojas and Macías had written to Don Venustiano, saying that, in order to avoid causing any further embarrassment to the First Chief, they had decided to retire from politics at the conclusion of the convention and not to accept any position in his administration (Luis Manuel Rojas and José N. Macías to Venustiano Carranza, December 23, 1917, in *Diario de los debates*, I, 921–922).

other. Leadership of both groups was almost nonexistent, although
Múgica is generally credited with having been floor leader of the
leftists. Discipline was weak, and each delegate appears to have hon-
estly spoken his views as he understood the matter being discussed and
to have voted according to his own judgment. Much has been made of
a basic cleavage in the convention, pitting the military against the
civilians, but this is not proved, as members of both categories could
be found arguing opposing sides of the same issue. Finally, a third
bloc of delegates, associated with neither rightists nor leftists, constituted the true independents of the assembly.

In reality, although pronounced differences existed between individual rightists and leftists, disagreement between the two factions was
more of degree than of substance. Both groups were highly nationalistic. They gave no thought to personal gain. All were determined to
write a constitution that would satisfy the national needs as they saw
them, for today as well as for tomorrow.[14] To Carranza's great credit,
he let these two factions vie in a showcase of democratic action, without interfering in the convention's deliberations, probably because he
realized he had little influence over the outcome.[15]

Although the convention produced a new national charter, one dif-
fering fundamentally from his recommendations, Carranza did everything he could to link it with the Constitution of 1857. His draft
proposals were titled reforms to that document. He even promulgated
the Constitution of 1917 on February 5, 1917, sixty years to the day
after the Constitution of 1857 had been officially proclaimed. The
delegates swore to defend a document that "reforms the one of 1857,"
but the authentic title of their work is the "Political Constitution of
the United Mexican States, 1917." There was no mention in this title
of the Constitution of 1857. Don Venustiano, however, was to have
the last word. He promulgated the new Magna Carta as the "Political

[14] Hilario Medina, "Carranza figura entre los primeros constituyentes," *Boletín Bibliográfico de la Secretaría de Hacienda y Crédito Público*, no. 432 (February 1, 1970): 5.
[15] "The independent spirit of this Convention has been a surprise to those who intended to manage it according to their wishes. Such a manifestation of independent strength is a hope for the country" (Alberto Román in Fernández Martínez Album).

Constitution of the United Mexican States Which Reforms the One of February 5, 1857," and this remained as its official title.[16]

Much has been written about Obregón and his influence on the Querétaro Convention. His followers have claimed that without the support of the doughty general, the writing of radical articles into the Constitution of 1917 would have been impossible.[17] Although strongly anticlerical, Obregón was far less radical than Múgica, Jara, Monzón, and other militant leftists who played prominent roles in the assembly.[18] There is evidence that Obregón's influence on the convention has been exaggerated.[19] He was not a delegate. As secretary of war, actively engaged in the campaigns against Villa and Zapata, he was only in Querétaro for brief periods during the convention. No report of either the First or Second Committee, both dominated by leftists, mentions Obregón. Alvarez y Alvarez, who during the debate on Article 3 had referred to the "Manco de León" as leader of the jacobins, affirms that Obregón never exerted pressure on these committees.[20] Rouaix, more responsible than any other single delegate for Articles 27 and 123, makes no reference in his *Génesis de los artículos 27 y 123 de la constitución política de 1917* to any influence exerted at any time by Obregón in the drafting of these great articles. In the albums of four members of the Querétaro Convention, containing more than four hundred testimonials from fellow delegates, there is not one reference to Alvaro Obregón. Finally, the *Diario de los debates* records only one instance of a *¡viva Obregón!* during the entire two months of the convention. In short, the Constitution of 1917 was

[16] Felipe Tena Ramírez in manuscript in possession of Lic. Antonio Martínez Báez, Mexico City. See also Antonio Martínez Báez, "La Revolución mexicana y la Constitución de 1917," *Debate*, Organo de la Asociación y Colegio de Abogados de Ciudad Juárez, A. C., no. 3 (May 1961): 36–37.

[17] Juan de Dios Bojórquez, "El espíritu revolucionario de Obregón," in *Obregón: Aspectos de su vida*, p. 157.

[18] For his anticlericalism, see David C. Bailey, "Alvaro Obregón and Anti-Clericalism in the 1910 Revolution," *The Americas* 26 (October 1969): 183–198.

[19] Adolfo Villaseñor Norman, interview, Mexico City, March 13, 1965; Col. Pedro Chapa, Mexico City, to author, July 11, 1966.

[20] José Alvarez y Alvarez, interview, Cuernavaca, Morelos, May 31, 1965. Obregón was called "Manco [one-armed] de León" because he had lost his right arm at the hacienda of Santa Ana del Conde, near León, Guanajuato, in June, 1915, while directing the battle against Villa.

the work not of Don Alvaro but of the delegates themselves. They built on the Carranza proposals but modified or repudiated them as necessary to give the document its distinctive features and revolutionary flavor.

Nevertheless, the political influence of Obregón was considerable, and, in the words of one delegate, it shook "the atmosphere of the Congress with violence."[21] Outwardly loyal as a military man to the head of the Constitutionalist movement, the politically ambitious Obregón had his eye too on the presidency.[22] Since he was an avowed enemy of the *renovadores*, delegates opposed to the seating of the controversial group in the assembly naturally looked to Obregón for support.[23] His military prestige, established in the campaign against Huerta and confirmed for all time in the bloody battles against Villa in 1915, made him very popular, especially among the delegates of military rank, his ardent supporters, who would have unconditionally seconded the general in a showdown against Carranza. Although he made no personal contribution to the writing of the Constitution of 1917, Obregón was closely linked to the radical liberal faction that bore his name, ironically labeled *obregonista* by President Rojas himself, thus causing Obregón to become romantically and undeservedly associated with the distinctive features of the Constitution of 1917.

21 Chapa to author, July 11, 1966.
22 Roberto Guzmán Esparza, *Memorias de don Adolfo de la Huerta según su propio dictado*, pp. 79–83.
23 Alfonso Taracena, *Venustiano Carranza*, p. 263.

8. In Retrospect

All the laws are written in the Constitution, but there is a law, the law of progress, that each citizen turns to in his field of endeavor. Our duty is to be progressive. Progress is simply nothing but improvement.

Lorenzo Sepúlveda
Pastrana Jaimes Album

Humanity is to be congratulated. The Mexican Constitutional Convention of 1916–1917 gives to our most humble citizens the means to bridge the gap that separates them from civilization. In this way the revolution pays its debt and justifies the blood shed on the soil of the fatherland.

Antonio Aguilar
Pastrana Jaimes Album

How did the delegates to the Constitutional Convention of 1916–1917 view their work? What were their thoughts as they labored to finish the great document and affix their signatures? From the testimonials previously referred to, it is clear that, while a few expressed disappointment or skepticism, the overwhelming majority sincerely believed that their work was good, that it gave hope for the future. At the same time there was sobering recognition that the constitution would mean nothing if its saving principles were not carried into effect, that the awful responsibility of being its chief apostles fell on the framers themselves. What gives these testimonials added significance is that they came from the silent majority of the convention, from those who rarely if ever participated in the debate but who made their presence known during the voting.

Would it satisfy the needs of the people? Most thought it would. According to Alvaro Alcazar, whose state, Morelos, had been the battleground most disputed between possessed and dispossessed, the constitution would serve because it had been written by "true revolutionaries who have understood the necessities and miseries" of the people.[1] In the opinion of brave Gen. Amado Aguirre (Jalisco), who had campaigned in the Division of the Northwest under Obregón since early 1914, the constitution might not seem technically perfect to the *científicos* who had found their way into the convention (a slur on the *renovadores* for their supposedly neo-Porfirian attitudes), but it did "satisfy to the fullest extent the greatest aspirations and necessities of the population [as] understood by the revolutionaries who saw them face to face . . ."[2] According to Rafael Márquez (Michoacán), who in March of 1911 had fought against Díaz and who had joined the Constitutionalist movement in April, 1913, "The laws given by the Constitutional Convention will be the salvation of our country."[3] According to Román Rosas y Reyes (Federal District), the new constitution "restored faith to our homes and made a Fatherland, bringing dignity to our children . . . making them men and women."[4] For Pedro Chapa the constitution would be "the basis for the building of a free and sovereign nation whose strength and vigor will be exemplary."[5] Santiago Ocampo (Tabasco) said that "in the cruelest winter of our life as a nation, the Convention has forged the Constitution that will maintain our Mexican Republic in continuous spring."[6] Pastrana Jaimes, a fervent nationalist, considered the assembly's work to be "a new point of departure for the effective progress and the 'Mexicanization of our fatherland.' "[7] According to Francisco Díaz Barriga (Guanajuato), grandson of a delegate of the same name from

1 Pastrana Jaimes Album.
2 Ruiz Album.
3 Pastrana Jaimes Album.
4 Alvarez Album.
5 Ibid.
6 Ruiz Album.
7 Alvarez Album.

Michoacán to the Constitutional Convention of 1856–1857, "the Constitution of 1917 will be the tombstone that forever buries the filth of the past Regime."[8] Hilario Medina, who had labored long and hard as a member of the Second Committee, said, "I sincerely believe that the Constitution of 1917 signifies that Mexico has found the definitive form of its political system and that from today on it will be free and prosperous through an organic peace."[9]

According to Alvarez y Alvarez, the candidates for election to the convention had asked the people what they wanted the most. In a telling reaction to the Porfirian strait jacket, to its meaningless practice of democracy, they had answered: liberty.[10] The delegates themselves showed a strong, almost passionate, dedication to freedom. Juan Espinosa Bávara (Tepic), a former teacher and civilian official in the Carranza administration, revealed his faith in the new charter by saying that it would "constitute the base of future democratic institutions and, therefore, the safeguard of the people!"[11] Ismael Pintado Sánchez (Hidalgo) expressed his beliefs as follows: "The principles of redemption and liberty dreamed of for so many years by our people have been realized by finding their place in the constitution . . . it will be the flag of legality, the standard of the Republic, and symbol of the spirit which creates the national unity."[12] At least three delegates equated liberty with the destruction of tyranny. For José L. Gómez, who considered himself one of the first to have disavowed the Aguascalientes Convention, the revolution had "demonstrated to the entire world that tyrants, sooner or later, suffer the deserved punishment imposed by noble peoples."[13] To Manuel Dávalos Ornelas, a teacher who had joined the revolution following Madero's assassination, the Constitution of 1917 would "always be an insurmountable wall against the ambitions of despots and tyrants."[14] Young Román Rosas y Reyes

[8] Pastrana Jaimes Album.
[9] Ruiz Album.
[10] José Alvarez y Alvarez, interview, Cuernavaca, Morelos, May 31, 1965.
[11] Pastrana Jaimes Album. The territory of Tepic under Article 47 of the constitution was incorporated into the state of Nayarit.
[12] Alvarez Album.
[13] Pastrana Jaimes Album.
[14] Ruiz Album.

professed his faith as follows: "Constitution of 1917! Slaughterer of idols, scourge of tyrants; product of a thousand struggles, anxieties and sorrows, you raised the countenance of the outcast which used to face downward . . . you have a name of sublime redemption to be loved and understood and that name is Liberty!"[15] Others expressed themselves less dramatically but with equal feeling. Giving credit to the radicals, Alfonso Mayorga (Hidalgo) said, "The liberal group of the Chamber, known as 'jacobin', saved the children, saved the liberties of the people, and will save the Republic."[16] Ernesto Meade Fierro believed that "only the love of liberty dignifies the soul of people."[17] Juan N. Frías believed that "only through the rule of law and order is the exercise made possible of that divine gift which man possesses and which is called Liberty. This is the objective of the Constitutional Convention on affirming the rights of man."[18]

Most of the delegates saw freedom as an inherent right and wished its blessings for the people. Some, however, preoccupied with finding solutions to socioeconomic problems, gravitated toward socialistic ideals. To them a political solution to national problems was forceless and incomplete. They sought to subject individual rights to those of society, to make the State the instrument to extirpate the Porfirian inheritance as completely as possible, to ensure it would never recur. Paradoxically, these two concepts of individual liberty and socialism would exist together in the Constitution of 1917.

A considerable number of delegates singled out particular articles as the salient ones of the constitution. It was appropriate that Articles 3, 27, and 123 should receive special praise. In the words of Cándido Avilés (Sinaloa), "With only the resolution of the Agrarian and Labor questions, the work of the delegates will become immortal."[19] Antonio Gutiérrez, who had taken part in the discussions of the two most distinctive features of the new charter, wrote: "Without any doubt Articles 27 and 123 of the Constitution . . . contain the dearest ideals of the Mexican People in their social movement of 1910. These gave

[15] Alvarez Album.
[16] Pastrana Jaimes Album.
[17] Ruiz Album.
[18] Fernández Martínez Album.
[19] Pastrana Jaimes Album.

to that Supreme Code the value necessary to give us a page of honor in history."[20] If labor received its reward, Carlos Gracidas believed he knew to whom the credit was due: " . . . the success of the labor deputation had its origin, without doubt, in the support of the radicals."[21] The jacobins, of course, sang the praises of Articles 3 and 130. For some it was the last opportunity to take pot shots at their favorite target: the clergy. However, according to Jesús Romero Flores, an experienced teacher, the surest way to put into practice the "saving principles" of the Constitution of 1917 was through strict compliance with Article 3.[22]

Many delegates felt strongly obligated to live up to their oath to defend the new constitution, to ensure its observance, to undertake a crusade in its behalf if necessary. Since no plebiscite would be held to determine its acceptance, there was justification for such an attitude. And who would be better qualified for this task than the founding fathers themselves? According to José Rivera (Puebla), "The good will that we have shown in drafting the Constitution, once it is promulgated, must be converted into a titanic effort to sustain it as the redeeming banner of the Mexican people."[23] Others felt the same way. Matías Rodríguez (Hidalgo) stated that "if we have made a bulwark for the oppressed with the Constitution of 1916–1917 it is our duty to preserve it and comply with it, even at the cost of our lives."[24] To Marcelino Cedano the task was a sacred one: "We have taken an oath: to look after and defend the new Code that we have signed today. Our duty is to comply with that pledge and to continue our struggles, begun before 1910, with the same motto: to overcome or die!"[25] Jairo R. Dyer (Zacatecas), a respected country doctor who had practiced medicine in Sombrerete, Zacatecas, from 1895 to 1916, stated it this way: "We who signed the Constitution of 1917 contracted the obligation to be its staunchest propagandists and sustainers

[20] Alvarez Album.
[21] Fernández Martínez Album.
[22] Pastrana Jaimes Album.
[23] Ibid.
[24] Ibid.
[25] Alvarez Album.

so that the Mexican people get the benefits that we want [for them]."[26]

Finally, some delegates, mindful of past experience, sounded warnings for the future. As Rafael Martínez Mendoza (San Luis Potosí) put it, "If we, the individuals who dictated the Constitution of 17, do not keep on fighting to maintain unharmed the principles of liberty and justice proclaimed in it, our work as delegates will be null and despicable, since it means nothing to give good laws to a people if one does not fight for their application and preservation."[27] Another lawyer, Juan Sánchez, was even more concerned: "If we are not united in maintaining the liberal and democratic principles approved [here] we shall head for disaster again."[28] Flavio Bórquez tempered his warning with optimism, expressed as follows: "If the Mexican people do not go to sleep again and [if] they require future *gobernantes* to obey the Constitution of 1917, I believe that Mexico will become the 'First Nation of Latin America.'"[29] Then there was Francisco Martín del Campo, also a lawyer, who believed firmly in the rule of law. This alone, however, was insufficient: "For the people to progress, good laws are not enough but good rulers [are also needed]. The present Convention has given the former; I hope that the Mexican people know how to give themselves the latter . . ."[30] Col. Adolfo G. García (Veracruz) feared that the revolutionary ideals would not be achieved because of the "reactionary element" in the convention.[31] Rafael de los Ríos was even more emphatic. Stating that the two great perils to liberty were the clergy and the military, he regretted that justice and the rights of man had not been freed from the "bonnets and from the swords of the praetorians."[32]

The men of Querétaro had struggled against formidable obstacles. Insufficient preparation, uncertainty, dissension, and the realization that so much had to be done in so short a time were all reasons for discouragement, especially during the early sessions. Yet the delegates

26 Ruiz Album.
27 Alvarez Album.
28 Pastrana Jaimes Album.
29 Ibid.
30 Alvarez Album.
31 Pastrana Jaimes Album.
32 Alvarez Album.

had not wavered in writing the design for national reconstruction. In spite of all the spoken rhetoric, at the end of the historic two months, the great majority were clearly satisfied with what they had accomplished. Initial pessimism had given way to optimism. If the future looked brighter, it was because the Mexicans had renewed their faith in themselves.

"Into the rude struggle of economic forces has been injected a force of conscious humanity." So concludes Helen Phipps in her monograph on the agrarian problem in Mexico.[33] It is a comment applicable with no less vigor to the Constitutional Convention of 1916–1917, for never before had the call for social and economic justice been so dramatically and positively answered. Never had so revolutionary a body written such radical reforms into Mexican constitutional law. Never had the cleavage between past and future been so clearly marked.

The ideas of a group of reform-minded delegates, led more by their instincts than by their knowledge, more provincial than sophisticated in their thinking, more pragmatic than theoretical in their outlook, crystallized into a definite constitutional program the ideology of the strife that had enveloped Mexico since 1910. Anticlericalism, labor welfare, agrarian reform, and humanitarianism were basic to their thinking. Underlying these goals was a strong spirit of freedom and of nationalism, a demand for emancipation from foreign control. As the delegates debated these matters, they kindled the fire of national consciousness that symbolizes the new Mexico.

In an atmosphere of complete independence, the delegates to the Querétaro Convention built on the rather strong anticlerical provisions of Carranza's draft of reforms. Whipped to a frenzy by rabid jacobins, they went further than an attack on the economic power of the Church. Convinced that the clergy exerted a pernicious influence on education and society, they wrote into constitutional law a series of provisions clearly aimed at removing the clergy and the Church from all nonreligious fields. The dividing line between anticlericalism and antire-

[33] Helen Phipps, *Some Aspects of the Agrarian Question in Mexico: A Historical Study*, p. 148.

ligion was not always sharp and clear. A subtheme was nationalism. Attack on the Catholic church as a foreign institution, an exploiter of Mexico and Mexicans, in no way connoted sympathy for Protestantism, an alien influence, mainly from the United States. Radical proposals which, if adopted, would have made the position of the Roman Catholic faith in Mexico untenable, were rejected in a final show of moderation and restraint. Nevertheless, in the opinion of the classical liberals of the convention, measures aimed at combatting the influence of the clergy in education trampled on fundamental freedoms and made a mockery of the individual rights granted by the constitution. It was an issue that stirred passionate debate and, in the end, resulted in a document of irreconcilable contradiction.

Applicable to the present as well as the future, the program of labor welfare formulated in the convention was both a declaration of proletarian rights and prerogatives and a body of limitations upon the abuse of workers under the prevailing capitalistic system. Liberal provisions manifested the paternal attitude of the framers, their humanitarian concern for the welfare of all who labored for wages, whether agricultural or industrial. Endowed with special powers to further the interests of the working class, the State would henceforth determine the complexion of employer-employee relations in Mexican industrial life. For the first time in history, detailed rules and regulations had been written into constitutional law, a corpus that would serve as a model for other developing nations in formulating their own labor codes.

The most distinctive article to come out of the convention was undoubtedly Article 27, a basic attack on vested interests, the most fertile expression in the whole constitution of the violent reaction to the Díaz system. It was, as Frank Tannenbaum says, the expression of a new theory of property, one neither communistic nor socialistic.[34] Basic to the new philosophy was the concept that property might be held by private persons as long as its use was subordinate to the public interest. The rights of society were made to prevail over the rights of the individual. Again the State was endowed with special powers to ensure a more equitable distribution of the national wealth. Again there was

[34] Frank Tannenbaum, *Mexico: The Struggle for Peace and Bread*, p. 112.

an expression of nationalism, as the ownership of natural resources was vested in the nation, as the acquisition and possession of real property by foreigners was limited. Above all, Article 27 contained a formula for the solution of a pressing agrarian problem. To the delegates this was the cardinal feature of the whole constitution. This is what they had come to Querétaro to write. The excessive detail and legal niceties of the wording meant little. The far-reaching significance of the revolution in property rights was probably understood by only a handful of delegates. Individually and collectively, however, they had laid the constitutional basis for the solution of the underlying problem of the revolution. From one end of Mexico to the other they had been witness to its evils, had seen the misery in which the rural inhabitants were hopelessly embedded, had seen the greed of the *hacendado*, his hold on the people and the land which they worked. More than any other problem, the agrarian problem had to be solved, or the Constitutional Convention would fail the people, would fail the revolution. It was this thought that hung over the conscience of the delegates from the first session until the glorious predawn triumph of January 30, when Article 27 was written into the constitution. It was then, and only then, that the delegates could breathe with ease.

Finally, the reforms of the progressive era that rocked the United States also found their echo below the border in the Querétaro Convention. Despite some measure of gain in municipal reform, the causes of prohibition, woman suffrage, and abolition of the death penalty were rejected as being too advanced or inappropriate for the Mexico of 1917. But it mattered little. The convention had already accomplished its main objectives. The others could wait until a later date.

The Constitution of 1917 is the legal triumph of the Mexican Revolution, the first great social upheaval of the twentieth century. To some it is the revolution. To the everlasting credit of the framers, strong disinterest in everything except the resolution of pressing national problems resulted in a famous document of social and economic change. If their hopes could be condensed into one expression, this might be stated as the demand for social justice, a demand for the redemption of the native race from the depths of wretchedness into which it had sunk. The work of the convention may be criticized for the haste in which it was performed, for inherent contradictions, for superfluous detail, for strong anticlericalism, for excessive idealism, or for altering the theory of the inviolability of private property, but it cannot be denied that it represented an honest effort by the delegates —the lawyers, doctors, generals and colonels, teachers, engineers, laborers, and others—to write a fundamental law that would provide the bases for a more just and equitable national future.

Altruism, a humanitarian spirit, an ennobling belief in the dignity of man, a conviction that the less fortunate elements of Mexican society were worthy of better treatment, were worthy of saving, all characterized the Querétaro gathering and distinguished it from previous Mexican constitutional assemblies more concerned with political issues than socioeconomic needs.

Almost unknowingly, certainly without intention, the Constitutional Convention of 1916–1917 produced a great document, one that brought fame to its framers as trailblazers in the development of a pragmatic philosophy of twentieth-century constitutional law. It would mean little if their fellow countrymen lagged in according them honor and recognition. By merely writing the constitution, by bringing it forth, by affixing their signatures, they had already assured themselves of an everlasting place of honor in Mexican history.

APPENDIX A
Article 130 of the Constitution of 1917

Article 130. The Federal Authorities shall have the power to exercise in matters of religious worship and outward ecclesiastical forms the intervention required by law. All other officials shall act as auxiliaries to the Federal authorities.

The Congress cannot enact laws establishing or prohibiting any religion.

Marriage is a civil contract. This and the other acts relating to the civil status of persons are within the exclusive jurisdiction of civil officials and authorities, in the manner prescribed by law, and they shall have the force and validity given them by the said laws.

A simple promise to tell the truth and to comply with obligations contracted subjects the promiser, in the event of a breach, to the penalties prescribed by law.

The law does not recognize any juridical personality in the religious groups known as churches.

Ministers of religious creeds shall be considered as persons exercising a profession, and they shall be directly subject to the laws enacted on such matters.

The State Legislatures shall have the exclusive power to determine the maximum number of ministers of denominations according to the needs of each locality.

Only a Mexican by birth may be a minister of any religious denomination in Mexico.

The ministers of religious denominations shall never, in a public or private meeting constituting an assembly, nor in acts of the denomination or religious propaganda, criticize the fundamental laws of the country, the authorities in particular or the Government in general; they shall have no active nor passive vote, nor the right to associate for political purposes.

In order to dedicate new places of worship open to the public, it is necessary to obtain permission from the Secretariat of Gobernación, upon the recommendation previously obtained of the Government of the State concerned.

Every place of worship must have a person in charge of it who is responsible to the authorities for compliance with the laws on religious worship within the said building and for the objects which belong to the denomination.

The caretaker of each place of public worship, together with ten other residents of the locality, shall immediately advise the municipal authorities who is in charge of the said place of worship. The outgoing minister accompanied by the incoming minister and ten residents of the locality, shall give notice of each change. The municipal authorities, under penalty of dismissal and fine, not to exceed 1,000 pesos for each violation, shall be responsible for compliance with this provision; under the same penalty, they shall keep a register of the places of worship and another of the caretakers of the same. The municipal authorities, through the Governor of the State, shall give notice to the Secretariat of Gobernación of each permission to open to public use a new place of worship, or of a change of caretakers. Donations in the form of movable objects shall be kept in the interior of church buildings.

Under no condition shall studies carried on in institutions devoted to the professional training of ministers of the denominations be given credit or granted any other dispensation or privilege which shall have for its purpose the accrediting of the said studies in official institutions. Any authority violating this provision shall be criminally liable, and the privilege or step referred to shall be null and void, and shall invalidate the professional title for the attainment of which the violation of this provision was incurred.

Periodical publications of a religious nature, whether by reason of their programs, their titles or merely by their general tendencies, shall not comment upon national political affairs, nor publish information regarding the acts of the authorities of the country or of private persons directly related to the functioning of public institutions.

The formation of any kind of political group, the name of which contains any word or indication whatever to any religious belief, is strictly prohibited. Meetings of a political nature shall not be held within places of public worship.

No minister of any religious denomination may inherit, either on his own behalf or through an intermediary, nor otherwise receive, any real property occupied by any association of religious propaganda or religious or charitable purposes. Ministers of denominations are legally incapable of inheriting by will from the ministers of the same denomination or from any private individual to whom they are not related by blood within the fourth degree.

The acquisition by private parties of personal or real property owned by the clergy or by religious organizations shall be governed by Article 27 of this Constitution.

Trials for violation of the preceding provisions shall never be by jury.

APPENDIX B
Article 5 Compared with Draft Proposal

Draft Proposal of Article 5 (Presented January 13, 1917, by Pastor Rouaix and others)

Article 5. No one shall be compelled to render personal services without due compensation and without his full consent, except labor imposed as a punishment by judicial authority.

Only the following public services shall be obligatory, subject to the conditions set forth in the respective laws: military service, jury service, service in public elective office, and service in connection with elections, which shall be obligatory and without compensation.

The State shall not permit any contract, covenant or agreement to be carried out which has for its object the restriction, loss, or irrevocable sacrifice of the liberty of man, whether by reason of labor, education, or religious vows. The law, therefore, does

Article 5 of the Constitution of 1917 (As approved in convention, January 23, 1917)

Article 5. No one shall be compelled to render personal services without due compensation and without his full consent, except labor imposed as a punishment by judicial authority, which shall be governed by the provisions of clauses I and II of Article 123.

Only the following public services shall be obligatory, subject to the conditions set forth in the respective laws: military service, jury service, service in municipal and other public elective office, whether the election be direct or indirect, and service in connection with elections, which shall be obligatory and without compensation.

The State shall not permit any contract, covenant or agreement to be carried out which has for its object the restriction, loss, or irrevocable sacrifice of the liberty of man, whether by reason of labor, education, or religious vows. The law, therefore, does not recognize monastic orders nor can it permit their establishment, whatever may be their denomination or the purpose for which they are intended.

not permit the establishment of monastic orders, whatever may be their denomination or the purpose for which they are intended.

Nor shall any person legally agree to his own proscription or exile, or to the temporary or permanent renunciation of the exercise of a given profession or industrial or commercial pursuit.

Identical.

A labor contract shall only be binding to render the services agreed upon for the time fixed by law, not to exceed one year to the detriment of the worker, and in no case shall it embrace the waiver, loss or restriction of any political or civil right. Noncompliance with said contract, as far as the worker is concerned, shall only render him liable for civil damages, without coercion being exercised against his person under any circumstances.

Identical.

APPENDIX C
Article 123 Compared with Draft Proposal

Draft Proposal of Article 123 (Presented January 13, 1917, by Pastor Rouaix and others)

Title VI
Labor

Article [no number]. The Congress and the State Legislatures, upon legislating on labor of a remunerative nature, in exercise of their respective powers, shall be subject to the following principles:

I. The maximum duration of a day's work shall be eight hours for labor in factories, mills and industrial establishments, in mining and related employment, in the construction and repair of buildings, on railroads, in harbor facilities, in land improvement and other engineering works, in transportation enterprises, in the loading and unloading of freight, in agricultural work, in commercial occupations and any other labor of a remunerative nature.

Article 123 of the Constitution of 1917 (As approved in convention, January 23, 1917)

Title VI
Labor and Social Security

Article 123. The Congress and the State Legislature shall make laws relative to labor with due regard for the needs of each region and in conformity with the following principles which shall govern the labor of skilled and unskilled workers, employees, domestic servants and artisans, and every labor contract in general.

I. The maximum duration of a day's work shall be eight hours.

II. The maximum limit of night work shall be seven hours, and it shall be absolutely prohibited for all women and for minors less than sixteen years of age in mills, factories and industrial establishments from ten o'clock at night to six o'clock in the morning.

II. The maximum limit of night work shall be seven hours. Unhealthy and dangerous occupations are prohibited for all women and minors under sixteen years of age. Night work in factories is likewise forbidden to them; nor shall they be employed in commercial establishments after ten o'clock at night.

III. The maximum limit of a day's work for minors over twelve and under sixteen years of age shall be six hours. The work of minors under twelve years of age shall not be made the subject of a contract.

III. Identical.

IV. Every worker shall enjoy at least one day's rest for every six days' work.

IV. Identical.

V. During the three months prior to childbirth, women shall not perform physical labor requiring excessive physical effort. In the month following childbirth they shall necessarily enjoy a period of rest and shall receive their full wages and retain their employment and the rights acquired under their labor contract. During the lactation period they shall have two special rest periods daily, of a half hour each for nursing their infants.

V. Identical.

VI. The minimum wage to be received by a worker shall be that considered sufficient, according to the conditions prevailing in the respective region of the country, to satisfy the normal needs of the life of the worker, his education, and his lawful pleasures, considering him as the head of the family.

VI. The minimum wage to be received by a worker shall be that considered sufficient, according to the conditions prevailing in the respective regions of the country, to satisfy the normal needs of the life of the worker, his education, and his lawful pleasures, considering him as the head of the family. In all agricultural, commercial, manufacturing, or mining enterprises the workers shall have the right to share in the profits in the manner fixed in clause IX of this article.

VII. Equal wages shall be paid for equal work, regardless of sex or nationality.

VII. Identical.

VIII. The minimum wage shall be exempt from attachment, setoff or deduction.

VIII. Identical.

IX. The determination of the minimum wage shall be made by special commissions to be set up in each municipality and to be subordinated to the Central Board of Conciliation which shall be established in each State.

IX. The determination of the minimum wage and of the rate of profit sharing referred to in clause VI shall be made by special commissions which shall be set up in each municipality, subordinate to the Central Board of Conciliation which shall be established in each State.

X. All wages shall be paid in legal currency and shall not be paid in merchandise, IOUs, counters or any other tokens intended as a substitute for money.

X. Identical.

XI. When, owing to special circumstances, it becomes necessary to increase the daily working hours, an additional one hundred percent of the wages fixed for regular time shall be paid as overtime. In no case shall the overtime exceed three hours nor occur three days consecutively. Men under sixteen years of age and women of any age shall not engage in overtime work.

XI. When, owing to special circumstances, it becomes necessary to increase the daily working hours, an additional one hundred percent of the wages fixed for regular time shall be paid as overtime. In no case shall the overtime exceed three hours nor occur more than three consecutive times. Men under sixteen years of age and women of any age shall not engage in overtime work.

XII. In every agricultural, industrial, mining or any other place of work, which is more than two kilometers from centers of population, the employers shall be obliged to furnish

XII. In every agricultural, industrial, mining or any other kind of labor, employers shall be obliged to furnish their workers comfortable and sanitary dwellings, for which they may

the workers comfortable and sanitary dwellings, for which they may charge rents that shall be equitable. They shall likewise establish schools, dispensaries and other services necessary to the community.

charge rents not exceeding one-half of one percent per month of the assessed value of the properties. They shall likewise establish schools, dispensaries, and other services necessary to the community. If the enterprises are located within population centers and employ more than one hundred persons, the first of the above mentioned conditions shall be complied with.

XIII. Furthermore, there shall be set aside in these same labor centers, whenever their population exceeds two hundred inhabitants, a space of land not less than five thousand square meters for the establishment of public markets, and the construction of buildings designed for municipal services and recreation centers.

XIII. Furthermore, in these same labor centers whenever the population exceeds two hundred inhabitants, there shall be set aside a space of land not less than five thousand square meters for the establishment of public markets and the construction of buildings designed for municipal services and recreation centers. No saloons nor gambling houses shall be permitted in these labor centers.

XIV. Employers shall be liable for accidents at work and occupational diseases arising in a particular industry or contracted by employees through the performance of their work; therefore, employers shall pay, in accordance with the provisions of the law, the proper indemnity, depending on whether death or disability, either temporary or permanent, has occurred. This liability shall exist even though the employer contracts for the work through an agent.

XIV. Identical.

XV. The employer shall be required to observe, within the premises of his establishments, all the provisions of the law regarding hygiene and health

XV. The employer shall be required to observe, within the premises of his establishments, all the provisions of the law regarding hygiene and health and to adopt adequate measures for the prevention of accidents in the use of machinery, tools and working materials, under penalties which the law shall determine.

and to adopt adequate measures for the prevention of accidents in the use of machinery, tools, and working materials, as well as organize the same in such way as to ensure the maximum guarantee possible for the health and safety of the workers compatible with the nature of the work, under the penalties which the law shall determine.

XVI. Workers as well as employers shall have the right to organize in the defense of their respective interests, by forming unions, professional associations, etc.

XVI. Identical.

XVII. The law shall recognize strikes and suspensions of work as the right of workers and employers.

XVII. Identical.

XVIII. Strikes shall be lawful when through the use of peaceful means, they seek to bring about equilibrium between the factors of production, capital and labor, in order to achieve a just distribution of the profits. In the case of public services, it shall be obligatory for strikers to give notice ten days in advance to the Board of Conciliation and Arbitration.

XVIII. Strikes shall be lawful when they shall seek to bring about a balance between the various factors of production, harmonizing the rights of labor with those of capital. In the case of public services, workers shall be obliged to give notice ten days in advance to the Board of Conciliation and Arbitration of the date set for the suspension of work. Strikes shall be considered unlawful only when the majority of the strikers engage in acts of violence against persons or property, or in the event of war when they work for establishments and services of the government. Employees of military manufacturing establishments of the Federal Government shall not be included in the provisions of this paragraph, inasmuch as they are a dependency of the national army.

XIX. The suspension of work shall be lawful only when the excess of production shall render it necessary to shut down in order to maintain prices at a level with the cost of production, subject to the approval of the Board of Conciliation and Arbitration.

XIX. Identical.

XX. Differences or disputes between capital and labor shall be subject to the decisions of a Board of Conciliation and Arbitration, to consist of an equal number of representatives of workers and of employers and one from the government.

XX. Identical.

XXI. If the employer shall refuse to submit his differences to arbitration or to accept the award made under the writ of arbitration, the labor contract shall be considered as terminated, and the employer shall be obliged to indemnify the worker by the payment to him of three months' wages and shall incur any liability resulting from the dispute.

XXI. If the employer shall refuse to submit his differences to arbitration or to accept the award rendered by the Board, the labor contract shall be considered as terminated, and he shall be obliged to indemnify the worker by the payment to him of three months' wages and shall incur any liability resulting from the dispute. If the workers reject the award, the contract shall be considered as terminated.

XXII. An employer who discharges a worker without justifiable cause or for having joined an association or union, or for having taken part in a lawful strike, shall be obliged, at the option of the worker, either to fulfill the contract or to indemnify him by the payment of three months' wages. He shall also incur the same liability when the worker leaves his employment on account of the lack of good faith on the part of the employer or because of ill treatment from him,

XXII. An employer who discharges a worker without justifiable cause or for having joined an association or union, or for having taken part in a lawful strike, shall be obliged, at the option of the worker, either to fulfill the contract or to indemnify him by the payment of three months' wages. He shall also incur the same liability when the worker leaves his employment on account of the lack of good faith on the part of the employer or because of ill treatment from him, whether to the worker or to his wife, offspring, parents, brothers and sisters. The employer may not evade this responsibility when the ill treatment is inflicted by subordinates who act with his consent or knowledge.

whether to the worker or to his wife, children, parents or brothers and sisters. The employer may not evade this responsibility when the ill treatment is inflicted by subordinates or agents who act with his consent or knowledge.

XXIII. Claims of workers for salaries or wages earned within the past year and for indemnity compensation shall have preference over any other claims in cases of receivership or bankruptcy.

XXIII. Identical.

XXIV. Debts contracted by workers and payable to their employers, or their employers' associates or agents, shall only be charged to the workers themselves, and in no case and for no reason shall payment be demanded from the members of the worker's family.

XXIV. Debts contracted by workers and owed to their employers, or to their employers' associates or agents, shall only be charged to the workers themselves, and in no case and for no reason shall they be collected from the members of the worker's family, nor shall such debts be paid by the taking of more than the entire monthly wage of the worker.

None

XXV. No fee shall be charged by municipal offices, employment agencies, or by any other public or private institution for finding employment for workers.

None

XXVI. Every labor contract between a Mexican and a foreign employer shall be legalized before the competent municipal authority and visaed by the consul of the nation to which the worker intends to go, with the understanding that, in addition to the regular clauses, it shall be clearly specified that the expenses of repatriation will be borne by the contracting employer.

XXVI. The following stipulations shall be null and void and shall not bind the contracting parties although stated in the contract:

a) Those which provide for an inhuman day's work because it is notoriously excessive, considering the nature of the work.

b) Those which set a wage which, in the judgment of the Board of Conciliation and Arbitration, is not remunerative.

c) Those which stipulate a term greater than one week before the payment of the daily wage.

d) Those which stipulate a place of amusement, an inn, café, tavern, bar, or store for the payment of wages, when the employees of such establishments are not involved.

e) Those which include the direct or indirect obligation of acquiring consumer goods in specified stores or places.

f) Those which permit the retention of wages by way of fines.

g) Those which constitute a waiver by the worker of the indemnifications to which he is entitled due to labor accidents or occupational diseases, damages from breach of contract or for discharge from work.

h) All other stipulations which imply a waiver of any right designed to favor the worker in the laws of protection and assistance to the workers.

None

XXVII. Identical to draft-proposal paragraph XXVI.

XXVIII. The laws shall determine what property constitutes the family patrimony, property which shall be inalienable, not subject to encumbrances or attachments, and which may be bequeathed with simplified formalities in the succession proceedings.

XXVII. Insurance covering old age, death, unemployment, accidents, and similar happenings is considered to be of social utility; the Federal Government as well as that of each State shall encourage the formation of institutions of this nature in order to instill and inculcate the idea of social security.

XXIX. Identical to draft-proposal paragraph XXVII.

XXVIII. Cooperative associations for the construction of low-cost, hygienic dwellings for workers, when they may acquire ownership within a specified period, shall likewise be considered of social utility.

XXX. Cooperative associations for the construction of low-cost, hygienic dwellings for workers, when designed to be acquired in ownership by them within a specified time, shall likewise be considered of social utility.

APPENDIX D
Carranza's Draft Proposal of Article 27

Article 27. Private property can not be taken for public use without previous indemnification. The need for or utility of the occupation shall be decided by the corresponding administrative authority; but the expropriation shall be made by judicial authority in case there is disagreement between the parties concerned over the conditions.

Religious bodies and communities, whatever may be their character, denomination, duration and purpose, shall not have legal capacity to acquire property or to administer more real property than the buildings designated immediately and directly for the benefit or purpose of the said bodies and communities.

Public or private charitable institutions for the aid of the needy, the diffusion of education, mutual aid to individuals who are members, or for any other lawful purpose, under no circumstances shall be under the patronage, direction, or administration of religious bodies nor of the ministers of any religious denomination, and they may have capacity to acquire real property, but only that which is indispensable and devoted directly and immediately to the objective of the said institution.

Likewise, they may make mortgage loans on real property at interest rates which shall, in no case, be higher than those fixed by law and for a period not to exceed ten years.

The *ejidos* of the villages, whether those maintained subsequent to the Ley de Desamortización, since restored to them, or which have been granted anew in conformity with the law, shall be enjoyed in common by their occupants while they are divided in accordance with the law to be expedited to that effect.

No other civil body may own or administer by itself real property or mortgage loans on said property with the sole exception of the buildings devoted directly and immediately to the purpose of the institution.

Civil and commercial companies may own urban property and manufacturing or industrial establishments within or without the centers of population, as well as mining operations, those relating to petroleum or any other class of substances which are found in the subsoil, the same as railroads or pipelines also; but they shall not acquire nor administer for themselves rural property greater in area than that which is strictly necessary for the establishments or for the fulfillment of their indicated objectives and which the Executive of the Union shall determine in each case.

Banks duly organized under the laws governing institutions of credit may make mortgage loans on rural and urban property in accordance with the provisions of the said laws.

APPENDIX E
Article 27 Compared with Draft Proposal

To show its close relationship to and derivation from the Rouaix proposals, Article 27, with paragraph numbers in parentheses, is compared with that draft.[1] Although there is some overlapping, paragraphs (1) through (6) concern the nature of property; paragraph (7), containing seven clauses (in Roman numerals), enumerates the ones who have a right to hold property and the nature of that right; and paragraphs (8) through (12) deal with the proposed solution to the agrarian problem. In the convention the paragraphs were discussed in numerical order.

Draft Proposal of Article 27 (Presented January 25, 1917, by Pastor Rouaix and others)

Article 27 (As approved in convention, January 30, 1917)

Article 27. Ownership of lands and waters within the boundaries of the national territory is vested originally in the Nation which has had, and has, the right to transmit direct title

Article 27. (1) Ownership of lands and waters within the boundaries of the national territory is vested originally in the Nation which has had, and has, the right to transmit title

---

[1] For comparison with corresponding paragraphs of the Rouaix draft proposals, the paragraphs of Article 27 are listed out of context.

thereof to private persons, thereby constituting private property.

Private property shall not be expropriated by authority except for reasons of public utility and by means of indemnification.

Legal capacity to acquire direct ownership of lands and waters of the Nation, their exploitation and the conditions to which private property will be subjected, shall be governed by the following provisions:

I. Only Mexicans by birth or by naturalization and Mexican companies have the right to acquire ownership of lands, waters and their appurtenances for the exploitation of mines, waters or mineral fuels in the Mexican Republic. The State may grant the same right to foreigners when they declare before the Secretariat of Foreign Relations that they renounce their status as foreigners and the protection of their Governments in all matters which refer to the said properties, remaining fully subject with respect to them to the laws and authorities of the Nation. Within a zone of 100 kilometers along the borders and fifty from the seacoasts, no foreigners shall under any conditions acquire direct ownership of lands and waters.

II. The Church, regardless of creed, shall in no case have legal capacity to acquire, hold or administer real property loans made on such real property. The places of public worship are the property of the Nation, as

thereof to private persons, thereby constituting private property.

(2) Expropriations shall only be made for reasons of public utility and by means of indemnification.

(7) Legal capacity to acquire ownership of lands and waters of the Nation shall be governed by the following provisions:

I. Only Mexicans by birth or naturalization and Mexican companies have the right to acquire ownership of lands, waters and their appurtenances or to obtain concessions for the development of mines, waters or mineral fuels in the Mexican Republic. The State may grant the same right to foreigners, provided they agree before the Secretariat of Foreign Relations to consider themselves as Mexican nationals with respect to such property, and accordingly not to invoke the protection of their Governments in regard to the same, under penalty in case of breach, of forfeiture to the Nation of property so acquired. Within a zone of 100 kilometers along the borders and fifty from the seacoasts, no foreigners shall under any conditions acquire direct ownership over lands and waters.

II. Religious associations known as churches, regardless of creed, shall in no case have legal capacity to acquire, hold or administer real property; all such real property or loans as may be at present held by the said

represented by the Federal Government, which shall determine which of them may continue to be devoted to their purposes. Bishops' residences, rectories, seminaries, asylums and religious schools belonging to religious associations, or any other building built or designed for the administration, propaganda or teaching of a religious creed, shall immediately, as of full right, revert to ownership by the Nation to be used exclusively by the Federation or the States, within their respective jurisdictions, for services to the people. The places of public worship which are erected in the future, shall be the property of the Nation, if constructed by public subscription; but if they are constructed by private persons, they shall be subject to the current laws on private property.

religious associations, either directly or through an intermediary, shall revert to ownership by the Nation, any person whosoever being authorized to denounce any property so held. Presumptive evidence shall be sufficient to declare the denunciation well founded. Places of public worship are the property of the Nation, as represented by the Federal Government, which shall determine which of them may continue to be devoted to their present purposes. Bishops' residences, rectories, seminaries, asylums, and schools belonging to religious orders, convents, or any other buildings built or designed for the administration, propaganda, or teaching of a religious creed, shall immediately, as of full right, revert to direct ownership by the Nation, to be used exclusively by the Federation or the States, within their respective jurisdictions, for the rendering of services to the public. All places of public worship which are hereafter erected shall be the property of the Nation.

III. Public or private charitable institutions for the needy, for scientific research, the diffusion of knowledge, mutual aid to members, or for any other lawful purpose, shall not acquire more real property than actually needed for their purpose and immediately and directly devoted thereto; but they may acquire, hold, or administer mortgages on real property provided the term thereof does not exceed ten years. Under no circumstances shall institutions of this kind be under the patronage, direc-

III. Identical.

tion, administration, charge or supervision of religious bodies or communities, or of ministers of any religious denomination or of their dependents, even though the former or the latter shall not be in active service.

IV. Properties held in common by co-owners, hamlets situated on private property, villages, communities, tribes, and other settlements which in fact or by law conserve their communal character, shall enjoy in common the ownership and possession of lands, woods and waters which belong to them, whether they have been maintained following the laws of disentailment, or whether restored to them in conformity with the law of January 6, 1915, or whether given to them in the future by virtue of the provisions of this article. The properties mentioned shall be enjoyed in common while they are divided in accordance with the law to be expedited to that effect, only the members of the community having the right to them, who shall not obligate nor transfer their respective rights to other persons, agreements and contracts made in violation of this provision being null and void. Laws that are made for the distribution shall include the necessary measures to keep the participants from forfeiting the portions that pertain to them and with which the community will be reconstructed, or from forming undesirable large estates.

V. Civil or commercial companies owned under the form of bonds payable to bearer shall not acquire, hold

VI. Properties held in common by co-owners, hamlets situated on private property, villages, communities, tribes, and other settlements which in fact or by law conserve their communal character, shall have legal capacity to enjoy in common the lands, woods, and waters which belong to them, or which may have been or shall be restored to them in accordance with the law of January 6, 1915, until such time as the manner of making the division of the lands only shall be determined by law.

IV. Commercial stock companies shall not acquire, hold or administer rural properties. Companies of this

or administer rural properties. Companies of this kind which may be organized to develop any manufacturing, mining, petroleum or other industry not agricultural by nature, shall be able to acquire, hold, or administer lands only in the amount that is strictly necessary for the establishments or adequate to serve the purposes indicated and which the Federal or State Executive shall determine in each case.

VI. Banks duly authorized under the laws governing institutions of credit may make loans on urban and rural property in accordance with the provisions of the said laws, but they shall not own or administer more real property than that actually necessary for their express purpose.

VII. With the exception of the corporations to which clauses III, IV, V and VI refer, no other civil corporation shall own or administer on its own behalf real estate or mortgage loans derived therefrom, with the single exception of buildings destined immediately and directly for the purposes of the institution. The States, the Federal District and the Territories, as well as the municipalities throughout the Republic, shall enjoy full legal capacity to acquire and hold all real estate necessary for the rendering of services to the public.

VIII. All proceedings, findings, resolutions and operations of demarcation, concession, composition, judgment, transaction, alienation, or auction which may have deprived

kind which may organize to develop any manufacturing, mining, petroleum or other industry not agricultural by nature, shall be able to acquire, hold, or administer lands only in the amount that is strictly necessary for the establishments or adequate to serve the purposes indicated, which the Federal or State Executive shall determine in each case.

V. Identical.

VII. Identical.

(9) All proceedings, findings, resolutions and operations of demarcation, concession, composition, judgment, transaction, alienation, or auction which may have deprived

properties held in common by co-owners, hamlets situated on private property, villages, communities, tribes and other settlements which still exist in communal form since the law of June 25, 1856, of the whole or a part of their lands, woods and waters, are declared null and void; and all the proceedings, findings, resolutions and operations which take place in the future and produce the same effects shall likewise be null and void. Consequently, all lands, woods and waters of which the communities mentioned above have been deprived, shall be restored to them in accordance with the decree of January 6, 1915, and other related laws to be issued in this regard, with the sole exception of the lands and waters to which title may already have been given in the divisions made by virtue of the cited law of June 25, 1856, or held in undisputed ownership for more than ten years when their area does not exceed 100 hectares. The excess over this area shall be returned to the community and the owner indemnified for its value. All laws of restitution enacted by virtue of this provision shall be of administrative character and immediately carried into effect.

properties held in common by co-owners, hamlets situated on private property, villages, communities, tribes and other settlements which exist since the law of June 25, 1856, of the whole or a part of their lands, woods and waters, are declared null and void; and all the findings, resolutions and operations which take place in the future and produce the same effects shall likewise be null and void. Consequently, all the lands, woods, and waters of which the above-mentioned communities have been deprived, shall be restored to them in accordance with the decree of January 6, 1915, which shall remain in effect as a constitutional law. In case the adjudication of lands, by way of restitution be not legal in the terms of the said decree, which adjudication may have been requested by any of the above-mentioned communities, those lands shall be given to them by way of grant, and they shall in no event fail to receive such as they may need. Only such lands, title to which may have been acquired in the divisions made by virtue of the said law of June 25, 1856, or such as may be held in undisputed ownership for more than ten years are excepted from the provision of nullity, provided their area does not exceed fifty hectares. The excess over this area shall be returned to the community and the owner indemnified for its value. All laws of restitution enacted by virtue of this provision shall be immediately carried into effect by the administrative authorities. Only the members of the community shall have the right to the lands to be divided and the rights to the same lands shall be inalienable while they remain undivided, as well as those held in ownership when the division has been made.

(3) The Nation shall at all times have the right to impose on private property such limitations as the public interest may demand, as well as the right to regulate the development of natural resources which are susceptible of appropriation, in order to conserve them and ensure an equitable distribution of the public wealth. For this purpose necessary measures shall be taken to divide up the large landed estates; to develop small landed holdings; to create new centers of rural population with the lands and waters that are indispensable to them; to encourage agriculture and to prevent the destruction of natural resources and the damages that property may suffer to the detriment of society. Villages, hamlets situated on private property, and communities which lack lands and water, or do not have them in sufficient quantities for the needs of their inhabitants, shall have the right to be provided with them from adjoining properties, always having due regard for small landed holdings. Therefore, all grants of lands made up to the present time under the decree of January 6, 1915, are confirmed. Private property necessary for the achievement of the above-expressed objectives shall be considered as taken for public utility.

IX. The Nation shall have at all times the right to regulate private property and to exploit the natural resources which are susceptible of appropriation, in order to conserve them and ensure a more equitable distribution of the public wealth. For this purpose necessary measures shall be taken to divide up the large landed estates; to develop small landed holdings; to grant lands to the existing villages, hamlets situated on private property and communities; and to create new centers of rural population with lands and waters that are indispensable to them, as well as to prevent the destruction of natural resources and the damages that property may suffer to the detriment of society. The acquisition of private property necessary to achieve this objective shall be considered as taken for public utility; therefore, the grants of land which have been made until now under the decree of January 6, 1915, are confirmed.

X. The Nation reserves for itself the direct ownership of all minerals or substances which in veins, layers, masses, or beds, whatever may be their form, constitute deposits whose nature is different from the components of the land; minerals and substances which at all times shall have the character of being inalienable and imprescriptible, and which only may be exploited by private persons or civil or commercial companies established according to Mexican law, by means of a concession granted by federal administrative authority and under the conditions which the corresponding laws shall establish. The minerals and substances which need a concession in order to be developed are the following: minerals from which metals and metalloids used in industry are extracted, such as platinum, gold, silver, copper, iron, cobalt, nickel, manganese, lead, mercury, tin, chromium, antimony, zinc, vanadium, bismuth, magnesium, sulphur, arsenic, tellurium, strontium, barium, and the rare metals; beds of precious stones, rock salt, and salt lakes formed directly by marine waters; products derived from the decomposition of rocks, such as asbestos, amianthus, and talc when they are in the form of veins, layers, or pockets and their exploitation requires underground work; phosphates which may be used for fertilizers, whether in their natural state or by means of chemical processes, coal and any other solid fuel which is found in veins, layers, or masses of any form;

(4) In the Nation is vested direct ownership of all minerals or substances which in veins, layers, masses or beds constitute deposits whose nature is different from the components of the land, such as minerals from which metals and metalloids used in industry are extracted; beds of precious stones, rock salt and salt lakes formed directly by marine waters; products derived from the decomposition of rocks, when their exploitation requires underground work; phosphates which may be used for fertilizers; solid mineral fuels; petroleum and all solid, liquid, or gaseous hydrocarbons.

and petroleum or any other solid, liquid, or gaseous hydrocarbon whether it gushes to the surface or is found in the ground and the water extracted from mines.

XI. The following are the property of the Nation and shall be under the control of the Federal Government: the waters of the territorial seas to the extent of and under the terms recognized by International Law; waters of lagoons and inlets of the seacoasts; waters of inland lakes of natural formation which are directly connected with flowing waters; the waters of principal rivers or tributaries with permanent current from the point where this commences; those of intermittent streams whose main branch traverses two or more States; the waters of rivers, streams, or ravines when they serve as the national boundary or that of States; and the waters running from mines. Likewise, there shall be the property of the Nation the river beds and beds and shores of the lakes and streams to the extent fixed by law.

(5) In the Nation is likewise vested the ownership of the waters of the territorial seas to the extent and in the terms fixed by International Law; waters of principal rivers or tribuseacoasts; waters of inland lakes of natural formation which are directly connected with flowing waters; the waters of principal rivers or tributaries from the points at which there is a permanent current of water in their beds to their mouths, whether they flow to the sea or cross two or more States; those of intermittent streams whose main branch traverses two or more States; the waters of rivers, streams, or ravines when they serve as the national boundary or that of States; waters extracted from mines; and the river beds and beds and shores of lakes and streams heretofore mentioned to the extent fixed by law. Any other stream of water not included in the above enumeration, shall be considered as an integral part of the private property through which it flows; but the utilization of the water, when its course passes from one property to another, shall be considered of public utility and shall be subject to the provisions prescribed by the States.

(6) In the cases to which the two foregoing paragraphs refer, the ownership of the Nation is inalienable and imprescriptible, and only shall

concessions be made by the Federal Government to private parties or to civil or commercial corporations organized under Mexican law, on condition that regular efforts be made to develop the resources concerned and that the legal requirements be complied with.

XII. The need for or utility of the occupation of a particular property shall be declared by the corresponding administrative authority in accordance with the preceding bases. The value which shall be set as compensation for the expropriated property shall be based on the sum recorded as the fiscal value in the tax assessment or collecting offices, whether this value has been declared by the owner or simply accepted by him by implication, as a basis for the payment of his taxes, with ten percent added. The increased value which the property in question may have acquired through improvements made subsequent to the date of the fixing of the fiscal value shall be the only matter which shall be subject to expert opinion and to judicial determination. This same procedure shall be followed when objects are concerned whose value is not recorded in the tax offices.

(8) Federal and State laws within their respective jurisdictions shall determine the cases in which the occupation of private property shall be considered of public utility; and in accordance with the said laws the administrative authorities shall make the corresponding declaration. The value which shall be set as compensation, etc. [from here on, identical to paragraph XII of the draft proposal].

XIII. From the day on which the present Constitution is promulgated, direct ownership by the Nation shall be invalidated by prescription over lands and waters held by private persons or communities permitted by the law, in favor of the same private

There is no similar paragraph in Article 27.

persons or communities, when the possession has been for more than thirty years, peaceful, continuous and public, whenever the surface held does not exceed the limit that is fixed for each State, which shall not exceed ten thousand hectares, and that the said lands and waters do not fall within the reservations of this article. The owners of lands and waters not in communal use shall have this same right in the future in order to invalidate ownership by the State or private persons by prescription.

XIV. The exercise of the rights belonging to the Nation by virtue of the provisions of this article, shall follow judicial procedure; but as part of this procedure and by order of the respective tribunals, which order shall be issued within the maximum period of one month, the administrative authorities shall proceed immediately to the occupation, administration, auction or sale of the lands and waters in question, together with all their appurtenances, and in no case may the acts of said authorities be set aside until a final decision has been handed down.

No similar paragraph in draft proposal.

(10) Identical to draft-proposal paragraph XIV.

(11) During the next constitutional term, the Congress and the State Legislatures shall enact laws, within their respective jurisdictions, for the purpose of carrying out the division of large landed estates, based on the following principles:

(a) In each State and Territory there shall be fixed the maximum area of land which any one individual or legally organized company may own.

(b) The excess of the area thus fixed shall be subdivided by the owner within the term set by local law and the subdivisions shall be offered for sale on conditions approved by the governments in accordance with the same laws.

(c) If the owner shall refuse to make the subdivision, this shall be carried out by the local Government by means of expropriation.

(d) The value of the subdivisions shall be paid in annual amounts that amortize principal and interest within a period of not less than twenty years, during which the person acquiring shall not alienate them. The interest rate shall not exceed five percent per annum.

(e) The owner shall be obliged to receive bonds of a special issue to guarantee the payment of the property expropriated. With this end in view, the Congress shall pass a law authorizing the States to issue bonds to meet their agrarian obligations.

(f) Local laws shall provide for the organization of the family patrimony, determining what property shall comprise it, on the basis that it shall be inalienable and not subject to attachment or encumbrance of any kind.

No similar paragraph in draft proposal.

(12) All contracts and concessions made by previous governments since the year 1876, which have had as a consequence the monopoly of lands, waters and the natural resources of

the Nation by a single individual or company are declared subject to revision and the Executive of the Union is authorized to declare them null and void when they seriously prejudice the public interest.

APPENDIX F
Biographic Information on Delegates Referred to in Text
(as of January 31, 1917)

Name	Age	State from which elected	Occupation, profession, or military rank
Adame, Julian	35	Zacatecas	
Aguilar, Antonio		México	
Aguilar, Cándido	27	Veracruz	General
Aguirre, Amado	53	Jalisco	General
Aguirre Berlanga, Manuel	30	Coahuila	Lawyer
Alcazar, Alvaro L.	30	Morelos	Held military rank
Alonzo Romero, Miguel	26	Yucatán	Physician
Alvarez y Alvarez, José	31	Michoacán	Colonel
Amaya, Manuel		Nuevo León	Businessman
Ancona Albertos, Antonio	33	Yucatán	Journalist
Andrade, Cayetano	26	Michoacán	Physician
Aranda, Manuel G.	47	Guanajuato	Mining engineer
Avilés, Cándido	35	Sinaloa	
Avilés, Uriel	32	Michoacán	Lieutenant colonel
Barrera, Antonio de la	32	Puebla	Lieutenant colonel
Bojórquez, Juan de Dios	24	Sonora	Agricultural engineer
Bolaños V., Gaspar	33	Jalisco	Public administration
Bórquez, Flavio A.		Sonora	
Bravo Izquierdo, Donato		México	Held military rank
Cabrera, Alfonso	34	Puebla	
Calderón, Esteban B.	40	Jalisco	General
Cañete, Rafael P.	60	Puebla	Lawyer
Cano, Nicolás		Guanajuato	Miner, labor leader
Castañón, Samuel	32	Zacatecas	Carpenter

Name	Age	State from which elected	Occupation, profession, or military rank
Castaños, Fernando		Durango	
Castillo, Porfirio del	32	Puebla	Colonel
Cedano, Marcelino	28	Territory of Tepic	Major
Cepeda Medrano, Manuel		Coahuila	Public administration
Céspedes, Eliseo L.	25	Veracruz	Lawyer, lieutenant colonel
Chapa, Pedro A.		Tamaulipas	Colonel
Colunga, Enrique	39	Guanajuato	Lawyer
Cravioto, Alfonso	33	Hidalgo	Lawyer
Curiel, Rafael		San Luis Potosí	
Dávalos, Marcelino	37	Jalisco	Lawyer
Dávalos Ornelas, Manuel	36	Jalisco	Teacher
Díaz Barriga, Francisco		Guanajuato	Physician
Dorador, Silvestre	46	Durango	Public administration
Dyer, Jairo R.	48	Zacatecas	Physician
Enríquez, Enrique A.		México	Lawyer
Espinosa, Francisco	52	Federal District	Lawyer
Espinosa, Luis	32	Oaxaca	Lawyer, major
Espinosa Bávara, Juan	40	Territory of Tepic	Public administration
Ezquerro, Carlos M.	51	Sinaloa	
Fajardo, Zeferino		Tamaulipas	Lawyer
Fernández Martínez, Luis	28	Guanajuato	
Figueroa, Francisco	44	Guerrero	Teacher, colonel
Frausto, Ramón		Guanajuato	General
Frías, Juan N.		Querétaro	
Gámez, Ramón	39	Nuevo León	Colonel
García, Adolfo G.		Veracruz	Colonel
Garza González, Agustín	43	Nuevo León	Physician
Giffard, Juan Manuel		México	Lawyer
Gómez, José F.	32	Oaxaca	Colonel
Gómez, José L.		Morelos	
Góngora, Victorio E.	42	Veracruz	Civil engineer
González, Alberto M.		Hidalgo	
González Galindo, Modesto	34	Tlaxcala	
González Torres, Salvador		Oaxaca	General
Gracidas, Carlos L.	28	Veracruz	Linotype operator, labor leader

Name	Age	State from which elected	Occupation, profession, or military rank
Gutiérrez, Antonio	33	Durango	
Guzmán, Salvador R.	28	Puebla	Physician
Herrera, Alfonso	46	Federal District	Teacher
Herrera, Manuel		Oaxaca	
Ibarra, Federico E.		Jalisco	Engineer
Ilizaliturri, Luis		Nuevo León	Lawyer
Jara, Heriberto	36	Veracruz	General
Lizardi, Fernando M.	33	Guanajuato	Lawyer
López Lira, Jesús	28	Guanajuato	Physician
Machorro y Narváez, Paulino	39	Jalisco	Lawyer
Macías, José Natividad	59	Guanajuato	Lawyer
Magallón, Andrés		Sinaloa	Lawyer
Manjarrez, Froylán C.	25	Puebla	Journalist
Márquez, Josafat F.	32	Veracruz	Public administration
Márquez, Rafael	32	Michoacán	
Martí, Rubén	38	México	Held military rank
Martín del Campo, Francisco	30	Jalisco	Lawyer
Martínez, Epigmenio A.		Puebla	
Martínez, Rafael	29	Federal District	Journalist
Martínez de Escobar, Rafael	27	Tabasco	Lawyer
Martínez Mendoza, Rafael		San Luis Potosí	Lawyer
Mayorga, Alfonso	30	Hidalgo	Police officer, held military rank
Meade Fierro, Ernesto	29	Coahuila	
Medina, Hilario	25	Guanajuato	Lawyer
Méndez, Arturo	49	San Luis Potosí	Physician
Monzón, Luis G.	44	Sonora	Teacher
Moreno, Bruno	49	Jalisco	
Moreno, Fernando		México	
Múgica, Francisco J.	32	Michoacán	General
Nafarrate, Emiliano		Tamaulipas	General
Navarro, Gilberto M.	39	Guanajuato	
Navarro, Luis T.	35	Puebla	Engineer, colonel
Nieto, Rafael	32	San Luis Potosí	Public administration
Ocampo, Santiago	42	Tabasco	
Ochoa, Rafael		Jalisco	
O'Farrill, Enrique	42	México	Lawyer

Name	Age	State from which elected	Occupation, profession, or military rank
Ordorica, Guillermo	39	México	Lawyer
Palavicini, Félix F.	35	Federal District	Engineer (topographer)
Palma, Juan de Dios		Veracruz	
Pastrana Jaimes, David	33	Puebla	Lawyer
Pérez, Celestino	28	Oaxaca	Lawyer
Perusquía, Ernesto		Querétaro	
Pintado Sánchez, Ismael		Hidalgo	Lieutenant colonel
Prieto, Manuel M.	28	Chihuahua	
Ramírez Llaca, Carlos	31	Guanajuato	
Ramírez Villarreal, Francisco		Colima	Lawyer
Recio, Enrique	32	Yucatán	
Reynoso, José J.	48	México	Mining engineer
Ríos, Rafael de los	26	Federal District	Journalist, public administration
Rivera, José	30	Puebla	Major
Rivera Cabrera, Crisóforo		Oaxaca	Lawyer
Robledo, Juan de Dios		Jalisco	
Rodiles, Saúl	32	Veracruz	Teacher
Rodríguez, José María	46	Coahuila	Physician
Rodríguez, Matías		Hidalgo	
Rodríguez González, José	36	Coahuila	Teacher
Rojas, Luis Manuel	46	Jalisco	Lawyer, journalist
Román, Alberto		Veracruz	Physician
Romero Flores, Jesús	31	Michoacán	Teacher
Rosales, Miguel		Puebla	
Rosas y Reyes, Román	26	Federal District	
Ross, Ramón	53	Sonora	
Rouaix, Pastor	42	Puebla	Civil engineer
Ruiz, José Pilar		Michoacán	Physician and surgeon
Sánchez, Juan	50	Oaxaca	Lawyer
Santos, Samuel M. de los	30	San Luis Potosí	General
Sepúlveda, Lorenzo		Nuevo León	Physician
Silva Herrera, José		Michoacán	Lawyer
Terrones Benítez, Alberto	30	Durango	Lawyer
Torre, Jesús de la		Durango	Held military rank
Truchuelo, José María	36	Querétaro	Lawyer
Ugarte, Gerzayn		Federal District	

Name	Age	State from which elected	Occupation, profession, or military rank
Vega Sánchez, Rafael	28	Hidalgo	Public administration
Victoria, Héctor	31	Yucatán	Journalist
Villaseñor, Carlos	41	Jalisco	Surgeon
Villaseñor Norman, Adolfo	28	Zacatecas	Engineer (hydrographer and topographer)
Von Versen, Jorge E.		Coahuila	Printer, labor leader
Zambrano, Nicéforo	54	Nuevo León	Businessman
Zavala, Dionisio	29	San Luis Potosí	Miner, labor organizer
Zavala, Pedro	40	Sinaloa	Engineer

GLOSSARY

abrazo: Mexican (and Latin American) embrace, used on greeting or taking leave of close friends and relatives.

adelante: Let's get going!

amparo: a unique writ of Mexican jurisprudence. It is a federal order granting relief to persons or corporations alike when a law or decree is considered to infringe on any of their individual rights under the constitution.

a votar: Let's vote!

ayuntamiento: municipal council, the legislative branch of the municipal government.

bachillerato: course of study followed upon completion of secondary schooling and prior to beginning professional studies on the university level. Called the preparatory level. Also, the name of the diploma awarded for successful completion of this course of study.

bravo: as an exclamation, "well done!"

Bravo: "Río Bravo," the Mexican's name for the Rio Grande.

brigada de intelectuales: brigade of intellectuals.

cacique: local or regional political boss.

campesino: a peasant, a rural worker of the lower social classes.

carrancista: supporter of Venustiano Carranza, leader of the Constitutionalist movement (1913–1920).

caudillo: regional chief who became a national leader, usually with dictatorial powers, in Latin American countries.

científico: member of a clique surrounding President Díaz. The *científicos*, who were guided by positivist thinking, sought order and material progress. They profited from lucrative concessions during the *porfiriato* (q.v.).

colegio: secondary school.

come fraile: "priest-eater"; a rabid jacobin.

condueñazgos: properties held in common by co-owners.

congregaciones: rural communities.

Congreso Constituyente: constitutional convention.

convivialidad: festive occasion with food and drink.

corralista: supporter of Díaz's hated vice-president, Ramón Corral (1904–1911).

criollo: Caucasian, mainly of Spanish descent, who has no Indian blood.

decena trágica: the "tragic ten days," February 9–18, 1913, which began with the uprising against President Madero by dissident military elements and ended with his arrest. During this period Mexico City was subject to needless and indiscriminate military action. Many civilians as well as combatants perished. The supposedly loyal Gen. Victoriano Huerta, plotting with rebel leaders, betrayed Madero, engineered his removal from office, and subsequently seized the executive power himself.

diputado: delegate to a constitutional convention or representative in Congress.

dominio directo: direct ownership.

duranguense: native of the state of Durango.

ejido: land held and worked in common by rural inhabitants.

envenenado: literally, "poisoned," but "sick" when used with reference to an alcoholic.

federales: troops of the federal government who fought against the Constitutionalist forces of Venustiano Carranza during the presidency of Victoriano Huerta (1913–1914).

fiesta de la raza: traditional entertainment.

Fomento, Colonización e Industria: Ministry of Development, Colonization, and Industry.

fuero: special privilege granted to clergy or military, under which they could be tried in civil and criminal cases by their own courts.

gachupín: derogatory term for a Spaniard.

garantías: individual rights.

Gobernación: "Government"; the most important ministry of the executive branch of the Mexican federal government. It has authority over state-federal relations, the regulation of religious denominations, election laws, political parties, federal crime prevention and punishment, immigration, and other important matters. For a brief enumeration of the responsibilities of this powerful ministry, see William P. Tucker, *The Mexican Government Today*, pp. 173–180.

gobernante: holder of a high governmental office, i.e., state governor or president, who is usually elected but who enjoys considerably more authority or power than that conferred on his office.

golpe teatral: theatrical stunt.

gonzalista: supporter of President Manuel González (1880–1884).

guanajuatense: native of the state of Guanajuato.

hacendado: owner of a large estate or hacienda.

huertista: supporter of President Victoriano Huerta (1913–1914).

ignorantes: ignorant or uninformed persons.

infalsificables: "noncounterfeitable" notes authorized by Carranza in his decree of July 21, 1915. They were supposed to be backed by metallic reserves. For a time they had an exchange value of twenty centavos (Mexican gold) for each peso of paper. When the promised metallic reserves did not materialize, however, the notes quickly depreciated, and by the end of 1916 they were worth less than one centavo.

ingeniero: "engineer"; the professional title awarded for the successful completion of a course of study in engineering. Abbreviated "Ing."

jacobinos obregonistas: "Obregón jacobins"; a bloc in the Constitutional Convention of 1916–1917 that was radical and anticlerical in its views and refused to accept without discussion the Carranza draft of reforms to the Constitution of 1857.

jamona: plump, middle-aged woman.

jefe político: an official, first provided for under the Spanish Constitution of 1812. Interposed between *ayuntamientos* (q.v.) and state authorities, he served as an agent of both state and federal governments in Mexico, exercising extensive control and supervision over administrative, political, and social matters in the municipalities of the district under his supervision. See J. Lloyd Mecham, "The Jefe Político in Mexico," *Southwestern Social Science Quarterly* 13, no. 4 (March 1933): 333–353.

joven núbil: girl of marriageable age.

latifundio: large estate (larger than a hacienda).

latifundista: owner of a large estate, i.e., *hacendado*.

Ley de Desamortización: the Ley Lerdo of June 25, 1856, which provided that no civil or religious corporation would be permitted to acquire or own real property and that such property would be sold to those who worked it at a price determined by law. The purpose of the law was to make real property more available for national development.

ley fuga: "law of flight"; justification for shooting a prisoner on the grounds of attempted escape.

liberales carrancistas: Carranza liberals; a bloc in the Constitutional Convention of 1916–1917 that supported Carranza's draft of reforms to the Constitution of 1857.

licenciado: licensed; one who has a license to practice a profession, usually law. Abbreviated "Lic."

magonista: supporter of Ricardo Flores Magón, Mexican radical of the 1906–1918 period.

mesa central: central plateau area of Mexico.

mescalitos: drinks of mescal, a liquor distilled from the maguey plant.

mestizo: offspring of the union of an Indian and a Caucasian.

mezcal: intoxicating drink distilled from fermented juice of certain species of the agave plant, especially the maguey.

Ministerio Público: Public Ministry; an agency for the administration of justice that represents the federal government as the organ of prosecution in cases before federal courts.

municipio: principal unit of Mexican local government. Comparable to an American county or township, it consists of a *cabecera municipal* (seat of government of the *municipio*) and a surrounding area, which may include towns, villages, and other communities.

municipio libre: goal of advocates of political autonomy for the *municipio*.

muy bien: very good or very well.

norteño: northerner, i.e., a native of a northern Mexican state.

oficial mayor: chief clerk in an office of the state or federal administration.

Padre: "Father"; title used in addressing priests.

patria: fatherland or native country.

pelado, peladito: Mexican of the lowest social class.

pensión: boarding house.

población: town or village.

poblano: native of the state of Puebla.

porfiriato: the period when Porfirio Díaz was the strong man of Mexico (1876–1911). Díaz was president for the entire period except the years 1880–1884 when Manuel González, his supporter, was chief executive.

porfirista: supporter of Porfirio Díaz, Mexican president.

presidente municipal: presiding officer of an *ayuntamiento* (q.v.); mayor, or chief executive, of a *municipio* (q.v.).

previsión social: social security.

profesor: teacher.

provincia: collective term for all Mexico outside the Federal District.

Proyecto de Ley sobre Contrato de Trabajo: draft of a law, or proposed legislation, on the labor contract.

pueblos: villages.

pulque: fermented, undistilled juice of the maguey plant.

pulquería: place where *pulque* is sold.

rancho: small farm.

rancherías: hamlets.

rebanada de melón: slice of cantaloupe.

refaccionario: "auxiliary bank" for the promotion of agricultural, industrial, and mining enterprises. For a discussion of Mexican banking terms of this period, see Walter Flavius McCaleb, *Present and Past Banking in Mexico*, pp. 97–112.

renovadores: "reformers"; a bloc of the Twenty-sixth Congress (1912–1913), which sought to pass measures of socioeconomic reform.

rurales: Mexican rural police force or constabulary, which obtained notoriety during the *porfiriato* as a law-enforcement arm of the federal government.

sí: yes.

tabasqueño: native of the state of Tabasco.

tahur: gambler; cardsharp.

tapatío: native of the state of Jalisco.

tienda de raya: company store.

tinacalito: wooden trough or vat used to make *pulque*.

trabajo: labor, work.

trabajo doméstico: household work.

tribus: tribes.

vaquero: cowboy.

vida alegre: dissolute life, one spent in the company of women of easy virtue.

villista: supporter of Gen. Francisco (Pancho) Villa, who opposed Carranza for the leadership of the Constitutionalist cause.

violación: deflowering; ravishment. See chapter 6, footnote 48, for a fuller explanation of this term.

viva: interjection usually translated as "hail!" or "long live!"

zapatero: shoemaker.

zapatista: supporter of Emiliano Zapata, leader of the armed agrarian movement in Morelos and surrounding states (1909–1919).

BIBLIOGRAPHY

Album de Autógrafos y Retratos de los Constituyentes de 1917, coleccionado en Querétaro por José Alvarez y Alvarez, Constituyente Michoacano. Secretaría de Educación Pública, Mexico City.

Album del Congreso Constituyente de 1917, Querétaro, JPR. Property of Dr. José Pilar Ruiz, Morelia, Michoacán.

Album of Lic. Luis Fernández Martínez. Partially published in *El Nacional*, February 5, 1937.

Alvarez Album. *See* Album de Autógrafos y Retratos de los Constituyentes de 1917, coleccionado en Querétaro por José Alvarez y Alvarez.

Alvarez y Alvarez, José. Interview. Cuernavaca, Morelos, May 31, 1965.

Bailey, David C. "Alvaro Obregón and Anti-Clericalism in the 1910 Revolution." *The Americas* 26 (October 1969): 183–198.

Becerra, Marcos E. *Palavicini: Desde allá abajo.* Mexico City: Talleres Linotipográficos de "El Hogar," 1924.

Bedau, Hugo Adam, ed. *The Death Penalty in America.* New York: Doubleday and Co., 1964.

Bojórquez, Juan de Dios [pseud. Djed Bórquez]. *Crónica del constituyente.* Mexico City: Ediciones Botas, 1938.

———. "El espíritu revolucionario de Obregón." In *Obregón: Aspectos de su vida.* Mexico City: Editorial "Cultura," 1935.

———. *Monzón: Semblanza de un revolucionario.* Mexico City: A. Artís, 1942.

Branch, H. N. "The Mexican Constitution of 1917 Compared with the Constitution of 1857." Supplement to the *Annals of the American Academy of Political and Social Science* 71 (May 1917).

Breceda, Alfredo. *México revolucionario, 1913–1917,* vol. 1. Madrid: Tipografía Artística Cervantes, 1920.

Brown, Lyle C. "Los liberales mexicanos y su lucha en contra de la dictadura de Porfirio Díaz, 1900–1906." In *Antología MCC, 1956*, pp. 89–136. Mexico City: Mexico City College Press, 1956.

———. "The Politics of Armed Struggle in the Mexican Revolution, 1913–1915." In *Revolution in Mexico: Years of Upheaval, 1910–1940*, edited by James W. Wilkie and Albert L. Michaels, pp. 60–72. New York: Alfred A. Knopf, 1969.

Callcott, Wilfrid Hardy. *Liberalism in Mexico, 1857–1929.* Stanford: Stanford University Press, 1931.

Cárdenas, Leonard, Jr. "The Municipality in Northern Mexico." *Southwestern Studies* 1, no. 1 (Spring 1963): 3–37.

Chapa, Pedro. Letter to author. Mexico City, July 11, 1966.

Cincuentenario de la ley de 6 de enero de 1915. Mexico City: Secretaría de Gobernación, 1964.

Cincuentenario de las adiciones y reformas al Plan de Guadalupe, del 12 de diciembre de 1914. Mexico City: Secretaría de Gobernación, 1964.

Clark, Marjorie R. *Organized Labor in Mexico.* Chapel Hill: University of North Carolina Press, 1934.

Cockcroft, James D. *Intellectual Precursors of the Mexican Revolution, 1900–1913.* Austin: University of Texas Press, 1968.

Codificación de los decretos del C. Venustiano Carranza. Mexico City: Imprenta de la Secretaría de Gobernación, 1915.

Computa general de la votación recogida en el cuarto distrito electoral para la elección de diputados propietario y suplente al Congreso Constituyente que se reunirá en la Ciudad de Querétaro el 20 de noviembre próximo. Comisión escrutadora. Archivo de la Cámara de Diputados, Mexico City.

Congreso Constituyente, Actas secretas, 1916–1917. Archivo de la Cámara de Diputados, Mexico City.

El Constitucionalista, no. 7 (February 5, 1915); nos. 23–24 (April 20–May 28, 1915). Veracruz.

El Constituyente, no. 2 (December 26, 1916); no. 4 (January 7, 1917); no. 9 (January 25, 1917); no. 10 (January 31, 1917).

Constituyentes—1917: Album de David Pastrana Jaimes. Property of Srta. Emma Villaseñor, Mexico City.

Cosío Villegas, Daniel. *La Constitución de 1857 y sus críticos.* Mexico City: Editorial Hermes, 1957.

———, ed. *Historia moderna de México.* 8 vols. Mexico City: Editorial Hermes, 1948–1965.

———. "The Mexican Revolution, Then and Now." In *Is the Mexican Revolution Dead?* edited by Stanley R. Ross, pp. 115–126. New York: Alfred A. Knopf, 1966.

Cueva, Mario de la. *Derecho mexicano del trabajo*, vol. 1. Mexico City: Librería de Porrúa Hnos. y Cía., 1938.

Cumberland, Charles C. *Mexican Revolution: The Constitutionalist Years.* Austin: University of Texas Press, 1972.

————. *Mexican Revolution: Genesis under Madero.* Austin: University of Texas Press, 1952.

————. *Mexico: The Struggle for Modernity.* New York: Oxford University Press, 1968.

Diario de los debates del Congreso Constituyente, 1916–1917. Ediciones de la Comisión Nacional para la Celebración del Sesquicentenario de la Proclamación de la Independencia Nacional y del Cincuentenario de la Revolución Mexicana. 2 vols. Mexico City: Talleres Gráficos de la Nación, 1960.

Dunn, Frederick Sherwood. *The Diplomatic Protection of Americans in Mexico.* New York: Columbia University Press, 1933.

Ejército Constitucionalista, División del Norte. *Manifiesto del C. Gral. Francisco Villa a la nación y documentos que justifican el desconocimiento del C. Venustiano Carranza como Primer Jefe de la Revolución.* Chihuahua: Imprenta del Gobierno, 1914.

Fernández Martínez Album. See Album of Lic. Luis Fernández Martínez.

Ferrer Mendiolea, Gabriel. *Historia del Congreso Constituyente de 1916–1917.* Mexico City: Biblioteca del Instituto Nacional de Estudios Históricos de la Revolución Mexicana, 1957.

Garza, Sergio Francisco de la. *El municipio, historia, naturaleza y gobierno.* Mexico City: Editorial Jus, 1947.

González Navarro, Moisés. "The Ideology of the Mexican Revolution." In *Is the Mexican Revolution Dead?* edited by Stanley R. Ross, pp. 177–187. New York: Alfred A. Knopf, 1966.

————. *El Porfiriato: La vida social.* Vol. 4 of *Historia moderna de México,* edited by Daniel Cosío Villegas. Mexico City: Editorial Hermes, 1957.

González Ramírez, Manuel, ed. *Planes políticos y otros documentos.* Fuentes para la Historia de la Revolución Mexicana, vol. 1. Mexico City: Fondo de Cultura Económica, 1954.

Grieb, Kenneth J. "The Causes of the Carranza Rebellion: A Reinterpretation." *The Americas* 25 (July 1968): 25–32.

————. *The United States and Huerta.* Lincoln: University of Nebraska Press, 1969.

Guzmán Esparza, Roberto. *Memorias de don Adolfo de la Huerta según su propio dictado.* Mexico City: Ediciones Guzmán, 1957.

La Herencia del Constituyente, Boletín de la Secretaría de Acción Social de la Asociación de Hijos de Constituyentes, no. 2 (October 5, 1963); no. 4 (December 5, 1963); no. 5 (January 5, 1964); no. 6 (February 5, 1964);

no. 7 (March 5, 1964); no. 8 (April 5, 1964); no. 9 (May 5, 1964); no. 10 (June 5, 1964); no. 11 (July 5, 1964); no. 12 (August 5, 1964); no. 13 (September 5, 1964); no. 14 (October 5, 1964); no. 15 (November 5, 1964); no. 16 (December 5, 1964).

Libro de actas de la Comisión Legislativa. Contiene doscientas hojas útiles y se abre hoy para su uso. México, marzo trece de mil novecientos dieciséis. Archivo de la Cámara de Diputados, Mexico City.

McCaleb, Walter Flavius. *Present and Past Banking in Mexico.* New York: Harper and Brothers, 1920.

Madero, Francisco I. *La sucesión presidencial en 1910.* San Pedro, Coahuila, 1908.

Manzano, Juan José, and Emma Villaseñor. Interview. Mexico City, March 27, 1965.

María y Campos, Armando de. *Múgica: Crónica biográfica (aportación a la historia de la Revolución Mexicana).* Mexico City: Compañía de Ediciones Populares, 1939.

Martínez Báez, Antonio. "La Revolución mexicana y la Constitución de 1917." *Debate,* Organo de la Asociación y Colegio de Abogados de Ciudad Juárez, A.C., no. 3 (May 1961): 25–41.

Martínez Núñez, Eugenio. "Don Rafael Nieto." *Boletín Bibliográfico de la Secretaría de Hacienda y Crédito Público,* no. 357 (December 15, 1966): 4–5.

Mecham, J. Lloyd. *Church and State in Latin America.* Chapel Hill: The University of North Carolina Press, 1966.

———. "The Jefe Político in Mexico." *Southwestern Social Science Quarterly* 13, no. 4 (March 1933): 333–353.

Medina, Hilario. "Carranza figura entre los primeros constituyentes." *Boletín Bibliográfico de la Secretaría de Hacienda y Crédito Público,* no. 432 (February 1, 1970): 4–6.

Melgarejo Randolf, L., and J. Fernández Rojas. *El Congreso Constituyente de 1916 y 1917. Reseña histórica de los debates a que dieron lugar las reformas a la Constitución de 1857, presentadas por el C. Venustiano Carranza, Primer Jefe del Ejército Constitucionalista, encargado del Poder Ejecutivo de la Nación, ante el Congreso Constituyente, reunido en la ciudad de Querétaro el día 1 de diciembre de 1916. Extracto de todos los documentos parlamentarios de la época y apuntes biográficos de los constituyentes más notables, precedidos del texto primitivo del pacto de 57 y de un estudio crítico del mismo.* Mexico City: Departamento de Talleres Gráficos de la Secretaría de Fomento, Colonización e Industria, 1917.

Memoria de la Secretaría de Gobernación correspondiente al período revolucionario comprendido entre el 19 de febrero de 1913 y el 30 de noviembre de 1916. (Formada por el C. Lic. Jesús Acuña, Sec. de Estado, Encargado del Despacho de Gobernación.) Para presentar ante el Soberano Congreso Constituyente. Mexico City: Talleres Linotipográficos de "Revista de Revistas," 1916.

Meyer, Jean. "Los obreros en la Revolución mexicana: Los 'Batallones Rojos.' " *Historia mexicana* 21 (July–September 1971): 1–37.

Meyer, Michael C. *Huerta, A Political Portrait.* Lincoln: University of Nebraska Press, 1972.

Molina Enríquez, Andrés. *Esbozo de la historia de los primeros diez años de la revolución agraria de México,* vol. 5. Mexico City: Talleres Gráficos del Museo Nacional de Arqueología, Historia y Etnografía, 1936.

———. *Los grandes problemas nacionales.* Mexico City: Imprenta de A. Carranza e Hijos, 1909.

Mondragón, Magdalena. *Cuando la Revolución se cortó las alas.* Mexico City: Costa-Amic, Editor, 1966.

Morales Jiménez, Alberto. *Hombres de la Revolución mexicana: 50 semblanzas biográficas.* Mexico City: Biblioteca del Instituto Nacional de Estudios Históricos de la Revolución Mexicana, 1960.

Morton, Ward M. "The Mexican Constitutional Congress of 1916–1917." *Southwestern Social Science Quarterly* 33, no. 1 (June 1952): 7–27.

———. *Woman Suffrage in Mexico.* Gainesville: University of Florida Press, 1962.

Múgica Velázquez, Francisco José. *Hechos, no palabras,* vol. 2. Mexico City: Talleres Gráficos del Gobierno Nacional, 1919.

La obra de una vida: Homenaje de admiración y gratitud al maestro José Rodríguez González. Maestros Distinguidos Coahuilenses. Mexico City, 1949.

Palavicini, Félix F. *Historia de la Constitución de 1917.* 2 vols. Mexico City, 1938.

———. *Mi vida revolucionaria.* Mexico City: Ediciones Botas, 1937.

———. *Política constitucional: Artículos y discursos.* Mexico City: Beatriz de Silva Ediciones e Impresores, 1950.

Pastrana Jaimes Album. *See* Constituyentes—1917.

Phipps, Helen. *Some Aspects of the Agrarian Question in Mexico: A Historical Study.* Austin: The University of Texas, 1925.

Plenn, Jaime H. *Mexico Marches.* New York: The Bobbs-Merrill Company, 1939.

Priestley, Herbert I. *The Mexican Nation, a History.* New York: The Macmillan Co., 1930.

Quirk, Robert E. *The Mexican Revolution, 1914–1915: The Convention of Aguascalientes.* Bloomington: Indiana University Press, 1960.

Rabasa, Emilio. *La constitución y la dictadura: Estudio sobre la organización política de México.* Mexico City: Tip. de "Revista de Revistas," 1912.

Ramírez Villarreal, Francisco. Interview. Cuernavaca, Morelos, May 31, 1965.

Recopilación de los circulares, reglamentos y acuerdos expedidos por las Secretarías de Estado adscritas a la primera jefatura del Ejército Constitucionalista. Mexico City: Gobierno Provisional de la República Mexicana, Imprenta de la Secretaría de Gobernación, 1916.

Records of the Department of State Relating to Internal Affairs of Mexico, 1910–1929. National Archives, Washington, D.C.

Romero Flores, Jesús. *La Revolución como nosotros la vimos.* Mexico City: Biblioteca del Instituto Nacional de Estudios Históricos de la Revolución Mexicana, 1963.

Rosenzweig, Fernando, et al. *El Porfiriato: La vida económica.* Vol. 7 of *Historia moderna de México,* edited by Daniel Cosío Villegas. Mexico City: Editorial Hermes, 1965.

Ross, Stanley R., ed. *Is the Mexican Revolution Dead?* New York: Alfred A. Knopf, 1966.

Rouaix, Pastor. *Génesis de los artículos 27 y 123 de la constitución política de 1917.* Mexico City: Biblioteca del Instituto Nacional de Estudios Históricos de la Revolución Mexicana, 1959.

Ruiz Album. *See* Album del Congreso Constituyente de 1917, Querétaro, JPR.

Salazar, Rosendo. *La Casa del Obrero Mundial.* Mexico City: Costa-Amic, 1962.

———, and José G. Escobedo. *Las pugnas de la gleba, 1907–1922.* 2 parts. Mexico City: Editorial Avante, 1923.

Saldaña, José P. Interview. Monterrey, Nuevo León, January 25, 1967.

Schmitt, Karl M. "The Mexican Positivists and the Church-State Question, 1876–1911." *A Journal of Church and State* 8 (Spring 1966): 200–213.

Simpson, Eyler N. *The Ejido, Mexico's Way Out.* Chapel Hill: The University of North Carolina Press, 1937.

Tannenbaum, Frank. *The Mexican Agrarian Revolution.* New York: The Macmillan Company, 1929.

———. *Mexico: The Struggle for Peace and Bread.* New York: Alfred A. Knopf, 1950.

———. *Peace by Revolution: Mexico after 1910.* New York: Columbia University Press, 1966.

Taracena, Alfonso. *Venustiano Carranza.* Mexico City: Editorial Jus, 1963.

Trueba Urbina, Alberto. *El artículo 123.* Mexico City: Talleres Gráficos Laguna de A. B. Arzate, 1934.

Tucker, William P. *The Mexican Government Today.* Minneapolis: University of Minnesota Press, 1957.

Vera Estañol, Jorge. *Carranza and His Bolshevik Regime.* Los Angeles: Wayside Press, 1920.

Villaseñor, Emma. *See* Manzano, Juan José, and Emma Villaseñor.

Villaseñor Norman, Adolfo. Interviews. Mexico City, March 3, 1965; March 13, 1965.

Villers, M. G. *El artículo 27 de la constitución mexicana de 1917.* Mexico City: Talleres Gráficos S. Galas, 1926.

Wilkie, James W. "Statistical Indicators of the Impact of National Revolution on the Catholic Church in Mexico, 1910–1967." *Journal of Church and State* 12, no. 1 (Winter 1970): 89–106.

————, and Albert L. Michaels, eds. *Revolution in Mexico: Years of Upheaval, 1910–1940.* New York: Alfred A. Knopf, 1969.

Womack, John, Jr. *Zapata and the Mexican Revolution.* New York: Random House, 1968.

INDEX

convention, 54; and prohibition, 196; quoted, 54 n.53

Andrade, Cayetano: as labor supporter, 106; background of, 106; on municipality, 174; and prohibition, 183–184, 185; on savage sports, 190–191

anticlericalism: of Reform period, 5; in debate on Article 3, 63, 67, 69–72, 74–76, 78–79; in debate on Article 24, 80–82, 83–85; in debate on Article 129 (later 130), 86, 88–94; in debate on Article 27, 94–97; in Articles 55, 59, and 82, 99; of Obregón, 223; of delegates, 231–232

Antirreeleccionista, El: 49

Aranda, Manuel G.: 45

Arizona: 113

Arredondo, Eliseo: 219

Arriaga, Ponciano: 5, 42

Arriaga, Chis.: 40

Article 3 (1857 Constitution): 62, 78

Article 3 (1917 Constitution): and church schools, 62; minority report on, 67, 79; Carranza's draft proposal on, rejected, 68; arguments opposing report on, 68–73; conflict of, with individual rights, 68–69, 73, 74, 77; and nationalism, 71–72; arguments favoring report on, 73–77; revised report on, 77–78; vote on, 78–79, 85, 217; and political division in convention, 221–222; praise for, 229, 230; mentioned, 37, 61, 101, 183, 184, 207, 208, 214, 216, 217

Article 4 (1917 Constitution): approved, 102, 185; proposed amendment to, 103; and prohibition, 181–182; mentioned, 184

Article 5 (1857 Constitution): 105

Article 5 (1917 Constitution): and Article 123, 97, 101, 109, 125, 131; anticlerical features of, 97, 98; First Committee reports out, 104–105; and Article 5 (1857), 105; debate on, 105–113, 116, 124–125; addition to, proposed, 109; Macías and proposal on, 116; proposal of Ochoa, Ríos, and Rodríguez on, 118; and Rouaix, 119, 137; revised report on, 124; amendments to, 125; reserved for voting, 125; approved, 131; mentioned, 102, 119, 181, 214

Article 9 (1857 Constitution): 103

Article 9 (1917 Constitution): 103–104

Article 13 (1857 Constitution): 98

Article 13 (1917 Constitution): 98, 126. *See also* transitory Article 13 (1917 Constitution)

Article 18 (1917 Constitution): 198 n

Article 20 (1917 Constitution): 88

Article 22 (1917 Constitution): 197–198, 200–206

Article 24 (1917 Constitution): First Committee report on, 80; discussion of, 80–85; approved, 85; analysis of vote on, 85, 89; mentioned, 87, 90, 214

Article 27 (1857 Constitution): 135

Article 27 (1917 Constitution): Carranza's draft of, 58, 94, 214; and Church property, 94–97; First Committee report on, 95; and Article 123, 101–102, 138; and Rouaix, 118; and 1917 Constitution, 134, 143; drafting process of, 136, 138; objectives of, 138–140; and property ownership, 139–140, 162–163; analysis of preface to, 141–142; Magallón and debate on, 143; Rojas asks deferral of discussion of, 143; discussion of, 144–164; rights of foreigners under, 147–150; and banks, 152–155; Rouaix draft of, 155, 158; veterans' benefits under, 163–164; judicial and administrative procedures under, 163; and monopolistic contracts, 164; and attention given by convention, 164; need for, 164, 233; significance of, 164–165; voted on, 164; indigenous to Querétaro Convention, 165; praise for, 228–229; and vested interests, 232; philosophy of, 232–233; mentioned, 133, 211, 215

Article 28 (1917 Constitution): 121–122

Article 33 (1917 Constitution): 98, 196–197

Article 35 (1917 Constitution): 208–209

Article 37 (1917 Constitution): 98–99

Article 39 (1857 Constitution): 29 n

Article 55 (1917 Constitution): 99

Article 59 (1917 Constitution): 99

Article 72 (1857 Constitution): 115

Article 82 (1917 Constitution): 99

Article 115 (1917 Constitution): first

clergy: limitations on, 4, 71; and Napoleon III, 5–6; as viewed by Carranza's followers, 61; supported Huerta, 61, 70; attitude of First Committee toward, 67; in education, 67, 69, 72, 73, 77, 231; influence of, 74, 100; hold of, on children, 75, 76; and State, 75; and confession, 80, 81, 84; marriage of, 80, 81, 84; papal control over, 85, 89, 91; as private citizens, 88; hold of, on people, 90; and the home, 90; foreign, 91, 92; of Philippine Independent church, 91; persecution of, 93; and financing of church construction, 95; property of, 96, 151; "dead hand" of, 96; and Article 5, 97; in Sonora, 97; expulsion of, 98; wealth of, 98, 151; political rights of, 99; restrictions on, 99; as undesirable influence, 100; as target of jacobins, 229; as peril to liberty, 230; and society, 231; mentioned, 16. *See also* anticlericalism; Church, the

Coahuila: Carranza governor of, 15, 26; and Constitutionalists, 17; municipal government in, 171, 172; mentioned, 19, 41, 66

cockfights, attempts to prohibit: 182, 197

Colima: 217

Colunga, Enrique: on delegates' unpreparedness, 43; and Committee on the Constitution, 63, 64; background of, 64; on workers' debts, 129; and Article 27, 141; on foreign capital, 150; on real property acquisition, 151; on banking, 153; and communal property, 157, 162–163; on small property holding, 160; on alcoholism, 184; quoted, 64 n. 7

Committee on the Constitution: 63–66. *See also* First Committee

Comonfort, Ignacio: 5

Comte, Auguste: 9, 10

Constitution, U.S.: 43, 207

Constitutional Convention (1823–1824): 36

Constitutional Convention (1856–1857): composition of, 4; draws up Constitution of 1857, 4, 5; length of, 36; religiosity of delegates to, 72; and Ignacio Ramírez, 110; and death penalty, 198; and Díaz Barriga, 226–227

Constitutional Convention (1916–1917): reflects spirit of times, 37; and secret sessions, 38; cost of, 58 n.61; and Church, 61, 231; political divisions of, 73–74, 132, 215–222; and education, 75–76; democratic action in, 100, 222; and labor, 110; and Zapata, 145; and capital punishment, 206; and woman suffrage, 207; souvenirs of, 213; independents in, 217; and albums, 223; and Obregón, 223–224; delegates to, 230–231; and social justice, 233; ideals expressed at, 234; mentioned, passim

Constitutionalist movement: beginning of, 15, 212; in northern states, 17; and Obregón, 17, 22, 224; and Villa, 18, 20–25 passim; strategy of, to defeat Huerta, 18; and reform program, 21, 22, 23, 30; division in, 23, 45, 215–216; support for, 23–25, 106–136; and convention delegates, 32; and *renovadores*, 45, 46; and Macías, 51; generally opposed by Church, 61; and Múgica, 66; and Jara, 87; and Méndez, 88; and Yucatecan labor, 107; mentioned, 216, 226

Constitution of 1824: 29, 91

Constitution of 1857: before Díaz, 4, 5, 6, 8; and Church, 5, 91, 99; under Díaz, 10, 11, 29; Carranza assumes leadership under, 15; Articles 121 and 128, 15 n.16; Carranza's government under, 21; Carranza and reforms to, 26, 36, 222–223; and individual rights, 27; Palavicini on need to replace, 27–29; Article 127 of, 28 n.43; Carranza on, 29, 56–57; Article 39 of, 29 n; and Constitutionalist movement, 30; requirements for election to Congress under, 31; reverence for authors of, 39; Carranza and revision of, 42; Macías and reforms to, 50; principles of, 56; Article 3 of, 62, 78; and Catholic religion, 99; anticlerical features of, 99; Article 72 of, 115; and labor contract, 124; Article 27 of, 135; compensation for expropriation under, 145; and municipality, 167; and death penalty, 198 n, 203; Carranza's attachment to, 222–223; and Constitution of 1917, 222–223; mentioned, 213, 221

Constitution of 1917: promulgation of, 4, 222; reform decrees incorporated into, 24; and Mexican Revolution, 30, 233; authors of, 39, 79; and Carranza's draft constitution, 58, 59, 214; distinctive features of, 58–59, 134; and Article 3, 77, 229; and restrictions on clergy, 99; Carranza takes oath under, 214; Calderón on, 217; and Constitution of 1857, 222–223; and Obregón, 223–224; various delegates on, 227, 229–230; paradoxical concepts in, 228; criticism of, 234; mentioned, 16, 143, 213

Constituyente, El: 38

Conventions. *See* Aguascalientes Convention; Constitutional Convention (1856–1857); Constitutional Convention (1916–1917)

corralista: 220

Cosío Villegas, Daniel: 11

Cravioto, Alfonso: and *renovadores*, 45, 46–47; and Martínez de Escobar, 46; defends Macías, 51; asks for harmony and cooperation, 55; attacks First Committee report on Article 3, 68–69; on clergy, 69; on jacobins, 69; and menace of Church schools, 72; asks labor code, 112; on death penalty for *violación*, 200; and Carranza's draft constitution, 216; mentioned, 205; quoted, 47 n, 69

Creel family: 159

Cuba: 40

Cumpas, Son.: 97

Curiel, Rafael: 45

Dávalos, Marcelino: 45, 211

Dávalos Ornelas, Manuel: 41, 227

death penalty: abolition of, 167, 197; arguments against, 198, 200–203; and penitentiary system, 198; defense of, 203–206; at Querétaro Convention, 233

Department of General Public Health: 187

Diario de los debates: 58, 94, 129, 131, 136, 140, 153, 156, 164, 169, 196, 207, 223

Díaz, Porfirio: dictatorship of, 4, 7, 12, 29; agrarian problem under, 7, 8, 9, 24, 139, 232; grievances under, 7, 12, 17, 166, 182; national development under, 7; labor under, 9; positivism under, 9, 10; politics under, 10, 11, 12, 167, 207; opposition to, 11–13, 40, 60; fall of, 12–13; and Huerta, 14; and Madero, 14; banditry under, 204; mentioned, 13, 14, 47, 48, 49, 54, 59, 65, 201, 203, 207, 226, 227

Díaz Barriga, Francisco: 226–227

Diéguez, Manuel: 215

Division of the North: 18, 19, 20

Division of the Northeast: 54

Division of the Northwest: 217, 226

Don Venustiano. *See* Carranza, Venustiano

Dorador, Silvestre: 120, 121, 138

draft constitution (Carranza's): articlerical features of, 61–62, 68, 97, 98, 99, 231; and secular education, 62, 70; Article 3, 62, 70, 79; vulnerability of, to attack, 78; Article 24 of, 80; Article 129 of, 86; and property of religious bodies, 94; and labor, 101–102, 103, 112, 117; and agrarian reform, 101–102, 135, 137; Article 27 of, 136, 137; and municipality, 168, 177; and choice of profession, 181; and death penalty, 197–198; and 1917 Constitution, 213–214; and needs of country, 214; Article 27 (1917) missing from, 214; Article 123 (1917) missing from, 214; Obregón on, 216; opposition to, 217; support for, 217; and reform of 1857 Constitution, 222; use of, in Querétaro Convention, 224

Durango (city): 17, 218, 219

Durango (state): 17, 86, 118–119

Dyer, Jairo R.: 229–230

education: under Juárez and Lerdo de Tejada, 6; and Aguascalientes Convention, 22; and church schools, 67, 68, 70, 72–76, 79, 231, 232; rational, 67, 74; and secular requirement, 68, 70–71, 73, 77, 166; freedom of, 68, 69, 71, 73, 74, 76–78; in municipality, 169–170, 172, 173–174, 178; and jacobins, 221

ejidos: and Madero, 14; under 1917 Con-

Nafarrate, Emiliano: 42, 211
Napoleon III: 5–6
National Agrarian Commission: 24, 137
national church: 91, 92
nationalism: in attitude toward foreign priests, 80; and removal of papal control over clergy, 85, 88–89, 91; and national church, 91; exploited by Palavicini, 92; and labor issue, 132–133; and Article 27, 147–150, 233; of Enríquez, 148; of Giffard, 148; of Reynoso, 149; of Pastrana Jaimes, 226; of Jara, 203; of delegates, 231; in attack on the Church, 232
National School of Medicine: 186–187
natural resources: 13, 145
Navarro, Gilberto M.: 41
Navarro, Luis T.: as *renovador*, 45; on division of estates, 144; praises Zapata, 144–145; on small property holding, 160; quoted, 134
New Mexico: 113
New York City: 114
Nieto, Rafael: 45, 152–153
Nuevo Laredo, Tam.: 87
Nuevo León: 18, 34, 35, 87

Oaxaca (state): 38
Obregón, Alvaro: and Constitutionalist movement, 17, 22, 224; and Sonora, 18; occupies Mexico City, 20; and Carranza, 36, 216, 217, 218–219, 220, 224; and Palavicini, 51; as reputed leader of jacobins, 217; and 1917 Constitution, 223, 224; and Querétaro Convention, 223–224; views of, 223; and *renovadores*, 224; and A. Aguirre, 226; mentioned, 19, 215, 216
obregonistas: 217, 224
Ocampo, Santiago: 226
Ochoa, Rafael: 118
O'Farrill, Enrique: 45
Opposition Constitutional party: 33
Ordorica, Guillermo: 45, 46, 47, 63

Palavicini, Félix F.: on need for new constitution, 27; familiarity of, with American institutions, 43; as *renovador*, 45; fight over credentials of, 46, 47, 48, 49–50; background of, 48, 49, 50; defends Macías, 51; and opinion of Recio, 64; and limitations on indi-

vidual rights, 69, 78; anticlerical views of, 70; views of, on Article 3, 70–71, 77; and foreign clergy, 92; on labor organizations, 122; favors Carranza's draft of Articles 27 and 33, 143; and municipality, 176; and death penalty for *violación*, 206; on woman suffrage, 208, 209; and Carranza's draft constitution, 216; and "Manifesto to the Nation," 220; mentioned, 177, 213; quoted, 48 n.40, 50, 71–72
Palma, Juan de Dios: 60
Paris, France: 48, 187
Parras, Coah.: 184
Pastrana Jaimes, David: on divorce, 88; and clergy, 88–89; and the Church, 91; on Article 5, 109; and Article 27, 138; on acquisition of real property, 151–152; fears violation of state sovereignty, 188; mentioned, 42, 111, 152; quoted, 226
peonage: 16, 120, 129
Pérez, Celestino: 76
Perusquía, Ernesto: 192–193
Philadelphia: 114
Philippine Independent church: 91 n.52, 92
Phipps, Helen: 231
Piedras Negras, Coah.: 219
Pino Suárez, José María: death of, 14; resignation of, 45, 46–47, 54; mentioned, 216
Pintado Sánchez, Ismael: 227
Plan of Ayala: 20
Plan of Guadalupe: writing of, 15–17; terms of, 16; and Múgica, 17, 47, 66, 212–213; and Lucio Blanco, 18; in oath of delegates, 32; seating of *renovadores* under, 216; mentioned, 18, 23, 212, 214
Plan of San Luis Potosí: 13
porfiriato: 7, 61, 94
porfirista: 220
positivism: 9, 10
preconstitutional period: and decree of December 12 (1914), 23–24; and decree of January 6 (1915), 24, 135–136, 137, 142, 145, 155, 158, 161; and decree of January 29 (1915), 24–25; and decree of December 25 (1914), 25, 167; need to end, 26; and Carran-

DATE DUE

FE